GW00319396

THE BEDFORDSHIRE
HISTORICAL RECORD
SOCIETY
1997

Frontispiece: Brass of William Cobbe, smith, of Sharnbrook, showing also his wife Alice and their son Thomas. William died in 1522, and his will is no. 3 in this volume.

Thomas Fisher

THE PUBLICATIONS OF THE BEDFORDSHIRE
HISTORICAL RECORD SOCIETY
VOLUME 76

Bedfordshire Wills
1484–1533

Edited by

Patricia L. Bell

PUBLISHED BY THE SOCIETY   1997

ISBN 0 85155 059 2
First published in 1997 by the Society

This volume has been published with the help of grants from Bedfordshire County Council and Bedford Borough Council

Cover design by Ian Davies, Park Farm Studios Ltd., Riseley Road, Bletsoe, Bedford MK44 1QU

Printed and bound by
Stephen Austin and Sons Ltd., Hertford

CONTENTS

ILLUSTRATIONS

The lithographs of monumental brasses are taken from Thomas Fisher's *Monumental Remains and Antiquities in the County of Bedford*, published in 1828.

INTRODUCTION

The first surviving wills in the probate records of the Court of the Archdeacon of Bedford, dating from 1480, are to be found in the first registers of wills and testaments proved by the Archdeacon or his commissary. These were deposited with other local probate material in the Bedfordshire County Record Office in 1950. For later years original wills survive as well as the registered copies. Original wills begin in 1536, though few survive for that year, but by 1560 probably most original wills copied into the registers have survived, and can be found stored in bundles arranged under the date of probate.

Wills are an invaluable source for local, family and social history, and abstracts of the 396 wills in the first Bedford archdeaconry probate register, ABP/R 1, which date between 1480 and 1526, were published by this Society in 1957 and 1966 as volumes 37 and 45.[1] Only those people with at least a little property made a will, and so such local probate records relate to the more prosperous husbandmen, yeomen and tradesmen and their widows, and also to the parish clergy and some minor gentry. Such a person would use the parish priest or another literate person to write down in proper form what he or she wanted done with their property, and after death those named as executors took the document to the Archdeacon's Court for probate, and then, armed with the probate copy, they could execute the testator's wishes.

People of higher rank or with extensive estates used the Prerogative Court of Canterbury. Mrs Margaret McGregor edited a volume of P.C.C. wills between 1383 and 1548 of people connected with Bedfordshire which was published by this Society in 1979 as volume 58.[2] She notes that two wills proved in the P.C.C. were also registered, though not proved, in the Bedford archdeaconry court, one being no. 9 in this volume, John Hardyng of Harlington, which was no. 94 in volume 48. A full account of all probate courts and probate records covering Bedfordshire can be found in the introduction by Christopher Pickford to the *Index of Bedfordshire Probate Records 1484–1858*.[3]

In the present volume we are continuing the publication of wills proved in the court of the Archdeacon of Bedford, and include all the wills in the second probate register, ABP/R 2, and some from the third register, ABP/R 3. ABP/R 2 contains 219 wills, most of which were proved between 1510 and 1530, though there is one of 1484 and one of 1533. The contents of this register are not in date order. It would seem that loose sheets or foldings were used by the Archdeacon's clerks for

1

copying wills and testaments and these were then allowed to pile up on the shelves for a number of years, until a decision was made to have them bound into a volume. ABP/R 1, containing 396 wills between 1480 and 1526, seems to have been put together in a similar somewhat haphazard fashion. However the third register, ABP/R 3, appears to have been in volume form before its use for registration, and in this register the wills are entered more or less in the date order of probate. From ABP/R 3 I have included material from folios 1 to 36, which are wills proved from early 1529 to the end of 1530. Thus we might hope that abstracts of nearly all surviving Bedfordshire probates up to the end of 1530 are now available in print. Several wills were printed *in extenso* in vols. 37 and 45, and so none are included in this volume. Year dates from 1 January to 24 March are given in double form.

This volume owes much to two very able voluntary helpers at the Bedfordshire County Record Office, John S. Thompson and his wife, Isobel. Isobel was already a regular helper in 1957, when I joined the staff of the Record office, and on John's retirement from his work at the RAE aeronautical research establishment at Thurleigh he began to come regularly, and took to archives with great enthusiasm. He preferred to exercise his problem-solving talents on medieval sources, especially those with palaeographic obscurities, and a great deal of his work was published by this Society in 1990 in volume 69. However, he also produced an abstract of ABP/R 2, and Isobel worked on ABP/R 3, and it is because of the preliminary work of these two capable and valued helpers that I have been able to produce this volume in a very limited time.

The methods used in volumes 37 and 45 have been used here. The testator's name comes first, then the parish or place of burial, date of will and then date of probate, and after that the volume (ABP/R 2 or 3) and folio number. Nearly all the wills began with the usual "In the name of God Amen", followed by the bequest of the testator's soul to Almighty God, Our Lady, and to all the saints in heaven, and this has been omitted from the abstract, unless there is a variation from the formula, as in no. 54. After that there comes the place of burial, and if this is to be inside the body of the church it would appear that the fee was usually 6s. 8d. Invariably a sum was left to the high altar for any tithes that might inadvertently have been left unpaid by the deceased. Then came the mortuary or principal, a required donation to the parish priest, generally the best of the testator's goods. After these came the spiritual or charitable bequests made for the health of the testator's soul. Nearly all testators left money to the church bells and to the torches for lighting the church. All included a donation, often 2d., to the cathedral at Lincoln, and money was left for a mass to be said for the soul of the testator, or for a number of masses, perhaps a trental (thirty masses). The money sometimes went to a secular priest, but very popular beneficiaries were the various orders of friars. Occasionally a prosperous testator would leave funds for a priest to sing for a year, or for several years. Many people left a small endowment, perhaps a rent charge on a building, to pay for an obit or anniversary mass, usually on the day of the testator's death. There were often gifts to the church building or furnishings, and to the many lights before images of saints in the church. There are some charitable gifts to the poor, and very often gifts to bridges and for the repair of highways, which were then considered charitable causes.

A man had control over what was to be done with his goods and chattels, and these he could dispose of in his testament. Before the Statute of Wills, 1540, in theory a man had no such jurisdiction over his land, and so the will was a separate document which stated what he wished to be done with land. However, a surprising number of testators had already transferred their land to feoffees to uses, and in the will the testator would instruct his feoffees what they should do. Some probates still kept the distinction between will and testament, as in nos. 9 and 28, but on the whole this was disregarded, and one document covered both areas.

Provision was usually made for widows and children, if the testator's means permitted. Cattle and sheep are frequently mentioned, and sometimes horses, and measures of barley or malt were useful legacies. In the wills of widows we find details of clothing, and of household utensils. At the end come the names of the executors, and then of the witnesses who were present when the deceased declared that the document contained what he wished to be done. Sometimes the probate shows that one or all of the executors decided that the task was going to be too difficult, and so he or they refused to act. If all refused, then letters of administration would be granted to a relative to deal with the estate.

Such a mass of material will always have points of interest for a local historian. For instance, we find the Skevington family already well established in Turvey, where they remained as leading inhabitants for several centuries, and where the name survives to this day. Potton, as a centre for education, first appeared in volume 58, where we find that Sir John Gostwick, knight, born c. 1480–90, had been educated at Potton, and in a will made in 1545 Robert Burgoyne mentioned George Gifforde "Whome I finde at scoole at Potton". In this volume William Hale of Marston (no. 244) who made his will in 1529, required his executors to keep his grandson Thomas Hayle to school at Potton for two years. On another subject we have the will of John Slade of Blunham, made in 1528, with the bequest to the church of Little Barford of "all my play bookes and garmentes" and all the properties and other things belonging to the same (no. 218). This is the only evidence so far for plays being performed in Bedfordshire parish churches in this century.

Unfortunately the will comes at the end off the volume ABP/R 2, and some parts have been rubbed away. There are two bequests towards the making of a Palm Cross in the churchyard at Dunton, a cross usually sited in the churchyard on the north side of the church and at the east end.[4] We have more evidence of people with Welsh names living in the Chicksands area of the county. In volume 37 there was Owen Vap Jenkyn, otherwise called Humfrey Gough of Chicksands, 1515 (p. 70) and in this volume we have Agnes Johnson of Chicksands in 1521 (no. 115); and David and Alice Jones of Haynes, 1514 and 1528 (nos. 133 and 154). George Joye, the Protestant reformer of Peterhouse, Cambridge, is mentioned in the will of his father John in 1521 (no. 198). In the will of the widow Margaret Parcell of Riseley, made in 1521 (no. 210), we seem to have one of the last members of the ancient Pertesoil family of Riseley, who after three hundred years were selling their manor and estates to the St. John family, and in this will we have some vivid descriptions of women's clothing more decorative than utilitarian, and also of jewellery other than the usual pair of beads.

With one exception all the wills in this volume are for people living in or very near to Bedfordshire, and the exception is no. 16, the will of Robert Whitstone of Watton in Yorkshire, made in 1519 and proved in 1520. No one has suggested an explanation for this stray.

With the present renewed interest in the course of the Reformation in England, it is possible that probates are one of the few sources for discovering the attitudes of ordinary people, and for this reason if for no other, it would be good if the Society could continue the publication of wills to cover those made until at least the early years of the reign of Queen Elizabeth I.

Patricia L. Bell

NOTES

1. *B.H.R.S.* vol.37. English Wills, 1498–1526, *edited by* A. F. Cirket, 1957.
   B.H.R.S. vol.45. Bedfordshire Wills, 1480–1519, *edited by* P. L. Bell, 1966.
2. *B.H.R.S.* vol.58. Bedfordshire Wills proved in the Prerogative Court of Canterbury, *edited by* Margaret McGregor, 1979.
3. *The Index Library* Index of Bedfordshire Probate Records 1484–1858, *compiled by* A. F. Cirket, *edited by* Joan Stuart and Peggy Wells, *with an introduction by* Christopher Pickford, F. S. A., The British Record Society, London, 1993.
4. The Stripping of the Altars, *by* Eamon Duffy, Yale U.P., 1992, p. 23.

ABP/R 2

1.

pr. 15 Nov. 1522. (ABP/R 2: 1)

—- for their labours 10s.; residue of goods between children by minds of three indifferent honest men —-

Witnesses Matthew Colman, Thomas Childerhowse, sir Robert Bisshopp.

2.

Johan Wynne now abiding in Steventon. 28 Aug., pr. 8 Nov. 1522. (2: 2)

Burial in the churchyard of Our Lady in Steventon before the image of St. Kateryn; her mortuary after the custom of the town; to the cathedral church of Lincoln 2d.; to the high altar 12d.; to the rood loft a sheep; for a priest to say mass for the testator's soul each year 4d.; to the Grey Friars of Bedford to be prayed for each year 4d., these payments to be made by son George Wyffe during his lifetime. Son George Wiffe to distribute yearly on Good Friday 8d. to poor people.

Residue to son.

Executors son George Wyffe and son-in-law Henry Parker. Witnesses John Walgrave, William Tawer, John Bak—-.

3.

William Cobbe/Cobb senior of Schernebroke. 14 Oct., pr. 25 Oct. 1522. (2: 3)

Burial in church of St. Peter in Scharnbroke for which 6s. 8d. to the church; his mortuary as customary; to the mother church of Lincoln 6d.; to high altar of the parish church for tithes forgotten 2s.; to the bells 2s.; to the sepulchre light 2s.; to the torches 2s.; to Our Lady's light 12d.; to the rood light 12d.; to the church of Bletsow 3s. and to the high altar of same 4d.; to Felmersham church 3s. and to the high altar 4d.; to Knottyng church 6s. 8d. and to the high altar 4d.; to Soldroppe church 3s. and to the high altar 4d.; to Wodell (Odell) church 3s. and to the high altar 4d.; to Wemington church 3s. 4d.; he wishes a priest to sing for one year in the parish church of Schernebroke for the souls of himself, his wife, his father and mother; to the friars of Bedford for a trental 10s..

To Clenyogges bridge 20d.; to Harwold bridge 2 bushels of barley; to Stafford bridge 2 bushels of barley.

If the parish of Schernebroke will begin again the brotherhood of the

Trinity then it is to have 6s. 8d..

To his wife Alys all lands, tenements, meadows and pastures in the parishes of Scharnebroke, Bletsowe and Felmersham for life, reversion to son William and his heirs and assigns for ever.

After the deaths of testator and his wife, his daughters Elizabeth Maryett and Jone Carter are to have 40s. each. Daughter Annes Meryell to have £3 paid her within 3 years, that is 20s. a year. To every grandchild 3 sheep, and to every godchild one sheep. To servant Nicholas Kyng a sheep; to servant Thomas Clarke a one year old bullock; to Margaret Varnam the daughter of Thomas Cobbe a two year old heifer.

Residue to be divided between wife Alys and son William.

Exors. son sir Richard Cobbe vicar of Felmersham, son William Cobbe and Robert Carter, who are to have 6s. 8d. each. Witn. master Hardwyke, John Negus, Nicholas Kyng.

Probate granted to one executor, reserving power of the other.

4.
William Butteler of Litlyngton. 4 Oct., pr. 31 Oct. 1522. (2: 4d)

Burial in churchyard of parish church of All Saints Litlyngton; to the high altar for tithes and offerings negligently forgotten 8d.; to mother church of Lincoln 12d.; to bells 8d.; to the mending of the steeple there 6s. 8d..

To his son Henry the house he dwells in with appurtenances and horses and cart and plough, 3 kine (cows), 3 calves, 2 steers. To wife Agnes a cow and a calf. To son Robert the house the testator lives in with appurtenances.

Residue to wife and to son Henry to dispose of for testator's and all Christian souls.

Exors. wife and son Henry; supervisor master Thomas Dekons. Witn. sir Richard—- (?Forthe), master James Button, Thomas Dekens, John Kaynow, John Davy.

5.
Thomas Caryngton of Dunton. 14 Oct. 1522, pr. 10 Jan. 1522/3. (2: 5)

Burial in churchyard of Our Blessed Lady of Dunton; to high altar 12d.; for his principal as is customary; to the sepulchre light 12d.; to the rood light 12d.; to the bells 12d.; to the torches 12d.; to mother church of Lincoln 4d.; son Gerard to pay son Richard x —- within a year after testator's death; to the ringers at the time of his dirige 6d.; son Gerard or whoever holds his property to keep every year testator and wife Margaret's names in the bede-roll with dirige and mass once a year, and each year for ever to give 12d. in bread to the poor where there is most need.

His son Richard to have "a certeyn frewte yearly" if there is sufficient at discretion of son Gerard; son Gerard to have all lands and tenements in town and fields of Dunton and Millow with their appurtenances, to hold to him and his heirs male, in default to son Richard and heirs male, in default to son William Caryngton and heirs male, in default to the next heir male.

Wife Margaret to have all lands given to son Gerard during her life-time, and she may fell a tree or two for the fire if she so needs. After the death of his mother son Gerard to make no waste in felling of the wood, but only to have wood to repair his houses, or loppings for his fire. If he does make such waste then the property to revert to son Richard.

Residue to wife Margaret.

Exors. wife Margaret, sons Gerard and Richard, each to have 6s. 8d..
Witn. William White priest, Thomas Caryngton, Peter White.

6.
Henry Feyry of Shefforth. 3 Jan., pr. 24 Jan 1522/3. (2: 6)
Burial in churuchyard of All Hallows in Camelton (Campton); for his principal as is customary; to high altar of Camelton for tithes and obla-tions forgotten 12d.; to mother church of Lincoln 2d.; to the mainte-nance of the bells in Camelton 12d.; for two new torches there 10s.; for two new torches for chapel of St. Michael in Shefforth 10s.; to Dane (Dom) John Rackett subprior of Chyxsand (Chicksands) to sing a trental for testator 10s.; to the friars of Bedford 10s.; to cousin [?]Gromon a friar of Dunstaple for a trental 10s.; for a vestment to maintain the service of Almighty God in the chapel of Shefforth 33s. 4d.; for a convenient priest to sing for testator in Camelton church for half a year 4 marks.

Wife Beterys to have tenement in Shefford where testator lives for her life, reversion to his daughter Johan and the heirs of her body, in default to the use and maintenance of the chapel of St. Michael in Shefforth, and his feoffees are instructed to hold his properties to these uses.

To daughter Johan 2 chaffing dishes, a latten bason, a pewter pot, a salet, a little posnet, a pair of cobbards, 4 pewter dishes, 3 brass pots and a posnet, a great brass pan and another brass pan with a band of iron, a "Tynkkers" kettle, 4 candlesticks, a featherbed, a mattress, a salt-ing trough, a table and a form, a plain coffer, a bedstead, 2 coverlets one yellow the other with flowers, a chair, a painted cloth, a pair of sheets "flexen and harden", 2 table cloths, 2 towels and an aumbry. The residue of his household stuff to his wife Beterys.

Exors. wife Beterys and William Stockes, to whom his residue. Witn. sir Alyn Ewe, parson of Camelton, sir John Woodward priest, George Flynders, Edward Johnson, Thomas Warner.

7.
Robert Laurence, Nether Stondon, Shitlyngton (Shillington), singleman.
6 Feb., pr. 14 Feb. 1522/3. (2: 7)

Body for burial in the churchyard of All Hallows in Shitlyngton; for his mortuary as customary; to mother church of Lincoln 2d.; to high altar for tithes forgotten 6d.; to the brotherhood of Jesus a quarter of barley; to the bells 4d.; to the torches 4d.; to the sepulchre light 2d.; to the light before Our Lady of Grace a bushel of barley; to the light before All Hallows a bushel of barley; to the light before Our Lady of Pity a bushel of barley; to the upkeep of the lights in the church 12d.; for a trental of masses to be said in Shitlyngton church for testator and friends 10s.; testator's portion of the goods bequeathed to him by his father to be used to find a priest to pray for him and his friends as long as the money lasts; a cow is to be let out along with his father's two beasts to keep his yeartide at the same time as his father's yeartide for ever.

To godson William Lille a sheep; to brother Richard Laurence the bullock that was testator's by bequest of his father; to brother Richard Laurence his black coat; to Alys Sheppard a young sheep; to John Sheppard junior a weaning bullock; to the 4 children of William Laurence of Peggisden (Pegsdon) a cow bullock of 2 years of age.

Residue to brother William Laurence of Peggisden, who is to be the executor and John Sheppard of Peggisden to be supervisor and he to have 3s. 4d. for his work. Witn. Thomas Childerhows and Robert Bisshopp parish priest of same town.

8.
William Lecher of Careleton. 1 Feb., pr. 21 Feb. 1522/3 (2: 7d)

Body to be buried in churchyard of St. Mary of Careleton; to mother church of Lincoln 2d.; to high altar for tithes forgotten 4d.; to sepulchre light 4d.; to the bells 4d.; for his mortuary as the custom of the town.

To his son Thomas 3 acres in the fields of Felmersham and to Thomas' daughter an aumbry and a bushel of barley. To his daughter Elizabeth half of testator's goods and to her daughter a bushel of barley. The residue to his wife Alys for life.

Exors. wife Alys and son Thomas. Overseer sir Robert, testator's ghostly father. Witn. John Grene, Robert Fox, John Harper, George Gale.

9.
John Hardyng of Harlyngdon Woodend. made 12 Apr. 1523, but no note of probate. (2: 8)

Testament His body to be buried in the church of Our Blessed Lady in Harlyngdon in the middle space of the said church; his mortuary as is customary; to the high altar for tithes forgotten 3s. 4d.; to said church for his burial place 6s. 8d.; to mother church of Lincoln 4d.; to church of St. Laurence in Stepingley 3s. 4d.; to church of Mary Mawdlen in Westonyng 3s. 4d.; to the upkeep of Harlyngdon bells 3s. 4d.; to the torches there 3s. 4d.. His executors are to sell the house once of William Lincoln with all lands and use the money from the sale to hire for 9 marks yearly an honest priest to say masses and suffrages in church of Our Blessed Lady in Harlyngdon for soul of testator for as long as the money lasts. 9 marks sterling are to be paid to the said priest to say masses and suffrages immediately after testator's death for one year, which sum to come from his moveable goods. To every godchild 4d.. To mend the highway in Hoorde lane 20d.. To Alys Hardyng daughter of testator's son William Hardyng £3 6s. 8d..

Residue to wife Agnes Hardyng to be used for health of testator's soul.

Exors. wife Agnes Hardyng, William Kirk senior, Richard Rudde of Lilly in the county of Hertford. Supervisor Dr. Edward Sheffeld vicar of Luton. Witn. sir Thomas Jamys vicar of Harlyngton, John Jenkyns, Thomas Aylbourne.

Will To his wife Agnes Hardyng for life all testator's lands and tenements in Harlyngdon, Westonyng, Todyngton and Tyngriff, both free and copyhold. On death of wife to William Hardyng the son of William Hardyng deceased two tenements, the one called Hardynges Place the other Acles in Harlyngton, with all their lands, when he comes of age. Should Agnes die before William comes of age, the executors are to have the guiding of him "to sett hym to scole gyvyng hym his fyndyng competently to his statue duryng the said nonage" and until he comes of age the executors are to give yearly accounts of their expenditure to testator's feoffees on St. Katerin's day in Harlyngton church, and executors to have 6s. 8d. each annually for their work, any surplus income to be used by feoffees in work for testator's soul.

Should William Hardyng die without heirs of his body, then William Akirk the youngest to have testator's place in Woodend for ever, and John Davy, testator's godson, to have the tenement at the Church End late Robert Acle. Should both William Akirk and John Davy die without heirs, then all to go to testator's right heirs held of chief lord by the service due. The reversion *[sic]* of all the estate to his wife Agnes Hardyng to give or sell.

10.
Matthew Arnold of Shitlyngton. 14 Apr., pr. 9 May 1523. (2: 9d)

Burial in churchyard of All Hallows in Shitlyngton; to mother church of Lincoln 4d.; for his mortuary as custom of the town; to high altar for tithes forgotten 3s. 4d.; to every light in the church a pennyworth of candles; to the brotherhood of Jesus 3s. 4d.; to the torches 20d.; to the sepulchre light 12d.; to every godchild 4d.; to a priest to say mass for half a year for testator and friends in Shitlyngton church £3; four of his milk beasts are to be let out annually at 20d. a head to keep his yeartide for ever with mass and dirige for testator, his wife and friends.

Testator's son Richard to have the beasts in his keeping for his lifetime, then they are to be let by the churchwardens to an honest man in the parish who must enter into a bond to ensure that the number is kept up.

To his wife Margery the place which is called Brekles House with the close and pightles for her life, his son Richard doing all repairs at his own expense. Wife to have also 3 loads of wood from Richard, also 3 sown acres of land each year one sown with wheat, one with barley, and one with peas or beans all the work to be done by son Richard. She is to have also 3 of his best milch beasts and 6 couple of ewes and lambs, also 2 heifers and all household stuff not bequeathed elsewhere.

To his son Richard a brass pot that goes on the fire every day; all tables and forms in testator's said place with testator's own mattress, the copyhold called Shitlyngton Bere with all appurtenances and testator's part of the farm in the parish of Mepersall; to Elizabeth Arnold daughter of testator's son Richard ten quarters of malt; to son Richard all cattle and corn not already bequeathed; to Alice Hokkill daughter of Roger Hukkill of Henlow a bullock 2 years old; to Laurence Inge (?Juge) a quarter of malt; to Margery Yong a quarter of malt.

If wife Margery be in great need or poverty then the place called Brikles Hows to be sold and wife to have half the money.

Residue to executors who are wife Margery and son Richard. Witn. Robert Bisshopp priest, John Walen, Richard Huges, Thomas Thelderhoff.

11.

Robert Cooper of Temmysford. 28 Mar. 1522/3, pr. 22 May 1523 (2: 11)

Burial in church of St. Peter of Temmysford in the middle aisle before the rood; to high altar for tithes forgotten 6s. 8d.; to mother church of Lincoln 4d.; to the upkeep of every altar in the church of Temmysford 3s. 4d.; to the bells 6s. 8d.; to the sepulchre light 6s. 8d.; two wax tapers each weighing 4 pounds to be bought after testator's death one to go before Our Lady of Pity and the other before St. Peter in the chancel, to burn every holy day at the time of divine service; to the repairs of Eynysbury church 6s. 8d.; to the church of Barkford 6s. 8d.; to the church of Sandy 3s. 4d.; to the church of Northivell 3s. 4d.; to the parish church of Bikleswade 3s. 4d.; to the brotherhood of Jesus within St. Neots 13s. 4d. if his goods produce sufficient, otherwise 6s. 8d.; to the church of Everton 3s. 4d.; towards buying a vestment, 2 tunicles, a cope and a written massbook for Temmysford church £6 13s. 4d. "so that by Writyng set uppon the vestmentes aforesayd my sowle be prayd for"; towards the "mortyfyyng" (mortmaining) of the lands belonging to the guild of St. Katerin in Temmysford if it may by licence be obtained within a year of the testator's decease 5 marks, or if this cannot be done, then the money to be used by his executors in other charitable deeds for the benefit of the said town.

To every godchild one ewe sheep; to John Abbot his servant in addition to his wages 13s. 4d.; to niece Lucy Cooper 13s. 4d. and two sheep; to Thomas Cooke his servant 2 sheep; to Elizabeth his servant 2 sheep, a quarter of wheat and a quarter of malt; to Thomas Rame his servant one ewe; to Elizabeth and Agnes his brother's daughters a quarter of barley each; to Thomas son of Robert Butler a sheep; to his wife Agnes 4 kine and their calves, 3 acres of barley, one acre of wheat, one acre of rye, 2 acres of pease, 40 sheep with all household stuff and all her yarn and £40 in ready money, to be paid within a year of testator's death.

To the house of friars in Bedford for a trental of masses 10s.; to the house of Our Lady of Grace in Cambridge for a trental 10s.; to the Augustinian Friars in Cambridge for half a trental 5s.; to the house of Our Lady Friars there for half a trental 5s..

Testator wills that wife Agnes is to have for life the house testator lately purchased of Robert Butler/Boteler in Temmysford with all lands in the fields of Temmysford and Everton (except the lands purchased from the executors of the late William Tetworth) charged with an annual obit of 13s. 4d. to be performed on the day of testator's death in Temmysford church for the souls of himself, his wife, Richard and Agnes Cooper his parents, William Cooper his brother and all Christian souls. On death of wife the property to pass to testator's cousin Robert Butler charged with keeping the same obit, and on Robert's death testator's executors and feoffees to dispose of the property still charged with maintaining the obit. The lands purchased of the executors of William Tetworth to be sold immediately after testator's death (except for one rood mentioned below) and the money to be used to carry out this testament, and the residue to find a priest to sing mass for one year in Temmysford church for the souls listed above, and all Christian souls, any surplus to be spent in charitable deeds. The one rood of land (once of William Tetworth) lies in Little North Field at Bullys Bridge next to the Common way and is to remain to the township of Temmysford "forevermore toward and for thenlargyng of the same Way for the ease of such parsons as have recourse by the same". His executors are to put on his grave a marble stone four foot broad or thereabouts with testator's epitaph engraved on a plate, the work to be completed within four months.

If Agnes his wife tries to disturb the disposal of his property through claims for dower or jointure, then she to have none of the legacies mentioned above, except at the discretion of the executors. Residue to his executors to use for his soul.

Exors. Richard Stapilho and William Butler, each to have 13s. 4d.. Witn. Edward Tetworth, Richard Parken, John Butler, John Spryng, John Angold, Henry Tyngey.

12.
Elizabeth Munke of Elnestow (Elstow). 4 June, pr. 20 June 1523. (2: 13)
Burial in churchyard of Elnestow; mortuary as custom of town; to mother church of Lincoln 2d.; to high altar of parish church of Elnestow 12d.; to the bells a quarter of barley; to the torches a quarter of barley; to the lady abbess of Elnestow and the convent 10s. to be equally divided between them.

To every godchild a bushel of malt; to John Fanne her son a couple of steers; to Johan Purvey a quarter of barley; to Elizabeth Purvey a quarter of barley; to Thomas Malen 2 bushels of barley and 2 "ew pookes" [female sheep in their second year]; to brother Robert Legatt half a quarter of malt; to John, William and Robert Fanne 5 nobles in money each; to Robert Fanne 2 quarters of malt; to John Fanne of Kempston a brass pan, a quarter of malt; to William Fanne a quarter of malt.

Residue to Edward Fanne her son to dispose of for benefit of her soul and all Christian souls.

Exors. Edward Fanne her son, William and John Fanne. Witn. sir Thomas Harwar her curate, Richard Watson, Richard Bromley, George Felpott.

13.
William Pope. 10 Sep. 1522, pr. 28 June 1523. (2: 13d)
Body to be buried in churchyard of Campton; for principal "as it shall require"; to high altar for tithes forgotten 12d.; to mother church of Lincoln 2d.; to the torches of Campton 12d.; to the bells 12d.; a taper to be kept before the crucifix for the lifetime of testator's wife.

To his daughter Elen a mattress, a coverlet, a pair of sheets, a pot and a pan, half a dozen pewter vessels, 3 dishes, 3 plates. Wife Johan to have his house for life and if necessary she can sell the said house from which the said Elynor [sic] to have 20s.. Daughter Elinor to have a cauldron after her mother's death or on day on which wife remarries.

Residue to wife Johan and William Dere, who are executors, to dispose of for health of souls. Witn. sir Oliver Ew the parson of Campton, Robert Legat, John Billcot.

14.
Thomas Tapp of Felmersham. 19 Sep., pr. 26 Sep. 1523. (2: 14)

Burial in churchyard of St. Mary of Felmersham; to mother church of Lincoln 4d.; to the high altar for tithes forgotten 2 bushels of barley; to Our Lady light in the chancel a bushel of barley; to the bells a bushel of barley; for his mortuary as is the custom of the town.

To "John' Tayllor my Dou ———" 10s.; to John his eldest son 10s.; to John his youngest son 10s.; to daughter Agnes 10s. and a bullock; to son William 20s. and a bullock.

He wills that his wife Denes is to have his house and 3 acres of arable land for her life. On her death one of his four children (whichever is worth the most) is to buy the land with the house, and the purchase money is to be divided between all the children. If any child die, then their share is to be divided between the survivors.

All other goods to wife Denes.

Exors. wife Denes and son John the youngest. Testator's ghostly father to be the supervisor. Witn. John Tapp, Richard Cosyn, John Albery, Henry Smyth.

15.
Robert Cokk, Stageden. 3 Sep., pr. 26 Sep. 1523. (2: 14d)

Burial in churchyard of St. Leonard, Stageden; mortuary his best good after custom of town; to high altar for tithes forgotten 12d.; to mother church of Lincoln 4d.; to the rood loft 5s.; to the bells 12d.; to the torches 12d.; to an honest priest to sing for testator a quarter of a year 26s. 8d.; to the highway in Church End 20d.; to the highway in the North End 20d.; testator's tenement in West End called Cokkes to be charged with the cost of a lamp before Our Lady of Pity for ever, to be lit at the beginning of the service of God and to stay alight until the service is done on festival days. Daughter Elizabeth Lambert and John Mose her son to have a dirige said yearly for souls of testator and his good friends, and to pay for the bede-roll during Elizabeth's life.

To wife Alice one ewe, a bullock, a quarter of barley, 4 sheep.

His house and appurtenances in the West End called Russell to his daughter Elizabeth Lambert, and on her death the property to go to her son John Mose and his heirs, in default to revert to whichever of the children of the said Elizabeth as she and her son John Mose think best.

Residue to John Lambert and Elizabeth his wife.

Exors. John Cownton, John Lambert. Witn. sir Robert Skynner vicar, Richard Lilliot.

16.
Robert Whitstone. 13 Oct. 1519, pr, 9 May 1520. (2: 16)

(Latin) Burial in the churchyard of the parish church of St. Monagundes of Watton (Yorkshire).

To the parish church of Watton 3s. 4d.; for masses etc. on the day of testator's burial 10s..

Daughter to have all lands which lie in the fields of Driffield except that testator's wife Alice shall have 40s. from them annually for the term of her life.

Residue to wife Alice, who is to be executrix. Witn. sir Peter Jakson, curate, William Robynson, Thomas Warpley.

17.

Roger Aleyn/Alen. 1520, pr. 6 July 1520. (2: 16d)

Burial in churchyard of St. Mary of Eton (Socon); mortuary as is customary; to high altar for tithes forgotten 12d.; to brother William Alen and to Thomas Buntyng 6 sheep to make testator's obit and to keep him on the bede-roll for 40 years.

To brother William Alen the tilth of testator's land from this time to the feast of St. Michael a twelvemonth; also 3 horses, one cart, a plough and the things pertaining to it, for four years. Then William is to give to testator's brother Thomas Alen 3 horses of the value of 16s. each, a cart of the same price, and a plough and all the things pertaining to it. Thomas is to keep them until testator's son James Alyn is 17 years of age, when they are to be given to him.

To brother William Alen 6 acres of corn (4 of the best and 2 of breach corn), 4 acres of pease and 3 acres and a rood of oats.

To brother Thomas 6 acres of barley lying in the fields of Eton and 4 acres of pease.

The two brothers are to have 4 kyne until the child is 14 years of age, and then they are to keep the cattle on behalf of the child for the next 3 years, when if the child does not want them, they are to give him 10s. a piece. Brothers William and Thomas [words omitted] to testator's son James at 17 years either of them 2 acres of barley and 2 acres of pease.

To brother John 3 sheep and to son James 4 sheep.

To Roger London testator's father-in-law a quarter of barley and if the child should die, a cow and his best brass pot.

Residue to his father and mother to pay debts and to dispose for the health of his soul.

Exors. testator's mother and his brother William. Supervisor Thomas Buntyng who is to have an acre of barley. Witn. sir William Smyth priest at Eton, Henry Parson, Thomas Parson.

Probate granted to one executor, reserving the power of the other.

18.

John Wild of Bedford St. Cuthbert. 12 Sep. 1525, pr. 10 Jan. 1527. (2: 17d)

Burial in churchyard of St. Cuthbert in Bedford; to high altar there for tithes forgotten 12d.; to mother church of Lincoln 4d.; to torches of Yelden church 3s. 4d.; to the brotherhood of Yelden church 12d..

To son Henry Wild of Yelden all testator's land in Yelden Field both meadow, pastures and closes and all appurtenances. Son Harry Wild to pay every year to testator's wife, his mother Elizabeth Wild, for the tern of her life 16s. 8d..

Residue to wife Elizabeth Wild who is executrix. Witn. sir Nicholas Dynsey parson of St. Cuthbert's of Bedford, William Norres.

19.
John Virgylet. 29 Aug., pr. 26 Nov. 1524. (2: 18)
Burial in churchyard of Eton (Socon); to high altar of Eton 12d.; to church of Lincoln 4d..

To wife Margaret his house in the Ford for her life, reversion to son Thomas and issue, in default of issue house to be sold by the vicar of Eton and one half of the money arising to go the brotherhood of Eton and the other half to a priest to pray for testator and his wives and for his son Thomas.

To son Thomas a horse, 2 steers, 8 quarters of barley (to be delivered within 2 years), a pot, a pan of six gallons, a chair, 2 sheets, an acre of pease in Lynfield, an heifer, a chaffingdish, a table at the Ford, a bedstead, 3 ewes and 3 lambs and a bell candlestick.

To "Johan" Roger a red heifer, 4 quarters of barley, a pair of sheets.

To John Roger an axe, 3 "Wybillis" [wimble = auger], 2 ewes and 2 lambs. To John White one ewe and a lamb. To William Basse his godson a bushel of barley. To Thomas Barley a bushel of barley. To Thomas Bennet one ewe and a lamb.

Remainder to his wife, who with William Rainold are executors. Witn. James Stephynson vicar of Eton, Elizabeth Johnson and others.
Probate granted to one executor, reserving the power of the other.

20.
George Gilbert of Amthull. 24 Oct., pr. 10 Dec. 1524. (2: 18d)
Burial in the church of St. Andrew in Amthull in the space before the altar of St. George; his mortuary after the custom of the country; to the mother church of Lincoln 2d.; to the high altar of Amthull church 4d.; to the gilding of a tabernacle of Our Lady 20s.; to the upkeep of the bells 20d.; to All Souls light 20d.; to the torches 12d..

To wife Ame Gilbert the tenement where testator lives with appurtenances for her life; reversion to Edward Russell son of Thomas Russell for his life. After his death tenement to go to the next child of daughter Johan Russell, Edward's mother, if she has more children, otherwise to Edward's heirs, and if Edward should die without heirs of his body, then the house to be sold and the money disposed of for the souls of testator, his wives and his friends.

Residue to Ame Gilbert his wife, who is executrix, to use for his soul. Supervisor to be son-in-law Thomas Russell. Witn. sir James Grene curate, William Hamond, Rawff Fichett.

21.
Thomas Goodwin of Woorthyng in the parish of Flitt. 4 Jan. 1526/7. pr. 10 Jan. 1527/8. (2: 19)

Burial in the churchyard of St. John the Baptist in Flitt; for mortuary as is customary; to the high altar in the same church for tithes forgotten 4d.; to the mother church of Lincoln 2d.; to the bells in the church of Flitt 3s. 4d.; to the torches 4d.. Ten loads of stones are to be laid in Grenefield Street.

To son William 5 horses and a couple of oxen, a plough and plough gear, a cart and cart gear. Wife Margery to have as much corn or cattle or household stuff as comes to half the value of the items bequeathed above to son William, according to the judgement of Thomas Spark, Richard Samwell, Robert Spark and Thomas Manne. Wife Margery to have the rent of four acres of land in Maple Furlong for the 8 years after the testator's death. Son William to give his brother John 2 quarters of barley, 2 quarters of beans and pease, and he is to receive half next Michaelmas, and the other half at Michaelmas twelvemonth. To daughter Margaret Day a quarter of wheat and a quarter of rye next Michaelmas.

The residue to be divided between wife Margery and son William by the judgement of the four men listed above. If wife Margery remarry then her legacies to be divided into two parts, one part to her, and the other part to be shared by the children she had by the testator.

Exors. son William Goodwyn and Johan Lepar, who is to have 2s.——. Overseer Robert Spark of Grenefield. Witn. Henry Richardes vicar of the same place, Thomas Spak, William Farow, Richard Day, John Mylward.

22.
John Cok the younger of Stageden. 27 June, pr. 12 July 1522. (2: 20)

Burial in churchyard of St. Leonard in the parish of Stageden; mortuary best of his goods; to the high altar for tithes forgotten 2s.; to the mother church of Lincoln 4d.; to the repair of the rood loft 40s.; to the sepulchre light 3s. 4d.; to the bells 3s. 4d.; to the torches 2s.; to Our Lady light to buy a heifer to find a trendle before the light; to an honest priest to sing a trental for me 10s.; to a priest to sing 5 masses of the Five Wounds 20d.; 12d. to buy 2 cruets; to the rood light a sheep; to the sepulchre light a sheep; to St. Margaret's light a sheep; to the bells

2 bushels of barley; to Kempston church 3s. 4d.; to Hardmede church 3s. 4d.; to sir Robert Skynner to pray for testator 6s. 8d..

To Richard, the testator's eldest son, 2 steers, 2 heifers, a horse, 6 sheep and 20s. to buy him a cart; to Stephen the second son 2 steers, 1 heifer and 6 sheep. To dau. Alice a cow, a heifer, 6 sheep; to testator's mother-in-law 3s. 4d.; to brother Robert Cok 3 sheep; to god-daughter Alys a cow calf; to every godchild 4d.; to John Gardiner his servant 20d.; to Margaret Gid—- his servant 8d..

Testator's wife Elizabeth to have half the profit of his tenement and lands called Mables lying in Wekend with testator's eldest son Richard until Richard is of full age at 21 years, when property to go to Richard. If Richard should die without issue, the tenement is to go to testator's second son Stephen, and if Stephen die without issue, then to the unborn child carried by the testator's wife, if a son, in default to be sold to the nearest kinsman at 40s. below the cost to any other person, and out of the profits wife to have 40s. and daughter Alys 40s..

Exors. John Cownton, Richard Hawxford, each to have 5s.; supervisor his father Nicholas Cok, to have 5s.; residue to wife Elizabeth. Witn. sir Robert Skynner, Nicholas Cok.

23.
Thomas Knevett, Elnestow (Elstow). 1 June, pr. 10 Oct. 1523. (2: 21)

Burial in churchyard of Elnestow; mortuary after the custom of the town; to mother church of Lincoln 4d.; to the high altar 12d.; to the bells 12d.; to the torches 12d.; to my lady abbess a quarter of barley; to the convent a quarter of barley. A half acre of land in Long Peslyngton furlong is to ensure that testator will be prayed for perpetually in the bede-roll, and after the death of his wife the churchwardens are to have the oversight and rule of the half acre; his wife to find a taper to burn before Our Lady in service time on holydays for a year after testator's death, also a priest to sing for him for a quarter of a year, and five masses are to be sung at his burial.

To cousin Margaret Knevett a kettle, a brass pot and a platter; to Robert Mason half an acre of land in Pek Meadow Hole.

His wife Agnes to have the place where testator dwells with all lands, meadows and pastures in Elnestow or elsewhere for her life, then it is to be divided equally between the testator's two daughters Margaret Knevett and Johan, each of them to pay the convent of Elnestow 20s., and if one of them die then the survivor to have the whole and pay to the convent 20s., and if both die the churchwardens of Elnestow with the advice of 5 or 6 of the best of the parish are to sell the place and the land, and of the money arising 40s. is to go to the convent of Elnestow for prayers for the testator, and the remainder to be expended for the souls of the testator and his friends, part for a priest to sing mass, part for the upkeep of the highways, and part to the church for whatever is most necessary and should bring most comfort to his soul.

Residue to wife for life, then to his two daughters.

Exors. wife Agnes, Master Jurdan, Thomas Pike, each to have 20d. for their labour. Witn. sir Thomas Harwar, William Maryson, Richard Noresse.

Probate granted to wife, the other two declining executorship.

24.

William Hopkynson of Chixsand (Chicksands). 10 Sep., pr. 24 Oct. 1523. (2: 21d)

Burial in churchyard of monastery of Chixsand; for principal as customary; to high altar in Chixsand for tithes forgotten 2d.; to mother church of Lincoln 4d.; to every canon being a priest at Chixsand 4d..

To son Richard a gown; to Margaret [?]Gwylbon a jacket.

Residue to wife Agnes, sole executrix. Witn. Dane [Dom] Peter Husband curate, Jamys Done, William Broughton.

25.

Thomas Blith of Keysho. 4 Oct., pr. 24 Oct. 1523. (2: 22)

Burial in churchyard of Our Blessed Lady in Kayshoo; mortuary as custom of town; to mother church of Lincoln 6d.; to the high altar for tithes forgotten 12d.; to church of Keyshoo 40s. towards the building of St. Thomas' chapel; and if the chapel is not built the money is to be disposed of within the church as the parish sees fit; a trental to be said in Kayshoo church.

Testator's wife Margery Blith to have her house and the land that lies to the said house and all her household stuff as she brought to him; to wife 3 kine and 12 sheep; testator's son-in–law Henry Halle to have any goods remaining.

Exors. Harry Hall and Thomas Slade, who are to dispose of residue for souls of testator and all Christians and to have 3s. 4d. each. Overseer wife's brother John Hayne, who is to have 3s. 4d.. Witn. sir William Boydon vicar of the town, Gregory Day, William Jenkyn, Thomas Cranfeld, Nicholas Peck.

26.

Henry Abbot of Husbourne Crawley. 4 Nov. 1511, pr. 14 May 1522. (2: 23)

Burial in churchyard of St. Mary of Husborne Crawley; for principal as is customary; to high altar for tithes forgotten ½ lb. wax; to cathedral church of Lincoln 2d.; ½ lb. wax each to the light in the Lady chapel in the same church, the rood light, the lights of St. Nicholas and St. Katerin; to the upkeep of the bells 8d.; to the upkeep of the torches

4d.; to maintaining Our Lady light in the parish of Aspley Gise a rood of arable in that parish lying next to the Town Close or Pightle of Aspley on the west side; five masses to be said on day of burial for the health of testator's soul, namely of the Five Wounds of Our Lord Jesus Christ, of the Assumption of Our Lady, of the Holy Ghost, of the Trinity, of All Hallows, and each priest to have 4d..

To daughter Elizabeth the best pot and the best pan; to wife Agnes all lands in the parishes of Birchmore and Husbourne Crawley for her life, and then to whichever of his two sons his wife shall choose, either John or Nicholas, and the one taking the land to give his brother 20s..

Residue to his wife Agnes and his two sons who are to be executors, to be disposed of for the health of the souls of the testator, his friends and all Christians. Overseer brother-in-law Henry Carter, to have 12d.. Witn. John Carter, John Potter, Henry Draper.

27.
Robert Heythorn of Pulloxhill. 17 Oct. 1523, pr. 3 Sep. 1524.

Body to be buried "ther as it please God"; to high altar 8d.; to Pulloxhill church a torch; to the mother church of Lincoln 2d.; to Pulloxhill church a quarter of barley.

To son-in-law Thomas Franklin who is an apprentice in London a pan which the testator bought; his wife Elyn is to have his housing with all appurtenances in Pullokhill for her life, if she remains single, otherwise the property is to go to Marion "my suster doughter dwellyng in London shalhave that I dwell in"; to Henry his sister's son a sheep; to Henry his sister's son's son a sheep; to John Day his sister's son a cow.

Exors. wife Elyn and William Johnson, the latter to have 3s. 4d.. Residue to wife. Witn. the curate of the same town, William Smyth.

28.
William Stanton of Southivell. 16 Aug., pr. 17 Sept. 1524. (2: 24d)
Testament Burial in church yard of Southivell on the north side within the foundations of the aisle already begun, to which 6s. 8d. (if the aisle be made), otherwise this money to go wherever the church has most need; to the high altar of the church one strike of barley; to Our Lady of Lincoln 2d.; to brother Thomas a russet coat; to cousin John Stanton a russet coat; residue to wife Agnes and to John Stanton who are to be executors to dispose of for his soul. Witn. sir Richard [Smyth del.] Church, vicar, John Stanton jun., Sawnder Witticar.
Will Wife to have testator's house for life, reversion to John Stanton his executor and his issue, in default of such issue, the vicar and church-wardens of the town shall sell it and expend the money for the souls of testator "and of them it cam of".

To Sawnder Witticar and his issue the house at the gate, he giving to testator's wife for her life 16d. a year, and in default of issue, the house to be sold as above. Sawnder to have his Ingate and Outgate when he comes to the house, and "a garden plott bytwene my hall and the way as it is closyd and the space bytwene my chamber corner and the yate howse".

Probate granted to John Stanton, reserving right of Agnes.

29.
John Marton of Beston (Beeston). 19 July, pr. 20 Sep. 1524. (2: 25)
Body to be buried in churchyard of St. Swythyn of Sandy; mortuary his best beast according to custom; to the high altar of Sandy for tithes forgotten 2 bushels of barley or else the value in money; to the bells of Sandy 4d.; to the mother church of Lincoln 4d.; a priest is to sing a trental in the church of Sandy for souls of testator and his friends for 10s..

His wife Agnes to have the same goods as she brought hither or else others as good; to wife an acre of barley and half an acre of wheat with "a lond of ry more than a roode"; to wife the messuage once Thomas Carter's for her life, also 2 hogs and a pig and a half acre of pease, a cow and a bullock, all testator's hemp and flax, also 6 sheep as a gift as well as those she brought.

Alys Manley/Mauley, testator's daughter, and her children after her to have the messuage and 3 acres of land once Thomas Carter's, also 6 acres of land belonging to the said messuage charged with the payment to each of testator's two sons Thomas and Robert 33s. 4d.. Thomas is to have his payment within 2 years after testator's death, but Robert's share is to be given within the same 2 years to Robert Wadnoo to keep until Robert is 21 years of age. Should either son die before marriage, the other to have his legacy, and if both die before marriage, then the money to go to a priest to sing for testator and his friends in Sandy church.

Should daughter Alys Marten [sic] die without issue then the messuage and 9 acres of land sometimes Carters to be sold and the money expended for testator's soul in the parish church of Sandy. Daughter Alys or her husband to have £3 6s. 8d. allowed them which they paid to testator's sons Thomas and Robert.

Daughter Alys to pay for repairs of the messuage that testator's wife shall live in; the two sons to have all household goods both indoors and outdoors (except the share of wife) and he who has the best pot to have the worse pan, and he who has the worst pot to have the best pan.

Wife and son Thomas to have testator's tilth for 4 years or longer if they can agree; to son Thomas 2 acres of the best barley; Roger Wadnoo to have son Robert with his part of testator's goods as long as they can agree; to each godchild a bushel of barley; to Edmond

Valentyne a dun horse; to Agnes Spark a rood of barley and an ewe; to Richard Wilson a bacon hog; to Margery Fisshir a bacon hog with two bushel of pease; to Katerin Tabi an ewe; to Mylysent Tibi a lamb; residue between his two sons when they come of age.

Exors. Richard Manley and William Allen to whom 3s. 4d. each. Witn. master Burgayne clerk, John Philipp, John Bromsall senior.

30.
Edward Dermer of Cadyngton. 12 Dec. 1518, pr. 12 Jan. 1518/9. (2: 26)
   Burial in the parish church of Cadyngton; to mother church of Lincoln 4d.; to the high altar for tithes forgotten 6s. 8d.; to the rood light 12d.; to Our Lady light 12d.; to the other lights a pound of wax; to the torches 3s. 4d.; to the bells 3s. 4d.; to an honest priest to sing for testator's soul for a quarter of a year in Cadyngton church "to mayng-tayne goddes servis in the quier" 30s.; to the brotherhood of Luton 6s. 8d.; to the upkeep of Luton church 6s. 8d.; to the upkeep of Cadyngton church 3s. 4d.; for the upkeep of the highway from the Prebendar Lane to the Groove 5s..
   To every daughter I have one ewe 6s. 8d.; to Edward Darmer, Herry Davys' son-in-law, a shod cart; to John Dermer 6s. 8d..
   Testator's wife Elizabeth is to have a stone put over his body price 4 marks; wife is to have house where testator lives and land with appur-tenances, charged with 5 marks to be spent for his soul in the parish church of Cadyngton, that is to say every month after his death a *dirige* with priests and clerks costing 3s. 4d. until the 5 marks used up. Once this is done, his feoffees to deliver an estate in the house and lands for ever to wife Elizabeth. Wife to keep his burial day, month day, and year day.
   Residue to wife Elizabeth, executrix; supervisors William Thrall and Herry Dane, to each of whom 6s. 8d.. Witn. sir Thomas Elstone vicar, William Wolle clerk, Edward Darmer.

31.
Johan Butler widow of Temmysford. 23 Apr., pr. 26 Aug. 1525. (2: 28)
   To be buried in the church yard of St. Peter in Temysford; mortuary the best of her goods as customary; to mother church of Lincoln 2d.; to the high altar of Temmysford 8d.; to the Trinity altar 4d.; to St. Katerin's altar 4d.; to the sepulchre light 12d.; to the upkeep of the bells 8d.; to the friars of Bedford for a trental of masses for the souls of tes-tator and her husband Thomas Butler 10s..
   Son William Butler to have the messuage testator dwells in called Lombardes Place with all appurtenances in Temyford, 2 acres arable and 2 acres 1 rood of meadow in Temmysford, charged with keeping an obit for testator costing 3s. 4d. in Temmysford church on the Friday in

Whitson week for the souls of sir Thomas Bull clerk, William Bull junior, the testator and all Christians for ever.

John Butler testator's other son to have her crop lying at the south end of Temmysford, an acre and a rood of arable land and an acre of meadow with appurtenances of which one half acre is against Blownham Brige, a rood lies under Pease furlong, a half acre on Little Marsh and the acre of meadow lies in West Mede, charged with 12d. a year for an obit in the church of Temmysford, on the same Friday, for the souls of Thomas Butler and his wife Johan, John's father and mother, for ever.

Residue to son William. Exors. sons William and John, each to have 3s. 4d.. Witn. sir Richard the parish priest, Richard Staploo, John Malyn.

32.
James Greneleff made 27 July, pr. 2 Aug. 1525 (2: 29)

Burial in churchyard of Eton (Socon); to church of Lincoln 4d.; to high altar of Eton 16d.; to Eton church 3s. 4d.; for a priest to sing a trental for souls of testator, his father and mother 10s..

To wife Johan testator's house with appurtenances and his land in the fields for her life, then to his son Nicholas and the heirs of his body, in default to son William and the heirs of his body, on condition that whoever has his house shall keep an obit for the souls of testator, his "wivis" and his father and mother.

To son William 3 acres of barley, a young bullock, 2 ewes, 2 candlesticks, a brass pot, a red pan, a little pan with 2 ears, a frying pan, a great spit, a coffer, a red coverlet, a table cloth, a towel, 2 pillows, 2 pillowberes, a mattress, a pair of sheets, a basin of latten, 2 forms, 2 trestles, a "bofet" stool and a table.

Residue to wife Johan and son Nicholas. Exors. wife and son Nicholas. Witn. James Stephynson vicar of Eton, Richard Greneleff.

33.
Richard Toky of Harlyngton. 22 Dec. 1526, pr. 15 Jan. 1526/7. (2: 30)

Burial in churchyard of Harlyngton; mortuary as custom requires; to mother church of Lincoln 2d.; to high altar of Harlyngton 2s..

To son John Toky testator's house in Woodend with close and all appurtenances, charged with the payment to his brother William Tokey of £12 at the rate of 40s. on the feast of the Annunciation for each of the 6 years after the testator's death.

To son William Tokey a close called Gardrokes alias Bauntes with all appurtenances. "Item I will commaund the sayd William Tokey uppon my blessyng" never to sell the close except to his brother John Tokey. Also to William Toke a mattress, a pair of sheets, a pair of blankets, a coverlet, the best brass pot "save oon" and 2 pewter plates.

Residue to wife Elizabeth. The remnant of all other goods to son John Toky to dispose of for testator's soul. Made at Harlyngton.

Exor. son John Toky. Witn. sir Thomas Jamys vicar, William Mathew, John Tokey.

34.

Thomas Stephyns of Luton. 4 Jan., pr. 10 Feb. 1527/8. (2: 30d)

Burial in church of Our Lady in Luton; for his mortuary the best of his goods according to the custom of the lordship; to the high altar for tithes forgotten 20d.; to mother church of Lincoln 8d.; toward the renewing of the light before the rood in the middle of the church 4d.; to Our Lady in the chancel 4d.; to the maintenance of the lights before every saint in Luton church "that continually have light yerely renuyd afore them by old custome every light 2d.". For an honest priest to sing for testator and his good friends in Luton church for half a year under the oversight of master the vicar of Luton, £3. Towards mending of the highway at Norrebrigg 13s. 4d.. His executors to keep his obit with the whole quire for 10 years in Luton church.

To wife Johan £10 and her chamber "hole with all howshold stuff to bryng upp my children". To eldest son Thomas "he to sow my somer cropp and to have halff my cropp of almaner Graynys with my wiff and at Ester to have all my horsys with that longith to my husbondry, my best gowne and my best Jakit". To daughter Johan a bed, 3 pair of sheets, a brass pot, a pan, a kettle and 6 pewter vessels. To each of his other children 4 marks of lawful money, and wife to reward them at the oversight of his executors.

Residue to wife Johan and children, who with his executors are to expend it on "dedes and warkes of mercy and pite" for the health of the souls of testator and his friends and all Christians.

If a child should die before marriage, then their share of goods to be divided between the others.

Testator revokes all previous wills or testaments.

Exors. William Welsh, Edward Hill of Luton, and each to have 10s. and expenses. Witn. Thomas Petide, John Stephyns, Thomas Toolee, sir William curate of Luton. Written at Luton.

35.

Margaret Coore of Potton, widow. 14 May, pr. 9 Aug. 1527. (2: 32)

Testament Burial in the churchyard of Potton; to high altar 20d.; to sepulchre light 8d.; to bells 8d.; to the torches 8d..

To daughter Elysabeth all manner of implements "to my bakhows and bruhowse" and the best brass pot of three; the best featherbed with the appurtenances; the best beads; testator's best girdle, "and after the departyng of Elizabeth to Johan Crosse".

To son William Crosse best mattress, 2 pair of sheets, one coverlet, one pair of blankets, 2 pewter platters, 2 pewter dishes, one brass pot, 2 candlesticks, one latten basin. To cousin Simond Mathew priest and scholar of Cambridge the second featherbed with the bolster belonging to the same, a pillow and a pair of sheets. To Johan Crosse the daughter of William Crosse 26s. 8d. sterling, and if she die before marriage and Elizabeth is still living, then the gift is void.

Will Daughter Elizabeth to have for her lifetime the messuage where testator lives on condition that she keeps testator's obit in the parish church of Potton. Should Elizabeth ever be in need, she may sell the messuage, but this must still be charged with an annual payment of 6s. 8d. for testator's obit.

Residue to daughter Elizabeth, sole executrix. Supervisor Stephen Butler. Witn. sir William Atkynson, sir Robert Carter, Richard Fisher.

36.
Walter Butler parishioner and inhabitant of Blownham (Blunham). 12 Dec. 1521, pr. 5 July 1522. (2: 33)

Burial in churchyard of Blownham; for his mortuary his best beast; to high altar 2s. 8d.; to the brotherhood of Blownham half an acre of land in the North Field of Blownham on a furlong called Foracre, which son William is to hold for his lifetime paying yearly to the "tuters" 4d.; to the bells 12d.; to torches when they are new made 8d.; to the upkeep of the torches 6d.; for half a trental to be sung for testator in the parish church of Blownham by a secular priest not being in service, 5s..

To son John 46s. 8d. to be paid after his apprenticeship is finished.

To son William the house lived in by the testator with all buildings, lands and meadows. If he die without male issue then the house and land to go to son John and his heirs male. If John has no male issue then to go to Walter Butler testator's godson, for ever "to remayn to the next mankyng of the name of the said stok".

To Margaret Butler when she marries his greatest brass pot save one, a pan, a salt, a candlestick, a saucer, 4 pewter dishes, a pair of sheets, a coffer, and also 4 quarters of barley. To her also an acre of land for the term of her life, reversion to "my hows", and if the land is let, then to be let to William, testator's son.

To Elizabeth Butler on marriage 20s..

Residue to son William and to Walter Butler, his executors, to be disposed of for testator's soul. Witn. sir William Bell, Richard Toller.

37.
John Day, Suldropp (Souldrop). 13 Feb., pr. 25 Feb. 1524/5. (2: 34d)

"Beyng seke in bodie dredyng the parell of death to fall unto me" leaves his body for burial in the church of All Hallows in Suldropp for which he gives the church 6s. 8d.; for mortuary as customary; to high altar for tithes forgotten 12d.; to sepulchre light 12d.; to the bells 12d.; to the mother church of Lincoln 4d.; to the prior and convent of Newenham to pray for testator and his father and mother 6s. 8d..

To sister Elizabeth Rawlyns 6s. 8d.; to Lucy Day daughter of Robert Dey 6s. 8d.; to Elyzabeth and Elyn Dey daughters of Robert Dey 6s. 8d. between them.

To wife Elyn all lands and tenements, meadows and pastures with their appurtenances in the parishes of Suldropp, Sharnebrok and Knottyng for her life, and on her death the property to be divided equally between all his children then living. If none survive her, then the property to be sold and the money used for the souls of the testator, his father and mother and all Christians. He has made William Cobbe of Scharnebrok his feoffee to hold his property to the uses of his will.

Residue to wife Elyn.

Exors. wife Elyn and Thomas Sawnson of Scharnebrok, each to have 6s. 8d.. Witn. Thomas Youngham, John Ry —-, Richard Yong.

38.
John Ibatt. 18 Oct., pr. 19 Nov. 1524. (2: 35)

Burial in churchyard of St. Peter in Pertenhall; his mortuary after the custom of the town; to high altar for tithes forgotten 12d.; to mother church of Lincoln 6d.; to the sepulchre light 12d.; to the torches 12d.; to the bells 12d..

To his wife Alys Ibatt his house and the land belonging to it in Pertenhall for life, reversion to son Thomas Ibat, except for three half acres which are to go to son William, unless William would prefer a money payment of 20s.. To William also 40s. more from house and land that wife Alis has in Pertenhall, and also 6 beasts or bullocks, 6 quarters of barley or malt, 12 sheep and a sorrel colt. To son Bartilmew a house and three acres of land in Much Stockton (Great Staughton, Hunts.), and if Barthilmew should die before his marriage, then the property to be divided between testator's other children. To Bartilmew also 6 beasts or bullocks, 6 quarters of barley or malt, 12 sheep and a bay colt.

To Thomas Ibatt half the goods left when testator's debts and funeral expenses are paid, and the other half of his goods to go to his wife Alys, the division to be done "by the mynd of honest men".

Residue of goods to executors, wife and Geffray Myriell who is to have 6s. 8d., to dispose of for the health of the souls of the testator and of all Christians. Witn. William Sheppard, John Chandeler, John Peck and John Shepard.

Probate granted to Geoffrey Myryell, reserving powers of Agnes the widow.

39.
Thomas Rachell, Bromham. 13 Nov. 1525 No note of probate. (2: 35d)
Burial in churchyard of Bromham; to high altar for tithes forgotten 12d..

To wife Elyn his house and lands for the term of her life, reversion to son Thomas and his issue, in default of issue the property to be sold and half of the money be given to the church of Bromham where most need is in the opinion of his executors.

Exors. wife Elyn and son Thomas; supervisor Thomas Cownton. Witn. sir John Patenson vicar, Thomas Bay, John Margettes.

40.
William Mortymer. 22 Aug. 1525. No note of probate. (2: 36)
Burial in churchyard of St. Peter of Holwell; to church of Lincoln 8d.; to the high altar of Holwell 20d.; to the high altar of Ikilford 8d.. *[unfinished]*

41.
Agnes Butt of Elnestow. 11 Oct., pr. 17 Dec. 1524. (2: 37)
Burial "in the Conventuall church of Elnestow in the yle before our lady chapell dore evynly by the Wall if I fortune to depart at Elnestow"; mortuary as is customary; to cathedral church of Lincoln 6d.; to every lady and priest at her burial 4d. and to the clerks at the discretion of her executors.

Her executors are to have the house testator bought in Hichyn for 12 years after her death paying to testator's daughters, Dame Ellyn and Dame Elizabeth (now nuns in Elnestow) 13s. 4d. every year for the 12 years, and the executors are to keep her obit in Elnestow among the convent and priests for the said 12 years to pray for the soul of the testator, her husband, her father and mother, all her benefactors and all Christians. With the residue the executors are to pay the chief rent and repairs of the house so as to keep it as they found it "by the sight of their neighbours". After the 12 years the house is to pass to William Butt and the heirs of his body, but he may not sell it, as appears by indentures between the feoffees and the abbess of Elnestow and the prior of Chicheson. Should William die without heirs of his body then the house to be sold by the advice of her executors and of the lady abbess of Elnestow and the prior of Chicheson, and of the money arising half is to go to the upkeep of the monastery of Elnestow, and half to the nuns and prior of Chichson, both houses to pay 4 marks to the repairs of the church of Hychyn.

To son William Butt and his wife and the heirs of his body a close called Welgos Croft and also two acres of arable with their pightles, which the testator bought of John Hymyngton when she was a widow.

William Butt her son shall buy such lands and tenements as she holds as executor of John Willisbe (paying £5 for it) to hold to his wife Katerine and his heirs. If William die without heirs the land to be sold and used for the soul of the testator.

Executors are to pay £12 for the upkeep and ornaments of Amthull church. The churchwardens of Amthull are to enter on the meadow "plek" called Byhoyme in Grenefeld in the parish of Flitton between the lands of the prior of Dunstable on one side the common of Flittwik on the other, and the said churchwardens are to keep an obit for ever in the parish of Amthull for the souls of John Willisbe, John Snow, Walter Butt and Agnes, and for the souls of their wives and parents and all Christians, as appears in a deed indented between them and the convent of Elnestow. The obit is to be kept by three priests and every priest to have 4d., and the clerks of the church 2d. each, and the four children that read the lections 4d. and to the bederoll to keep there the names listed above 4d. every year. Also to the bells 4d. every year, and the churchwardens are to have 4d. each for their labour. The residue is to be bestowed in bread and ale in the parish church to the people who pray for the souls of John Willisbe and his benefactors.

To Alys the daughter of William Butt a pair of beads of coral with double "gawdies" weighing 2 ounces and more; a mazer with the knop weighing 8 ounces; 4 silver spoons weighing 4 and a quarter ounces which are marked with a cross on the back; a table cloth of diaper; a double towel of diaper; a plain table cloth and a plain towel and 6 napkins of diaper; 2 pair flaxen sheets; a pair of hempen sheets; 2 pillows that are marked; a latten bason and an ewer; 2 bell candlesticks "booth of oon sort"; "the chest that standith in my hall to put the stuff in to kepe untill she cum to xv yere of age". If she die without heirs of her body, the goods are to revert to the heirs of William Butt, and if she be a "relygowse woman to have the stuff to her promocion".

To Katerine wife of William Butt testator's "kerchiff coffer with halff my kerchiffis halff my rayllys and half my smokkes". She to have also a blue kirtle and testator's best gown, the coffer her rails lie in and her ivory beads.

To Dame Elyn and Dame Elizabeth Snow nuns in Elnestow Abbey the other half of her kerchieves, rails and smocks, and to each of them 2 silver spoons. To Dame Elyn a silver pot and to Dame Elizabeth a piece of silver.

To Johan Raynold testator's father's servant, an old kirtle and an old gown and a smock.

To William Butt a silver salt with a cover weighing 14 ounces.

To the high altar of the conventual church of Elnestow £10 "the which shall cum of a statute of Thomas Parissh to by an aulter cloth with 2 curtens to be on high on the aulter". ['Statute' = statute staple or bond]

The residue resting in her chamber to be divided between Dame Elen and Dame Elizabeth Snow and William Butt her son.

William Butt to have her featherbed and bolster, and to bring the lesser featherbed and bolster that he had of testator to Dame Elyn and Dame Elizabeth.

To Friar William Bell a student at Oxford £3 6s. 8d. to pray for testator and her benefactors for 2 years; to friars of Bedford 6s. 8d.; to friars of Dunstable 3s. 4d..

Her executors to have the lease in Houghton which she has of the prior of Chicheson for two years and a half, to help pay for her legacies to Ampthill church, felling no timber, and property then to revert to son William Butt.

Master Gascoyn to be overseer and to have 40s.; executors sir Henry Richardson vicar of Flitton and Robert Stukeley, to each 40s.. Witn. sir John Kyng parish priest, master Edward Walton.

Probate: the named executors refused to act, and administration granted to William Butt.

42.
sir William Howson, vicar of Litlyngton. 18 May, pr. 4 July 1517. (2: 39)

Burial in the chancel of Litlyngton; to the high altar two tapers of one lb. each; to painting the image of All Hallows and of Our Lady 40s.; to the All Hallows light 3s. 4d.; to Our Lady light in the chancel 20d.; to the light of Our Lady of Pity 20d.; to the rood light 3s. 4d.; to the sepulchre light 10 lb. of wax and to the lights before the other saints in the church 5 lb. of wax; to the bells 3s. 4d.; to the repair of the highways in Lytillyngton 20s.; to the monastery of Barkyng 4 marks "to have ther prayers"; to the Friars Minor of Bedford 20s. for two trentals for the souls of testator and of all Christians; to the friars of Dunstable 5s. to sing half a trental; to the friars of Hychyn 5s. to sing half a trental; to Agnes Houghson 10s.; to Johan Seton 6s. 8d.; to Anne Hewson 6s. 8d.; to each of testator's god-children 20d.; to Gret Geddyng church 20s.; to the torch lights in Litillyngton 3s. 4d.; to the mother church of Lincoln 12d..

To Thomas Houghson and Robert Capon, to be equally divided between them "such thynges as partayne to my kychyn as bras, pewter, laten and such other"; to Robert Capon the bed he lies on, that is to say a mattress with a bolster, a pair of sheets, a pair of blankets, a coverlet and a coffer "that his gere lyeth in", 13s. 4d; to Thomas Kely/Kelly a mattress with a bolster, a pair of sheets, a pair of blankets, a coverlet with the hanging that belongs to it, a quarter of malt, testator's worst gown, and 13s. 4d.; to Margaret Howson testator's featherbed, a pair of sheets, a bolster, a pair of blankets, a coverlet with the hangings; to Margaret Middelton his second long gown; to John Jelian the best short gown and a pair of sheets; to John Houghson 2 pair of sheets and a gown; to Johan Yelyan 6 couples of ewes and lambs, a weaned calf; to William Heuson 6s. 8d.; to my sister Johan his wife 6s. 8d.; to Margaret Ostok 6s. 8d.; to sister Joan Heuson the second short gown; to Robert Howson 2 couples of ewes and lambs.

To William Houghson son of Robert Houghson and his heirs and assigns for ever, testator's houses and lands with appurtenances in Mych Gyddyng in Huntingdonshire, and testator's feoffees are to deliver an estate in them when asked; to master William Hyghwey 3s. 4d.; "to Sir Peter, Mayster Dicons prest" 3s. 4d.; to sir John Newton 3s. 4d.; to William Houghson of Whitilsey 6s. 8d.; to Thomas Houghson his son 3s. 4d.; to the "childerne of my good Master Dicons" 3s. 4d. and "my Master servaunts" 3s. 4d. "for a poore remembrannce".

Residue "to poore prestes that is to say oon at much Geddyng an other at Litillyngton as the money may Stretch with other good Deedes after the discrecion of myn executors".

Exors.: Thomas Jelyan, John Middilton, and each to have 10s.; overseer William Houghson. Witn. William Heynson, John Bedcok, John Alen, John Sutton, John Clerk, Richard Franklyn, Rawff Smyth.

43.
John Skevyngton of Turvey. 12 Mar. 1522/3, pr. 17 Sep. 1523. (2: 41)
Burial in churchyard of Turvey; for mortuary as customary; to mother church of Lincoln 4d.; to the high altar of Turvey 12d.; to Our Lady light there 12d.; to the torches 22d.; to the bells 20d.; to the sepulchre light 12d.; to Turvey bridge 12d..

To John Rainold his servant 6s. 8d. and a cow; to Elizabeth Long his servant 10s. and a bullock; to Margaret Stephynson his servant a quarter of malt.

To Johan his wife for her life, and then to his executors, the house in the town and the lands which the testator bought from William Stephynson, which is to be made his obit house for ever, paying 6s. on his obit day for prayers for his soul and all Christian souls, with the rest of the rent to be used to keep the house in good repair. After his wife's death his executors are to give any surplus from the rent to Turvey church. After the death of his executors, the church wardens of Turvey "shalhave the order and gydyng of the foresayd obit and the hows landes and appurtenances"; a trental of masses to be sung at his month day; to sir Thomas Botolff parish priest of Turvey 20d..

To William Skevyngton a horse and a shod cart, and the residue to testator's wife Johan.

Exors. William Skevyngton and John Bychener, to have 20d. each; supervisor John Stephynson, to have 2s.. Witn. sir Thomas Botolff, John Chaundeler.

44.
William Wolmer the elder of Elnestow. 20 Apr., pr. 3 May 1526. (2: 42)
Burial in churchyard of Elnestow; his mortuary as is customary; to the mother church of Lincoln 2d.; to the high altar 4d.; to the bells 20d.; to the torches 20d.; to a lawful priest to sing in Elnestow church for souls of testator, his friends and all Christians 8 marks 3s. 4d.; to the ladies of Elnestow 8s..

To Alys Wolmer testator's wife for her life, testator's house with appurtenances, then to son John Wolmer, on condition that the son does not sell it but keeps it in repair, otherwise the "feoffees and rulys" of the house are to have it in their hands until it is repaired. Residue to wife Alys Wolmer.

Exors. John Wolmer (to whom 3s. 4d.); William Barford (3s. 4d.); supervisor sir Richard White (3s. 4d.). Witn. sir John Kyng, parish priest; Henry Markyat, William Jurden.

45.
Kateryn Bilcok of Houghton Conquest. 13 Apr., pr. 15 May 1518. (2: 43)
To be buried in churchyard of Houghton Conquest. "To the parson Franceys my best good for my mortuary as the custum of the cuntre is"; to the church of Lincoln 2d.; to the altar in Houghton 4d..

To Johan Hillis her daughter her house in Houghton Conquest, to keep an obit yearly for evermore for testator and her husband and all her good friends "unto the sum of 2s."; to wife of Thomas Barns a little brass pot; to god-daughter Christian Bilcok a shirt and a pewter dish.

To daughter Johan Hillis, executrix, the residue to dispose of her goods for souls of testator and all Christians. Witn. John Kychyn curate, Richard Bilcok, John Wheler.

46.
Richard Bechnar of Wotton. 22 May, pr. 29 May 1518. (2: 43d)
Burial in churchyard of Wotton; for mortuary best beast after custom of town; to high altar 6d.; to mother church of Lincoln 2d.; to the sepulchre light a bushel of barley; to the torches a bushel of barley; to the bells a bushel of barley.

To daughter Elizabeth after death of wife the 2 best candlesticks. To wife Mawde for life, the house in the Church End, then to son William Bechnar and his heirs, he paying to daughters Christian and Elizabeth 6s. 8d. each, and if William should die without heirs, then the house is to go to the two daughters equally between them.

Residue to wife Mawde who is executrix, to dispose of for good of souls of testator and all Christians. Witn. sir Thomas Harwar my curate, Thomas Writt, Thomas Nightyngale, Richard Standbrige.

47.
William Percell/Parcell of Thornecott in parish of Northivell. 13 Apr., pr. 29 May 1518. (2: 44)

Burial in churchyard of Our Lady of Northivell; for principal after custom of parish; to high altar 16d.; to the bells 12d.; to the torches a quarter of malt; to St. Annys chapel over the church door 20d.; to the friars of Bedford 2s.; to the friars of Hychyn 2s.; to the parish priest 12d.; to the parish clerk 2d..

To son Robert Parcell and to his heirs and assigns for ever, "my place in Thornecott that I dwell in" with lands, pastures and meadows "so that Johan Percell my wiff shall have my over Chamber her liff if she kepe her sole, and met and drynk and rayment of the forsayd Robert Parcell". To Robert Parcell also, until his son John Parcell is 22 years old, a messuage with an acre of land that once belonged to Harry Cokkes, when property to go to John and his heirs, and if he die without issue, to the next of the kindred of name of Percellis. Robert Percell is to fell no timber except "it be to bild uppon the same messuage". If John die before the age of 22, property to go to Robert, and if Robert die without issue, to go to the next heir of the name of Parcellis "and for lak of the name to the next of the blood or kynred".

Exor. son Robert Parcell, to whom the residue. Written by sir John Lyn, parish priest. Witn. Richard Pech', John Hawkyn.

48.
Simon Cawnell of Willishamsted. Translation of St. Richard the Confessor, 16 June, pr. 26 June 1518. (2: 45d)

Burial in the churchyard of All Hallows of Willishamsted; for mortuary "that is lawful to be had"; to the high altar 20d.; to Our Lady light 12d.; to the torches 12d.; to a new bell 3s..

Residue to wife Agnes and daughter Alys "to be parted in even porcions as conscience will require".

Exors. son John Cawnell and wife Agnes. Witn. sir Richard Purcer vicar of the same town, Nicholas Mylward, William Hebbys.

49.
Nicholas Wolhed/Wolleyd of Wotton. 9 Apr. 1517, pr. 15 May 1518. (2: 46)

Burial in churchyard of Wotton; for mortuary "best beast as custume and maner is"; to the high altar 2 bushels of malt; to mother church of

Lincoln 2d.; to the sepulchre light a bushel of malt; to Our Lady of Pity a bushel of malt; to All Hallows light a bushel of barley; to the torches 2 bushels of barley; to the bells 2 bushels of barley; to Wilkyn Burge a bushel of barley; to every godchild 4d.; to Wolled my brother 20d.; to William Witt 20d..

To wife Alys for life then to William Wolhed his son for life, testator's place, lands, meadows and pastures in the parish of Wotton. On the death of son William property to go to Harry Browne and Agnes his wife, and after their death to their heirs, making no waste and keeping the property as they found it, and if they die without issue, the feoffees are to sell the property and use one part of the money to hire a priest to sing for testator and his friends in the parish church of Wotton, and the other part "to be done in othere good dedes as it shalbe most nedefull to the church and to the towne and to high wayys".

Residue to wife Alys.

Exors. wife Alys, brother William Wolled, William Witt. Witn. sir Thomas Haywar curate, Thomas Adame, John Wolhed, John Barton junior.

50.

William Wyngat' of Sharpenow in the parish of Stretley. 11 July, pr. 8 Aug. 1522. (2: 47)

To be buried in the church "of Our Lady of Stretley afor the aulter of Saint Katerin ther"; to vicar for tithes forgotten 12d.; "to the lights of the torches" 3s. 4d.; to buy an antiphoner for the church 40s..

To Robert Wyngat testator's messuage in Stretley called Myddilstretes and Lygravis with all lands and appurtenances, paying for it £5 to John Wyngate testator's younger son.

Residue to son Robert Wyngat to dispose of for soul of testator.

Exor. Robert Wyngat. Witn. sir John Peck vicar of Stretley, John Norton, John Baker, William Norton, William Saltwell.

51.

Richard Fissher of Stephynton. 22 Apr., pr. 12 May 1522. (2: 48)

Burial in churchyard of Our Lady in Stephynton; to vicar for principal as custom of town. All his moveable goods are to be used to find a priest to sing for souls of testator and of all Christians as far as it will go.

His will concerning his "unmovable goods the which I have in the parisshe of Stephynton" that is a cottage with three roods of pasture; a close called Westcroft containing 2½ acres with hedge and ditch at the "hever hede"; 6 roods of arable which abutts on Shortcroft Grene; one acre lying by Cokkes lane; these to be charged with 3s. 4d. yearly to be distributed at his obit day "among prestes and clerkes and other poore people", and the property "I give to the towne of Stephynton they to rule it and govern the most profitable way for the helth of my sowle and all cristen sowlys and for the most profitt of the church".

Exors. sir William Grene vicar, Robert Tayllour, John Darlyng. Witn. James Bays, Robert Pake.

Probate granted to sir Richard [sic] Grene and Richard Darlyng, reserving powers of Robert Tayllour.

52.
John Bowstred of Luton. 30 July, pr. 2 Dec. 1523. (2: 49)

Burial in the north churchyard of Luton; mortuary after custom of town, to mother church of Lincoln 2d.; to the high altar 12d.; to an honest priest to sing a trental for souls of testator and his good friends in Luton church 10s.; to John Barne 2 quarters of malt; to master Thomas Lynd 13s. 4d.; to every godchild 4d.; to the friars of Dunstable 2s. a year charged on land called Hydons to keep a yearly obit "for my father's sowle and mother and for my sowle and all my good frendes sowlys". To wife Johan for life then to son Edward and his heirs male, all testator's lands, charged with payment to son Richard of £10. Should Edward have no heir male, land is to go to Richard and his heirs male, and if he has none, then the land is to be sold by his executors and the proceeds "disposed in prest song and sum ornament unto the church and in mendyng of the hy ways and other dedes of pitie as myn executors shall thynk best within the church and town of Luton".

Residue to wife Johan and Thomas Monyngham.

Exors. wife Johan and Thomas Monyngham, he to have 13s. 4d.; supervisor master Doctor Edward Sheffeld, to have 13s. 4d. for his labour. Witn. sir John Moselay parish priest; sir Roland Richardson, Thomas Oviall, William Marston.

53.
Johan Picok. 10 Apr. 1518, pr. 15 Nov. 1523. (2: 50)

Burial in churchyard of Our Blessed Lady in Kyshoo; for mortuary as customary; to mother church of Lincoln 2d.; to the high altar 12d.; to the torches 4d.; to the bells 4d..

Her will is that her "hows in the forde athisside Saint Neots bridge" is to be sold to her son Rainold for £4 sterling, to be paid within three years after her death, from which 20s. to go to Walter Picok, 20s. to Richard Picok and 20s. to Thomas Picok. To son Raynold the best brass pot, the best pan, the hangings of her hall, the hangings of her bed, the best coverlet, a great chafer and a pair of sheets; to Walter Pickok a blanket and a pair of sheets; to Elizabeth Dixy a land of her best wheat and a cow; to the wife of Richard Picok 4½ yards of violet cloth; to the wife of Walter Picok a russet gown; to the wife of Thomas

1. Brass of Dr. Edward Sheffelde, canon of Lichfield and vicar of Luton from
1502 to his death. His will, proved in the P.C.C. in February 1526, is
published in *BHRS* vol. 58. He is occasionally mentioned as Supervisor in
wills in this volume, as in no. 52. *Thomas Fisher.*

Picok a violet gown; to Alys Pycok the daughter of Walter Picok 10s., the second brass pot, and a coffer; to son Rainold "those goods that be left".

Exors. Rainold Picok, Thomas Skott, Thomas Canon who is to have 20d. for his work. Residue to exors. to dispose of for good of souls of testator, her husband and all Christians. Witn. Thomas Rolt junior, Walter Folbek, William Meryell, Gregory Day.
Probate granted to Rainold Picok and Thomas Scott, reserving the power of Thomas Cannon.

54.
Thomas Thody of Goodwik in the parish of Eton (Socon). 1 Dec., pr. 9 Dec. 1525. (2: 51)
Testament "Calling to remembraunce the transytery and uncertayn liff of this world forsakyng all myserable lyvyng submittyng my seliff oonly to the gret power and mercy of god trustyng veryly by the vertue of his blissed passion to be savid." Burial in the churchyard of Eton; mortuary as customary; to the mother church of Lincoln 2d.; to the high altar 12d.; to the bells 8d.; for a trental to be sung in the church 10s.; to son William Thody when he enters the farm and dwelling-place as described in the will following 2 horses, 2 kine, 6 sheep; to son William to be given him by wife Johan after the next harvest at Michaelmas a quarter of wheat, a quarter of oats, 4 quarters of barley, 4 quarters of pease; to John Awngell 6 sheep and a 2 year old bullock; to Richard Gray 2 sheep and a bushel of wheat; to daughter Cristyan a quarter of barley; to the prior of St. Neots 3s. 4d.; to each god-child 4d.; to daughters Elizabeth and Cicely immediately after testator's death a cow; 10 sheep and a quarter of barley; to Honydon Way 8d.; to Goodwik Way 8d.; to four poor neighbours a bushel of malt next Christmas. Residue to wife Johan.

Exors. wife Johan and William Thody his son; supervisor Richard Fitzhew, and he to have "3s. 4d. for making of this my last will and testament". Witn. William Gore the elder, Rainold Picok, John Gore the younger.
Will He wills that his wife Joan is to have the place and land in Goodwik where testastor lives, until the harvest has been gathered, and then at the next fallow William is to enter and have the farm and place for himself and his assigns, with all appurtenances, leases and grants of land, wood and pasture belonging to it. When he has entered on the property, William is to pay his mother £8 within the next nine years, paying nothing the first year and £1 in each succeeding year. After this he is to pay her 6s. 8d. a year for her lifetime.

His wife is to have his tenement in Honydon and both the tenements in Eton for her lifetime, making no waste and keeping them in repair, and on her death son William is to have them.

55.
John Foster of Clifton. 10 Mar. 1526/7, pr. 15 July 1527. (2: 52)

Burial in the churchyard of All Hallows in Clifton; for his principal as customary; to the high altar 2 bushels of barley; to the mother church of Lincoln 4d.; to Our Lady light in the chancel a "Prilce" (pricket); to the bells 2 bushels of barley; to the torches 12d.; to repairing Clee Bridge a ewe sheep; to daughter Marion two ewes and two lambs; to daughter Agnes a great brass pot, a ewe and a lamb; to daughter Awdre a cow; to Johan Gold a ewe and a lamb.

To William Loryng and Elizabeth his wife and the heirs of their bodies, testator's tenement in Clifton with a croft and 2 acres and 3 roods of arable "lyyng by parcellys in the feldes of Clifton", they to find a priest to sing for testator's soul for half a year.

Residue to executors to dispose of for the good of testator's soul. Exors. William Loryng, Edward Thredar. Witn. sir William Pitman, curate, Thomas Warner.

56.
John Bechner of Turvey. 1527, pr. 29 July 1527. (2: 52d)

Burial in the churchyard of All Hallows of Turvey; to the high altar 12d.; to Our Lady 12d.; to the bells 20d.; to the bridge 12d.; to Bidnam (Biddenham) Bridge 12d.; to wife Alys 3 of the best kine, all household stuff not bequeathed elsewhere, 4 horses with their harness, the best cart, and 20 sheep; to five of testator's children, that is John, William, Richard, Beatrix and Alys an acre of barley and an acre of pease each "The payyng the rent of so many acres within my ferme at Pikkshill"; to son Robert an ox, 4 horses with their harness, the second best cart, and a plough; to daughter Joan a cow, the new pot, a bed, that is to say a mattress, coverlet, blanket, bolster, with a pair of flaxen sheets; to daughter Elizabeth 2 quarters of malt. A trental to be said for souls. Residue to testator's wife and children in equal shares.

Exors. wife Alys Bechnar, son Robert; supervisors John Geffray, John Hyllys. Witn. sir Thomas Mullisworth, priest, John Geffray, John Hillys.

57.
Thomas Barre of Nether Deane. 14 Mar. 1520, pr. 22 June 1520. (2: 53)

Burial in the churchyard of All Hallows in Over Deane; for his mortuary his best good; to "the hows of Lincoln" 4d.; to the high altar 3s. 4d.; to repairing Our Lady altar 3s. 4d.; to the brotherhood guild two lamb hoggs; to St. Thomas' altar 20d.; to St. Katerin's altar 12d.; to the bells 6s. 8d.; to the torches 6s. 8d.; to sir Jamys Tunstall 20d.; to repair the stone bridge in Nether Deane 3s. 4d..

He wills that his son Richard shall have Cokkes Close and 7 acres of land when he reaches the age of 20 years, or if he die before them, it goes to the next eldest son, or if he too should die, then to testator's youngest son at the same age, and if all die before the age of 20, then the property is to be sold after death of testator's wife and the money disposed of for the good of the souls of testator and all Christians. Residue to wife Alys.

Exors. wife Alys and Henry Freman, who is to have 16d. for his work; supervisor Richard Oliff. Witn. Jamys Tunstall, sir John Dixy, William Bulley, John Hyway.

58.
Thomas Fayre. 10 Apr., pr. 7 May 1524. (2: 54)
Burial in the churchyard of Flitton; to Lincoln cathedral 2d.; for his mortuary as customary; to the high altar 8d..

To wife Alys for life, then to son John Fayre and his heirs, testator's tenement or house in Flitton, with its appurtenances, they to keep a yearly obit in the parish church of Flitton for the souls of testator and all Christians. Residue to wife Alys.

Executrix wife Alys. Witn. Henry Richardes vicar, William Parrisse, John Parrisse.

59.
William Fossey of Kingishoughton. 8 Apr., pr. 7 May 1524. (2: 54d)
Testament Burial in the churchyard of Houghton; to the high altar there half a quarter of wheat; to the rood loft 2 lb. of wax; a pound of wax each to Our Lady light, St. Thomas, St. Anne, Our Lady of Pity, St. Martin, St. Margaret, St. Katerin, Mary Maudlen, King Henry and St. Sunday; to the brotherhood of Luton 10s.; to the brotherhood of Luton [sic] 6s. 8d.; to the brotherhood of Leighton a quarter of malt; to the friars of Dunstable a quarter of malt; to the friars of Bedford a quarter of malt; to the friars of Hychyn a quarter of malt; to the churches of Tillisworth, Pottisgrave, Badlesden, Stanbrige, Egyngton half a quarter of malt each; to the chapel of St. Thomas at Lynbury and to the chapel of St. Barthelmew at Chalton half a quarter of malt each; to the painting of the rood at Harlyngton 6s. 8d.; to the church of Kingishoughton to buy a chalice and a pyx £6 13s. 4d.; for a trental for souls of testator, his friends and all Christians in Houghton church 10s. a year for 5 years; to each god-child 12d.; to wife Emme 46s. 8d. every year for life, half testator's crop and half his household stuff; to son William all the horses and their harness, all the carts and ploughs, and half the crop; to daughter Margaret £6 13s. 4d.; to every child of daughter Margery 10s.; to Joan Fossey his son's daughter £13. 10s. 8d.; to John and William the sons of Thomas Hardyng 40s. each; to the children of William Hardyng 26s. 8d. each.

Will He wills that his feoffees should hold his property to the following uses, that is his son William and the heirs of his body shall have all
lands and tenements in Kingishoughton, Dunstable, Chalton or elsewhere, freehold and copyhold, and if William has no such heirs, the
property is to be sold by his executors and supervisor and feoffees, or
failing these by the church wardens of Kynges Houghton, and one half
of the money is to be given to the children of his son and of his daughter in equal shares, and the other half is to be given to a priest to sing
for testator's and all Christian souls, and in other deeds of charity.
Residue to son William to use for the health of testator's soul.

Exors. son William Fossey, Thomas Hardyng and John Whitlok, to
whom 20s. each; supervisor William Fossey, vicar, to have 20s.. Witn.
sir Richard Blew, priest, William Perott, John Eme the elder.

60.
Thomas Archer of Litlyngton. 10 July 1521, pr. 22 Apr. 1523. (2: 56)

Burial in churchyard of All Hallows in Litlyngton; to the high altar
10s.; to mother church of Lincoln 4d.; to mending the steeple in
Litlyngton 13s. 4d.; to Our Lady light in the chancel 2 kine; for a trental
for testator's soul 10s.; to his brother's son Richard Archer 20s. and to
his sister Agnes Archer 20s.; to master vicar of Litlyngton 3s. 4d. to pray
for testator's soul; to all god-children 4d. each; to Margaret Houghson
a cow; to Henry Archer his brother's son a bullock; to Christian Archer
a cow; to his wife Agnes all household stuff "my copie and corne".

He wills to wife Agnes for life, and his son Henry "to pay my ladies
rent" his house at Badlesden, with a close and pightle and 6 acres of
land and 2 acres of mead in Westmede, and 7 kine. Residue to son
Henry Archer to dispose of for his soul.

Exors. Thomas Julyon (to whom 3s. 4d.), and son Henry Archer.
Overseer Rawff Smyth (3s. 4d.). Witn. sir Peter Dent, sir Richard
Firtho, John Mydilton.

61.
Elizabeth Burne of Litlyngton, widow. 13 Dec. 1527, pr. 27 Jan. 1527/8.
(2: 56d)

Burial in the church or churchyard of Litlyngton; for mortuary her
best good; to mother church of Lincoln 4d.; to Litlyngton church 40s.
and to Wotton church 40s., both sums to be paid before Christmas
twelvemonth; to Besse Deane 5 marks "to her marriage". Residue to
sons John and William Burne to be bestowed for "my sowle helth".

Exors. John Burne, William Burne. Witn. Thomas Tayllour, John
Writh'.

62.
Thomas Norrett of Kingishoughton. 23 Mar 1524 [sic], pr. 2 Apr. 1524.
(2: 57)

Testament   Burial in the church of All Hallows of Kingis Houghton "within the belfray there"; to mother church of Lincoln 2d.; to the high altar of Kingishoughton a bushel of wheat and a bushel of malt; to the rood light 6d.; to Our Lady light in the chapel 6d.; to "every light gathered for" 4d.; to Our Lady light in the choir 2d.; to the Trinity light 4d.; to St. Sunday's light 2d.; to "the light of the Immage of Kyng Henr' the vjth" 2d.; to St. Elege called St. Loy 2d.; to St. Erasmus light 2d.; to St. Anthony light 2d.; to the lights of St. Michael, St. Sith (Osyth), St. Christopher and St. George 2d. each; to the light of the 12 Apostles 4d.; to the torches 3s. 4d.; to the Friars Preacher of Dunstable, a quarter of malt to pray for testator and his friends; to the friars of Bedford a quarter of malt; to the brotherhood of Luton a quarter of malt; to every godchild 2d.; to the brotherhood of Kingishoughton his best maser "to have it and occupie it for ever to the use of the sayd brotherhood new fowndid and toward the mayntenyng thereof and to be prayd for".

Will   He wills that his feoffees are to stand enfeoffed in all his property in Kingis Houghton, Dunstable or elsewhere to the uses of this his will. His wife Alys is to have during her life his two tenements in Houghton, the one the testator occupies and the one Gobyn dwells in "with all gardyns closys hegges dichis pastorys medows woodes londes and all other thynges what so ever it be to thies ij tenements belongyng" with all other lands in Kingis Houghton purchased by his ancestors and lying in the fields of Kingis Houghton. She will occupy them on condition that she continues to live in his house and maintains the property in repair, and keeps a yearly obit to the value of 5s. at which prayers are to be said for testator, his friends and for all Christian souls on a certain day each year, with dirige "over evyn" and she is to have a trental of masses said each year.

If she fails in these conditions, or if she falls into poverty, then the property is to go to the church-wardens of Kingis Houghton, who are to pay a third of the income to testator's wife and to keep the obit to the value of 3s. 4d.. The rest is to be used to provide the stipend of an honest priest to pray for souls of testator, his wife, his friends and all Christians for 99 years. If it happens that "the said prestes salary or stipend cannot be mortest nor licence gotten of the Kyng to be made sure for ever" then the property is to be sold after 99 years by the vicar and churchwardens for the best price, and the money arising used "to by an ornament which shalbe thought most necessary for the church of Kingishoughton aforesayd".

His house in Dunstable which he bought from master Lynd, sometime bailey (bailiff) of Dunstable, shall be sold, and the money used to pay debts and perform his last will.

The house and land that was once Henry Skegg's, his wife's father, in Dunstable, and the lands in Houghton fields, shall remain according to Henry Skegg's will. Testator's wife is to pay the £10 which he laid out for the marriage of the daughter of Henry Skegg's son, to the church-wardens, or cause it to be paid after her death by her executors, other-wise the house and land are to be sold by testator's executors, and the money is to be used to maintain the brotherhood founded there.

Regarding the house, close and land in Houghton which testator has on lease from the prior and convent of Dunstable, his wife and John Walys are to have the net profits of this lease which they are to bestow each year upon the highways about Kingishoughton. Residue to wife Alys.

Exors. master William Fossey, vicar of Kynges Houghton, to have 20s., and John Walys, to have 13s. 4d.; supervisor George Acworth esq. of Todyngton, to have 13s. 4d.. Witn. William Fossey the elder, Master Battisford Master of Arts, John Clerk, John Brigges of Kyngishoughton.

63.
Edmond Galaway of Pery in the parish of Much Stoughton. 14 Feb. 1525/6, pr. 19 Nov. 1526. (2: 59)

Burial in church of Much Stoughton; to mother church of Lincoln 2d.; to high altar 6d.; to ornaments of the altar 12d.; to the Trinity altar 4d.; to the ornaments of Our Lady altar 4d.; to the torches 6s. 8d.; to repairing Brosse bridge 12d.; to the rood loft 16d.; to the tapers of the rood loft 2d.; to a priest to sing for his soul for one quarter immediately after his death 26s.; to the friars of Huntingdon 20d.; to Bissemede Priory 12d.; to John Bareff, to Emme Bareff, to John Bareff and Margery Bareff, children of John Bareff, a sheep or a lamb each; to each of his god-children 2d.; to poor people on the day of his burial "byside the queer ordered after good heneste" 40s.; to be bestowed in bread, cheese and ale to poor people at his 7th day 10s.; and in like manner at his 30th day 10s.; to keep an anniversary or year day for souls of testa-tor, his wife and his father and mother 16d. to be paid yearly "out of my capitall or hed place where I now dwell in"; to the purchase of a cope for the said church 20s.; to a lamp in the high choir 4d. a year for evermore "to be takyn of an acre lond with medow lyyng agayn the medew agayn Groffham brig".

To son-in-law John Bareff, Edmond Bareff his daughter's son and Letice Jamys his daughter, all his household stuff remaining in his hall, kitchen and chamber, "evynly and indifferently to be devided betwene them iij by the sight and jugement of Edmond Parell of Stoughton aforesayd"; to each of Edmond Bareff's children a sheep; to Edmond

Bareff the 20 nobles he owes testator, the said Edmond to pay 20s. toward buying a chalice for the church; to sir John Lee 12d..

He wills to Edmond Bareff his daughter's son and to his heirs and assigns, testator's tenement, once Roger Cookkes, with its land, meadows and closes, on condition that the same Edmond shall pay "to the parformacans of this my testament" £8 of lawful English money in the following way: 20s. on the feast of the Purification of Our Lady next to come, and so yearly on the same day until the whole £8 is paid. If Edmond fail in any payment then testator's son-in-law John Bareff or his assigns are entitled to distrain on the said messuage or any part of it, and to "lede cary or drive away and then to hold and enioy unto the sayd somme or sommys so by the sayd Edmond unpayd be satisfyyd and payd and content".

To a priest to sing for the souls of testator and of Cokkes and all Christians 40s. of the said £8; to Stoughton church 20s. of the £8 to buy a cross and 20s. of the £8 to buy 2 banner cloths; to Letice Jamys his daughter 20s. of the said sum; to repair Brosse bridge and all the bridges 13s. 4d.; to a priest 26s. 8d. for a quarter's service in the said church.

He wills that his feoffees in the tenement called Cookkes with appurtenances are to deliver the estate to the persons named by his executors when they shall be required to do so by the terms of this will.

To son-in-law John Bareff 2 beasts; to Letice Jamys a cow; to testator's daughter's son Edmond Bareff a cow; to god-son Edward Bareff a bullock one year old; to daughter's son Edmond Jamys a bullock one year old; to each of John Bareff's children a sheep; towards making a "fenestre" (small window) in the church 6s. 8d..

Residue to son-in-law John Bareff and to daughter's son Edmond Bareff to dispose for the health of testator's soul. Provided that all lands both entailed and fee simple, unbequeathed, be equally divided between his daughters Isabell and Letice and their heirs.

Exors. John and Edmond Bareff, each to have 20s.; overseer master William [?]Reed, vicar of the said church, to have 6s. 8d. for his labour. Witn. sir John Lee priest, Edmond Parell of Stoughton, Richard Jamys of Bukworth; Edward Tayllor of Stoughton, Robert Hatley of St. Neots.

64.
Richard Flecher alias Cooke of Northivell, senior. 4 Aug. 1522, pr. 26 Aug. 1525. (2: 61)
Testament Burial in church of Northivell; mortuary best beast as customary; to mother church of Lincoln 8d.; to high altar 6s. 8d.; to upkeep of the bells 3s. 4d.; to the torches 3s. 4d.; to upkeep of the church 20s.; to the master of the College of Northivell 20d.; to every brother of the same 12d.; to the 2 quiresters of the same 4d.; to the abbot of the

monastery of Our Blessed Lady of Wardon 6s. 8d.; to the college of Northivell to pray for testator 20s.; to son Thomas 40s. to be spent at his discretion; to wife Elizabeth half his moveable goods "to be devided by the same Elizabeth and she to take and retayne to her owne use that part of my goodes as shall like her best, without lett, interrupcion or controlment of myn executors or any of them"; to son William Flecher the other half of his goods; to each god-child except Richard Hardyng 12d.; to be distributed to the people by executors on the day of his burial for the wealth of his soul £6.

Exors. wife Elizabeth and son William Flecher, each to have 3s. 4d. for their labour.

Will He wills to the abbot and convent of the monastery of Wardon "in pure and perpetuall almes" his messuage in the West End of Southivell with the land, all of the value of 10s. a year; to son Richard Flecher and his heirs and assigns for ever all messuages and lands in the towns and fields of Sandy, Girtford, Everton and Temmysford; to his wife for the term of her life the annuity of £6 13s. 4d. charged on his lands in Northivell, Beston, Hach', Thornecott, Calcott, Ikewell, Bikleswade and Shefford, which testator granted by a deed dated 3 August 1522 to his feoffees (Nicholas Hardyng gent., John Lyn chaplain, Robert Percell and Thomas Bromsall) for the life of testator Richard Flecher the elder and his wife Elizabeth. The feoffees or their heirs are to pay the annual rent of £6 13s. 4d. to wife for life.

To wife Elizabeth for life the house testator dwells in, and after her death house to go to son William Flecher for life, then to Nicholas Flecher and his heirs for ever.

To William Flecher and his heirs for ever all his lands, tenements, rents, reversions and services not before bequeathed in Northivell, Beston, Hach', Thornecott, Calcott, Ikwell, Bikleswade, Southivell, Shefford, and he is to pay testator's wife "the sayd annuite as is byforesayd".

Witn. Nicholas Hardyng, sir John Lyn, Robert Butler, Richard Numman, John Stokes Master of Arts, William Flecher.
Probate granted to one executor, reserving power of widow Elizabeth.

65.
John Crawnfeld/Cranfeld of Cardyngton, husbandman. 27 Mar., pr. 9 Apr. 1524. (2: 63)
Burial in the churchyard of Cardington; mortuary his best horse; to mother church of Lincoln 4d.; to the high altar 8d.; to the bells 4d.; to the torches 4d..

His two sons Thomas and William are to have his two "tenantries" one in Coople and the other in Cardyngton, with their lands, closes, meadows and pastures. Thomas the elder son is to have the holding in

Cardyngton, except for 6 acres of land purchased by the testator's father, which 6 acres are to go with the property in Coople. If Thomas should marry, he is to give his wife a jointure from the Cardyngton property for her life, and after her death it is to pass to his heirs. If he should die without issue, the property goes to William and the heirs of his body but William should continue to give Thomas' widow her jointure.

William is to have the holding in Coople, and if he should marry, he is to give his wife a jointure from the Coople property for her life, and after her death it is to go to his heirs. If he die without issue, then it goes to Thomas, who should continue to give William's widow her jointure.

If both sons die without issue, then all the property is to be sold. One part of the proceeds is to go to hire a priest to sing certain years for the souls of the testator, his wife, his father and mother, his grandfather and grandmother, and all Christians. The other part is to go to the mending of highways "where the substaunciall men of the towne shall thynk it most nede".

Neither son shall sell any part of the land, "but if they wold that then it shall be leefull for the lord of the towne of Cardyngton with the churchwardens to entre uppon it and sell it and fulfill my mynd accordyng as I have before rehersed".

An honest priest is to sing a trental for his soul in Cardyngton church.

All his moveables are to go to his sons Thomas and William to be divided between them by the "overlooking and discrecion" of William Craunfeld the testator's cousin, and William Bawdwyn his neighbour.

Exors. the two sons. Overseers William Crawnfeld and William Bawdwyn. Witn. sir Thomas Dykenson vicar of Cardyngton; William Crawnfeld; William Bawdwyn, John Bull, John Shittyngfeld.
Probate granted to Thomas Cranfeld, power of William Cranfeld reserved.

66.
John Rolt of Bedford. 1524, pr. 22 Apr. 1524. (2: 64)

To be buried in the parish church of St. Powlys "in the aly before Saint Jamys"; to the high altar 2s.; to the mother church of Lincoln 4d.; to the friars for a trental 10s.; to daughter Agnes Rolt "when she is maryable" after the death of her mother and at the time of her marriage £10 and the testator's great pan in the work house and her mother's best girdle; to wife Alys all the moveables "that God hath sent me" and the close at the Friars Stile called Adys "to give and sell for evermore". To servant John Sutton testator's violet gown that is furred with black lamb; to Jees his servant a pair of sheets.

Exors. wife Alys and John Longg. Overseers Thomas Rounth, Richard Waymunn. Witn. master Thomas West, John Longg.

67.
John Wales of Kynges Houghton. 22 Nov., pr. 2 Dec. 1527. (2: 64d)

Burial in churchyard of All Hallowes; to mother church of Lincoln 2d.; to the high altar 12d.; to All Hallows light 2d.; to Our Lady's light 3d.; to St. Martin's light 2d.; to "every gatherid light" in the church 2d.; to the upkeep of the torches 2s..

To each of his children 3 sheep and a quarter of malt "of the sort that it is now". To his eldest son: a long cart, with the best shod wheels, the cart leather and ropes; a plough with its share, coulter, chains and other things; and "all such stuff as shall make hym a duncart".

Wife Elizabeth is to have all testator's house and land, meadows, leys and pastures in Kingis Houghton for 20 years, except Gromys and the new barn with their lands, which she is to have until testator's eldest son is 16 years old. During these 20 years Elizabeth shall keep the property in repair, making "no stupe nor wast". At the end of the 20 years the property is to go to son Thomas and his heirs, or failing heirs it is to revert to son William and his heirs, in default to son John and his heirs, in default to son Robert and his heirs, in default to daughter Alys and her heirs.

If all his children die without issue, the property goes to wife Elizabeth for her lifetime, and after her death "to the next of my bloode". Failing this, all the copyhold land is to be sold to the highest bidder, and half the proceeds to be spent on highways about Houghton and the other half to buy an ornament for the church.

Residue to wife Elizabeth except "my standards naylid and pynnid belongyng to the sayd howses" (the fixtures). Exors. wife Elizabeth and John Clerk, he having for his labour [*blank*]. Witn. William Straunger, John Eme of the Grene.

Probate granted to John Clerk, reserving power of widow Elizabeth.

68.
William Eton of Willishamsted. 16 Dec. 1521, pr. 2 Dec. 1527. (2: 65d)

Burial in the churchyard. To wife Joan for life his house and the close within the gates "except I have nede to help my selff within the same hows". "After our livis my hows shalbe sold, if that I may forbere it, to the profite of the church and the highways", and the money arising to be used also for a trental to be said for testator and his friends. To every god–child 4d.; to the bells 2s.; to the torches at his burial and month's mind and at the twelve months 2s.; to the high altar 12d.; to mother church of Lincoln 2d.; residue to wife Johan to be used for souls.

Executrix wife Johan. Overseer John Cawnell. Witn. William Snow of Elnestow, John Cawnell of Willishamsted, John Preste, John Astlyn, William Eyer, sir Thomas Heyward vicar, John Palmer.

69.
William Bird of Turvey. 2 Sep., pr. 24 Sep. 1527. (2: 66)

Burial in churchyard of All Hallows of Turvey; to mother church of Lincoln 4d.; to the high altar 12d.; to the bells 12d.; to the torches 12d.; to Turvey bridge 12d..

To his wife for her life, the house where testator lives, after the death of his mother. After his wife's death then house to go to testator's eldest son John Bird, and then to testator's children "oon after another as long as any of them shall live", and if they all die without issue, the house is to be sold and the proceeds used for souls of testator, his mother and father, and all Christians.

All the land which testator has purchased in Turvey is to be sold and the money divided equally between his children, and he would prefer that his eldest son should buy it.

To whatever child occupies his house a shod cart and 4 horses to be given him by testator's wife for 53s. 4d.; to 6 of his youngest children 20s. each "when they cum to theyr discrecion, that is xvj yere old"; to sir Thomas the testator's ghostly father 20d.; and the residue to his wife.

Exors. wife and Nicholas Tayllour. Witn. sir Thomas Mullesworth priest, John Geffray, John Hodill.
Probate granted to Nicholas Tayllour reserving power of widow.

70.
William Kent of Clopham. 20 Aug., pr. 23 Sep. 1527. (2: 67)

Burial in Okeley churchyard; to mother church of Lincoln [*blank*]; to the high altar of Clopham church 12d.; to the bells 8d.; to the torches 8d.; to Okeley church 4d.; for his mortuary "my best horse"; to John Barton of Clopham 12d.; to wife Agnes his house and land and moveable goods to pay debts and perform will.

Exors. wife Agnes, John Barton; overseer Robert Gerard of Stageden. Witn. sir John Wion vicar of Okeley, William Stoke the elder, John FitzRychard.

71.
Thomas Nott of Tilbrok. 24 Aug., pr. 23 Sep. 1527. (2: 67d)

Burial in church of All Saints in Tilbrok; for his mortuary as customary; to mother church of Lincoln 4d.; to the high altar 6d.; to the church ornaments 6d.; "to the brokyn bell toward the makyng of a new bell" 6s. 8d.; to the sepulchre light a pound of wax; to the Guild of Our Lady in Kynbolton 20d. "to the use of what thyng is most nedefull".

To Alys Thomson a red bullock; to son Thomas Nott 3 acres and 3 roods of arable land; to son Richard testator's house called Lekes, with all lands and meadows with "hevedon" pertaining to the same, with the intent that a yearly obit shall be kept by him and his heirs for ever to the value of 3s. 4d.. In default, the property is to go to Thomas and John, testator's sons, who are to keep the obit in Tilbrook church for ever for the souls of testator, Agnes his wife, his father and mother and good friends, and all Christians.

To son John and his heirs and assigns testator's house called Richards with all meadows etc. in Tilbrok, and all goods moveable and unmoveable, and he is to pay funeral expenses and is to have all the profits of houses and lands for one year after testator's death, at which time each of the sons to have his inheritance.

Exors. sons Thomas Nott, John Nott, Richard Nott. Witn. sir Robert Gurnell parson of Tilbrok, sir John Pury curate there, William Stoughton of Kymbolton, Simond Wright, Robert Sheppard of Tilbrok, Thomas Lane, John Mahew.

72.
John Wales of Langford. 30 Jan., pr. 25 Feb. 1526/7. (2: 69)
Testament Burial in churchyard of the Holy Apostle St. Andrew of Langford; for mortuary his best horse; to the high altar of Langforth 12d.; to mother church of Lincoln 4d.; to the church 40s. "to the byyng of a vestment for the holyday"; to Richard Awbere a bullock; to Katerin Wales a bullock; to Margaret Rawley a bullock; to servant Emme half an acre of barley "to be sown at my cost and charge"; to son Edward 4 of best horses "after my mortuary be chosen", 2 of the best oxen, 3 of the best milch beasts, all the carts and all the hoggs.

Residue of goods after all paid to Rowland Clerk, John Bendoo and John Walys the elder to divide it equally between Richard Walys, Robert Walys and Edward Walys.

Exors. Richard Walys, Robert Walys and Edward Walys to dispose to the pleasure of Almighty God and to the health of testator's soul. Overseers: sir Rowland Clerk vicar of Langford; John Bendo; John Walys testator's brother.
Will He wills to eldest son Richard Wales and his heirs for ever all his tenements and lands in Brome or Southivell; to Robert Wales his second son testator leaves the house he himself lives in "with all such lond closys medows and pastures as I have lymytid thereto and surrendred in to the hands of John Wales my brother to the use of the sayd Robert my sonne and of his heyrys and assignes forever"; to Edward Wales the youngest son a messuage in Langford called Foxis, with all the free land testator purchased in Langford, Bikleswade and Holme, to the number of 16 acres more or less; also two copyholds, one held of the lord of the manor of St. John of Jerusalem consisting of a messuage next to William Wales with 10 acres of land; the other held of the lord of Langford manor consisting of the messuage next to Foxys with 20 acres of land, which testator surrendered into the hands of his brother John

Wales to the use of his three sons as above in the presence of sir Roland Clerk vicar and William Botteler bailiff.

73.
Richard Laudisdale of Stopisley in the parish of Luton. 27 Mar., pr. 16 Apr. 1526. (2: 71)
Burial in the parish church of Luton "within the north Ile"; to mother church of Lincoln 4d.; to the high altar of Luton 12d.; to the lights 5s.; "to the nedes of the sayd church" 12d.; to wife Johan 4 of his best beasts, all his household stuff, 20 quarters of barley, 6 quarters of wheat and all the corn growing on her own ground. To William Crawley, Thomas Crawley, Edward Crawley, John Spayne and Alys Crawley 20 young sheep each "to take them as they ryn"; to John Spayn two of the best young bullocks; to Edward Crawley a bullock; to Alice Crawley another bullock "at the sight of myn executors"; to Edward Chapman a bullock and 20s.; to Richard Crawley testator's best coat, his sword and buckler and 20s.; to Edward Crawley the house and land in Luton, lately purchased of Thomas Chapman "payyng to Richard Crawley v markes, so that he may suffer Henry Spayne to dwell therin payyng his rent to myn executors unto such tyme as he be xviij yere old", and if Edward Crawley should die before the age of 18, the house is to be sold and the money arising spent for the good of testator's soul by his executors and supervisor.

To John Crawley testator's gown; to William and Thomas Crawley the 2 youngest bullocks; to John Cawnfeld 2 quarters of barley; to godson Richard Crawley 2 sheep and 2s.; to each god-child in parish of Luton 8d.; to his mother £4; to Edward Thomasson 20d.; to William Sutton 10s. and testator's tawny coat; to Nicholas Bigg 3s. 4d. and the russet coat; to Thomas Lody 6s. 8d. and "a pety cote"; to William Dyer a quarter of barley; to sir Richard Fissher 3s. 4d..

Exors. John Crawley and Edward Chapman, to whom the residue, "they to bryng my bodie to Cristen buryall to kepe my monethis mynd yere mynd and to pay my dettes and to kepe an honest prest a quarter of a yere to syng and pray for me and such other of my frendes as I am specially bowndyn to pray for and otherwise to dispose for my sowle as they shall thynk most expedient in tyme comyng", and both to have 20s. and their costs. Supervisor Sir Henry Gray, knight, to have 10s.. Witn. sir Richard Fissher, Thomas Helder, John Cawnfeld, Henry Spayne, Edward Thomasson.

74.
William Amere of Bedford. 5 Jan., pr. 27 Jan. 1527/8. (2: 72)
Burial in the churchyard of St. Powlis in Bedford. To the high altar of the parish church 12d.; to the mother church of Lincoln 2d.; to the

rood light in the parish church 8d.; to St. Peter's church in the Feld 3s.
4d.; to St. Cuthbert's church 3s. 4d.; to wife Agnes his house and lands
in Thurly; to the friars for a trental of masses 10s.. Residue to wife
Agnes, part to be used for souls of testator and all Christians. Executrix
wife Agnes; supervisor sir Alexander Foscroft testator's curate, who is
to have 3s. 4d.. Witn. sir Alexander Foscroft, John Palmer junr.,
Thomas Ward, John Knight.

75.
John Edwardes of Willishamsted. Feast of St. Agnes Virgin and Martyr,
21 Jan., pr. 29 Jan. 1518/9. (2: 72d)
   Burial in churchyard of All Hallows of Willishamsted; to high altar
3s. 4d..
   To wife Johan 12 sheep, 3 kine, 3½ acres barley, one acre of pease,
half an acre of wheat and 5s.; to sons Thomas and Richard a cow each
and all household goods divided between them; to son Thomas a cow;
to son Richard another cow and 10 acres of land to him and his heirs
for ever, paying 10s. "to the fyndyng of a prest"; to Marion Day a ewe
and a lamb; to John Cooper a ewe and a lamb; to John Achurch a ewe
and a lamb.
   Exors. brother William Edward and son Thomas Edward. Witn. sir
Richard Purcer vicar, Robert Gilmyn, Nicholas Nicholl.

76.
William Crawley of the parish of Luton. 13 Nov., pr. 24 Nov. 1525.
(2: 73)
   Burial in the church of Luton; mortuary his best horse; to the church
of Lincoln 4d.; to the high altar of Luton 2s.; to repairing the church
12d.. A priest is to sing a trental of masses in Luton church.
   To his wife for two years after his death, all his house and land, which
is then to go to son John and the heirs of his body, on condition that
he keeps an annual obit for testator as long as he lives. If John should
die without issue, the property is to go to the next of the blood "and so
from oon to another for lak of issue".
   To his wife three score sheep and all the crops in the barn and in the
field; to each of testator's four children: John, Valentyne, William and
Alys, 20 sheep and 2 quarters of barley, and if any of them should die
before reaching the age of discretion, their share to be divided equally
between the survivors; to John Sprott 6 sheep; to daughter Alys a cow
and a bullock; to son John a horse, the brown cow and 2 quarters of
wheat; to son John also "the yerys that I have in Henry Pravys lond, so
that he tary with his mother by the space of ij yerys after my deth and
to be content to suffer her to have that ij yerys in my hows and lond
without gruge".

Exors. wife Godith and Thomas Bruse, who is to have 20d., to whom the residue. Witn. master Roger Bawdwyn, Thomas Crawley, Edward Crawley.

77.
Edmond Cosyn of Felmersham. 1 Jan., pr. 2 Mar. 1527/8. (2: 74)

Burial in the parish church "byfore the Trinite". For principal best good as custom of town. To the high altar 12d.; to the sepulchre light 12d.; to the torches 12d.; to the bells 12d.; to the mother church of Lincoln 2d.; to Stafford bridge half a quarter of barley.

To son William Cosyn the best brass pot and best pan; to son Richard Cosyn another great brass pot, "a brouner brasse", a brass pan; to each godchild 4d.; to John Guyn 40s. "to be payd of my goodes at the discrecion of Johan my wiff"; to Thomas Cosyn a chest standing in testator's chamber; to Edmond Cosyn a bullock.

To wife Johan for life testator's place in Felmersham with lands, meads and pastures, with an acre of mead in Bradmede, which lands and tenements are to go after decease of wife Johan to Richard Cosyn, testator's son, and to Alys his wife who will continue to have it after Richard's death, and then to Richard's heirs. In default he wills that the house and lands with the acre of mead go to son William Cosyn and the heirs of his body.

Residue to wife Johan. Exors. wife Johan and sons William and Richard Cosyn. Witn. Hugh Wynard priest, Harry Smyth, John Tapp the elder. *Probate granted to William and Richard Cosyn, reserving the power of Johan.*

78.
John Albany of the parish of St. Powlys, Bedford. 16 Feb., pr. 2 Mar. 1527/8. (2: 74d)

Burial in "Our Lady chapell in my parissh church"; to the mother church of Lincoln 8d.; to the high altar of the parish church 2s.; to son Henry, the house testator dwells in, and for this he is to hire an honest priest to sing for the souls of his father and of all Christians for four years after father's death; to son William, the house by the Waterside; to daughter Alys, house adjoining the house testator dwells in; to daughter Johan the house that Robert Gilbert dwells in; to daughter Elizabeth £6 13s. 4d. to be paid without delay; to testator's son sir Robert a featherbed and all that belongs to it; son Henry to have "for implementes to his hows and all such thynges as longith to the occupacion of a baker". The residue to be divided equally between testator's children William, Elizabeth, Alys and Johan, and if any should die before they are married, then their portion to be divided among the survivors.

Exors. sons sir Robert Albany, Henry Albany. Overseer Thomas

West. Witn. sir Alexander Foscroft, Thomas Routh the mayor of
Bedford, Thomas West, Edmond Johnson.

79.
William Harvy of parish of St. Powlys, Bedford. 7 Feb., pr. 2 Mar.
1527/8. (2: 75)
Burial in churchyard of St. Powlys, to high altar 12d.; to mother
church of Lincoln 4d.; to the brotherhood of St. John 3s. 4d. "in my
parissh church" to be paid within three years of his death; to the friars
of Bedford 3s. 4d.; to son Robert "ij payr of sherys next best that longith to my occupacion" and 12 pairs of "handillys"; to wife Elene house
where testator lives for her life, and after her death this to go to daughter Alice, if she outlive her mother. Residue to wife Elene.
Executrix wife Elene. Overseer Thomas West. Witn. sir Alexander
Foscroft, Richard Harpyngham, Nicholas Burdon.

80.
William Cokyn of Bury Hatley [Cockayne Hatley]. 3 Feb., pr. 2 Mar.
1527/8. (2: 75d)
Burial in the church of Hatley "by the sepulchre of my wiff"; to
"tithes forgotten" 10s.; to Hatley church 26s. 8d.; to Potton church 20s.;
£10 to be bestowed "at my buryall, vij day, moneth day, by the discrecion of myn executors"; to seven persons on the day of his burial seven
black gowns at 3s. 8d. the yard; to the friars of Bedford 10s. to sing a
trental; for a trental to be said at "Scala Celi at the Savage" 10s.; to the
Black Friars of Cambridge 10s. to sing a trental; to the church of
Lincoln 12d.. "I will that the halff of the money which I bestowed of
the bell in the stepill be levyd and gathered of the townshipp and so to
be bestowed and delivered to the church advauntage".
His feoffees to be seized in all his lands in Hatley and other places to
the yearly value of 20 marks to the use of Katerin testator's wife for the
term of her life, and they are to be seized in all other lands and tenements to the uses of this will. A priest is to sing for testator for seven
years in parish church of Hatley. To daughter Elizabeth Cokyn £40
towards her marriage. If wife Katerin should be with child, son or
daughter, this child is to have £40 at full age, and is to be brought up
at the cost and charge of his wife. To son Chadde £40 when he comes
to full age, and if any child should die before they come to full age, their
share to go to the survivors.
To sir John Hopkyns 10s. to pray for testator; to master vicar of
Tadlow 20d.; to master vicar of Potton 6s. 8d. to pray for testator; to
Walter Woorlich 6s. 8d. and a black gown; to four poor men four gowns
at 6d. a yard; to the church six torches.
His executrix is to sell 2 acres of wood towards the charge of the

2. Brass of William Cokyn esquire of Hatley Cockayne, and of Dorothy and Katherine his wives, with sons and daughters. His will, proved in March 1528, is no. 80 in this volume. *Thomas Fisher.*

funeral expenses. "I will that xx yere after the Michaelmasse my wiff pay yerely to her brother Humfrey Savage xxs.". To Alys Savage testator's mother-in-law 40s.; to brother John Cokayn, to Edmund Coken, to Jane a servant 20s. each; to sister Anne 10s..

"I will that Katerin my wiff have the kepyng of my childerne and that she fynd my son Chad to scole and other convenient lernyng duryng xx yerys next after my decease".

"I will that myn exequutrix shall cawse a stone of Marble with oon Image of a Man and ij Images of a Woman and iiij childrene with scripture after the discrecion of myn exequutrix".

Executrix wife Katerin, to whom residue. Supervisor Sir Michael Fissher, knight, and he to have 40s.. Witn. Sir Michael Fissher knight, Nicholas Hardyng, Walter Woorlich gent., John Hopkyns parson of Hatley Port and testator's ghostly father, John Castelyn, William Cloke, Humfrey Savage.

81.
Thomas Aulaby esquire at Dunstable "having in his good mynd goyng by Ways and stretes". 26 May 1525, no note of probate. (2: 76d)

Burial in the Black Friars of Dunstable "by the grave of my lady my mother byfore the Image of St. John Baptist"; to the friars for my grave 6s. 8d.; to their repairs "as is most nede" 10s.; to them for a trental 10s.; to be sung between burial and month's mind "As many massis of Scala Celi as the days will serve"; to the high altar in the Priory church 12d.; to every of the altars in the parish church 12d. each; to the mending of Podyll Hill where most need is 23s. 4d..

To daughter Margaret 20 marks to her marriage "her chamber and her kychyn of every thyng apart"; to younger daughter Agnes as much as her sister Margaret; to Ame, after her mother's death, as much as one of them. If any die, her share to be divided among the others. To daughter Jane 40s. "in money or in stuff".

Residue to wife, executrix. Overseers: his two sons each to have 20s. for their labours. "They have cost me ynough byfore and so I give them all Goddes blessing and myn".

Wife is to pay debts due, and receive debts owing to testator "they be writen in my long booke". Sword and harness to be divided between testator's sons. If wife should marry again, the principal "standers" (fixtures) of the house are to be left to the heir. If after wife's death, testator has no male heirs, then the land in Yorkshire that his brother John Aunaby gave him with the "evydencys" are to go to nephew John Aunelby and his heirs.

To Sisle Camp a mattress and a pair of sheets; to every god–son 12d.; to Thomas Griffyng 40s..

Witn. John Markham curate, Thomas Bentley, John Kent.

82.
Robert Coole of Potton. 21 Oct., pr. 10 Nov. 1524. (2: 78)
Burial "within the porch of the sowth side" in the parish of Potton; to church of Lincoln 6d.; to the sepulchre light 3s. 4d.; to the high altar 3s. 4d.; to the upkeep of the bells 20d.; to the torches 20d.; to the "plough light" 20d.; to the friars of Bedford 10s.; to the White Friars in Cambridge 10s.; to sir Richard his son 40s. to be paid when executors have sold testator's house and lands, on this condition "that if the sayd Ser Richard hereafter at any tyme do troble vex or alter ony thyng contaynyd in this my last will, that then my sayd bequest of xls. toward hym assigned and willid to be as voyd".
To daughter Elizabeth 40s. to be paid on day of her marriage; to daughter Ide 20s. to be paid "when myn executors shall thynk necessary"; to Margaret the daughter of Ide 20s. on the day of her marriage; to Agnes daughter of the said Ide 3s. 4d., and if Margaret or Agnes die before marriage, their legacies are to be void.
To buy a vestment of green damask £3; toward a hearse cloth 26s. 8d.; "To be bestowid upon a marbill stone to ly uppon me" 26s. 8d..
To wife Margaret for life, testator's messuage and lands in Potton. Executors are to sell the reversion of the property, and after payment of debts and legacies, the remainder to be disposed in deeds of charity for souls of testator and his friends.
Residue to wife Margaret "towards the payments of my dettes and preferment of Elizabeth my daughter".
Exors. wife Margaret, Thomas Coole, Richard Ficher. Supervisor Walter Woorlich. Witn. John Tayllour, John Wright, John Benet, Richard Yo.

83.
sir Richard Purcer, vicar of Willishamsted. Day of St. Gregory, 12 Mar. 1523/4. No note of probate. (2: 79)
Burial in the chancel of All Hallows of Willishamsted; for mortuary as is lawful; to Lincoln cathedral 6d.; to abbess of Elnestow and the convent 10 —-; to the friars of Bedford 10s.; to the bells 3 —-; to the torches 3s. 4d.; to Our Lady light 3s. 4d.; to the highway of Willishamsted 6s. 8d.; to a priest 8 marks and 3s. 8d. "to syng massys and pray for me and for the sowlys that I had charge of oon yere within the church of Willishamsted".
To Thomas Hich' of Bedford a featherbed, a coverlet and the hanging over it, the counter standing in the hall, 2 quarters of malt; to John Purcer and Richard his son, testator's books; to Philipp Purcer 6 silver spoons. Residue to John Purcer and Philipp Purcer equally between them.
Exors. Nicholas Nicholl, Thomas Hich' of Bedford, John Purcer. Witn. Philipp Purcer, John Colnell, Richard Fordemyll.

84.
John Samwell the elder of Malden. 2 Apr., pr. 12 Nov. 1524. (2: 79)

Burial in churchyard of Our Blessed Lady of Malden; for his mortuary his best good as customary; to mother church of Lincoln 2d.; to the high altar 12d.; to the torches 20d.; to the bells 20d.; to All Souls light 12d.; to the church of Malden 2 rochets for 2 children.

To son John the head place which testator dwells in, with the mill belonging to it and all his lands in Malden. If John should die without issue, then the mill and lands are to go to son Richard for his lifetime and after his death to Richard's son Harry and then to his male heirs. If there are no male heirs, the property is to be sold "and done for me and my frends".

To son Richard testator's three tenements in Water Ende in Malden, with one acre of mead in the Est Mede near Clophill bridge, a holm near Holyngden bridge, 2 acres of land in the close by Wardon and an acre of land on Thirley. To William Harper testator's tenement in the More End, sometime Dryvers, with the yard and one close "which buttith the brach' with oon hempwik lyyng bytwene Woodcokks howse and Margaret Niton". Residue to executors, to dispose for health of testator's soul.

Exors. sons John and Richard and William Harper. Witn. sir Edmond Londisdale, Richard Faldoo, Thomas Samson, William Lenton.

85.
John Archer of Litlyngton. 1518, pr. 9 Oct. 1518. (2: 80)

Burial in the churchyard of All Hallows in Litlyngton; to high altar 4d.; to mother church of Lincoln 2d.; to wife Christian for term of her life, testator's house with all the lands, and after her death to go to Richard Archar, testator's eldest son, and if he should die without issue, then to Herry Archer, Richard's brother, and if he has no issue, to Agnes Archer, testator's daughter, and if she has no issue the property is to be sold and the money used for the good of the souls of testator and his father and mother. Residue to wife Christian.

Executrix wife Christian. Witn. sir Peter Dent vicar of Litlyngton, Rawff Smyth, John Cooper, John Sutton.

86.
John Benett of Potton. 1521, pr. 20 Sep. 1521. (2: 81)

Burial in the churchyard of Our Lady of Potton; for his principal his best beast; to the high altar 12d.; to the sepulchre light 12d.; to the torches 12d.; to the bells 12d.; to the friars of Bedford 10s. for a trental; to the ringers for their labour 6d..

To wife Johan Benet for her life his place with all lands, meadows and pastures, to lop and crop on every ground, and after wife's death his son John Benet is to have the house with the mill and the close belonging to it and the close at the church, to hold to him and his heirs, making no waste nor sale of any part of it. To son John Benet "a litle stripe of mede lyyng on the north side of the high way to the churchward".

To son Robert and his heirs, after death of wife, testator's meadow plot next the church on the south side of the "cawsy" towards the church, which plot cannot be sold, and also testator's arable lands.

If wife should be in need, she can sell the mills "for to help her selff with all".

Son John is to have the place testator dwells in and a close at the church, and if he is not content with these, then Robert is to have the place, and John the close and the arable land.

His annual obit to be charged on his meadow next the "loo". the residue to sons John and Robert to be divided between them after the death of his wife.

Exor. Richard Potter, to have 3s. 4d. for his labour. Witn. sir William Atkynson, vicar of Potton, John Waren.

87.
Thomas Santon of Cadyngton. 12 May, pr. 30 June 1518. (2: 82)
Burial in the churchyard of Todyngton [*sic*]; to mother church of Lincoln 4d.; to high altar in "the sayd church of Cadyngton" 20d.; to the rood light 4d.; to Our Lady light 4d.; to the repair of Cadyngton church 16d..

To son William the house that William Preston lives in called Pollyns, with 3 acres of land on the backside of it, paying 12d. a year to the house where testator lives called Herberdes. William is to enter on the property when he reaches the age of 18 years.

To son Jamys 26s. 8d.; to Johan Houghton 26s. 8d., or the house she lives in for four years, whichever she wishes; to daughter Cicely his best brass pan, best brass pot, a "chaffer" of brass and a chest of spruce board, which are to be given her on the day of her marriage.

To wife Elizabeth for life all testator's houses and lands in Bedfordshire called Herberdes and Malyns, with 12 acres of land in Hertfordshire, that is 6 acres enclosed and 6 acres in the common fields, paying the lord's rent and keeping it in repair. After the death of wife the property is to go to son Harry and the heirs of his body for ever. If any of his children die without issue, then "I will ich child be others heyer", and if they all fail, then the property is to be sold "to fynd a prest to syng a yere for them that they cam of", and the remainder to be used for Cadyngton church under the direction of the vicar and church wardens. A trental to be sung for testator in Cadyngton parish immediately after his death. Residue to wife Elizabeth.

Exors. wife Elizabeth and William Preston, who is to have 3s. 4d. for his labour. Witn. sir Thomas Elston vicar, John [?]Nith', William Eliott, Geffray Abyngton, Thomas Houghton.

88.
William Hayward/Heyward of Dunstable. 25 Mar., pr. 30 June 1518. (2: 83)
Burial in "the parissh yard of Dunstable Peter and Pawle"; to the canons of the Priory Church 10s. for a trental to be sung; to the friars of Dunstable 10s. for a trental; to mother church of Lincoln 4d.; to the high altar of the Priory church 12d.; to the Trinity altar in the parish 8d.; to St. John's altar 12d..

To his wife for life an acre of land in Houghton field between Mr. Dyve's lands on the east side, and the lands of Saint John the Baptist on the west side, and abutting on Ykelyng Street. After her death this land is to go to Saint John the Baptist for ever. Residue to wife Alys.

Exors. wife Alys and John Neele, he to have 3s. 4d. for his labour; supervisor Richard Birton who is to have 3s. 4d. for his labour. Witn. sir Roger Geffray parish priest, sir Robert Cotton, Robert Harryson, Thomas Hill.

89.
Thomas Davy of Dunstable. 14 Feb. 1517/8, pr. 29 June 1518. (2: 84d)
Burial in churchyard of St. Peter and St. Paul of Dunstable; to mother church of Lincoln 2d.; to high altar in Priory church 12d.; to son Thomas testator's best brass pot; to Margaret Chapman a mattress, a coverlet, a pair of sheets.

To wife Elizabeth and her heirs and assigns for ever two acres of land in Houghton fields. Residue to wife Elizabeth to use for herself and for their children.

Exors. wife Elizabeth and John Fossey; supervisor Benet Davy testator's brother. Witn. sir Roger Geffray, Elys Hosbourne, Thomas Knightley.
Probate granted to widow, the other executor refusing to act.

90.
Robert A Lee (Alee) of Dunstable. 1 Sep., pr. 6 Sep. 1518. (2: 85)
Burial in the church of St. Peter of Dunstable. For his mortuary 40s.; to the high altar in the Priory 10s.; to sir Mychaell Chanon the £5 "which remayneth in the hond of Mr. George Cavdissh".

To Robert Bentley 40s.; to the canons of Dunstable 40s. for four trentals for testator's soul; to wife Agnes "all my stuff within my chaumber she to do with it what she will".

To wife Agnes for life a tenement and close in the south end of Dunstable, and after her death it is to go to the new chapel in the Priory which sir John Wastell has lately new built.

All the covenants and bargains made between testator and his wife and Richard Jakson and Elizabeth Jakson his wife shall stand for ever, as they appear more plainly in a pair of indentures made between them.

To Richard Jakson three and a half acres of land in Houghton fields and all testator's other goods, money, corn and cattle, with all other goods in the realm of England.

Exors. Richard Jakson, sir John Warwik vicar of Toternow who is to have 10s. for his labour. Witn. sir Roger Geffrey, John Holdern, John Awdley.

91.
Robert White vicar of Podyngton. 29 July, pr. 9 Aug. 1521. (2: 86)
Burial in the chancel of Podyngton before the high altar; for his principal "that thyng that the law requirith and askith of right".

To kinsman George Whit testator's horse, harness, carts, ploughs with all appurtenances, 16 "neat" (cattle) young and old; the pease field whole; all the wheat in the High Field and half the barley, household stuff and 60 sheep.

To John Gray a cow; to "Masteres" Jane Odell two sheep; "To the woman that kept me in my secknes my bed that I departed in"; to Podyngton church £3 6s. 8d. "to help to by them a book"; to mother church of Lincoln 4d..

Exors. sir William Eliott parson of Farndissh, William Burton, John Lews (or Laws), John Cornyssh of Podyngton, to whom the residue of his estate "to bear my charges and to dispose them for the wele and profit of my sowle". Witn. John Heyward, Henry Drage, Thomas Burton.

92.
Thomas Patwyn [*margin* Patwik] of Markyate in the parish of Stodham. 13 July, pr. 9 Aug. 1521. (2: 86d)
(*Latin*) Burial in churchyard of St. Mary of Stodham. To mother church of Lincoln 2d.; to wife Alice all tenements and lands while she remains unmarried, and if she remarries, then testator's best tenement with appurtenances to son Richard, the second tenement with appurtenances to son Thomas, and a meadow in the fields of Dunstable Houghton to daughter Agnes. Residue to wife Alice.

Exors. wife Alice, son Richard. Witn. Thomas Chessam, Thomas Pays, John Tomlynson.
Probate granted to wife Alice, son Richard Patewik refusing to act.

93.
John Hawkyns of Kynges Houghton, 29 July, pr. 9 Aug. 1521. (2: 87)
Testament Burial in the churchyard of All Hallows in Houghton; to the

high altar for tithes and offerings forgotten a bushel of barley; to every light in the church "that custumably the parisshons use to gather for" a bushel of barley; to the making of the tabernacle of All Hallows 6s. 8d.; a trental of masses to be sung immediately after death for souls and self, friends and all Christians; to the maintenance of the torches 2 bushels of malt; to the Friars Preacher of Dunstable a quarter of malt to pray for souls of testator and his friends; to the maintenance of the town priest in Houghton 6s. 8d. yearly, as long as the parishioners maintain him.

To eldest son Richard 3 horses, a plough and its gear, a cart and its gear; to son Robert a plough with 3 horses and all its gear, and a cart with its gear; to wife Marion the rest of the horses; to sons Richard and Robert 3 score sheep each; to daughter Margaret forty sheep; to each god-child a ewe or else a ewe pugg; to wife Marion the rest of the sheep; to sons Richard and Robert "all my boordes and cletes" to be divided between them.

Wife Marion is to have "mete and drynk and her dwelling with Richard my Sonne duryng her naturall liff' and he to give her yerely iiij quarters malt"; and if son Richard and Marion cannot agree, then Marion is to live with Robert instead, and Richard is to give her 6 quarters of malt yearly.

To son Richard 30 quarters of barley; to son Robert 20 quarters of barley and two beasts; to son Richard and wife the rest of the beasts, divided equally between them.

Residue to be disposed of by exors. for good of soul.

Will To eldest son Richard and the heirs of his body, the house testator dwells in and a close called Wulfes, with woods, lands, meadows, pastures, rents and services; to son Robert and the heirs of his body a messuage called Gobyns and Killyngworth, with lands, woods, meadows, pastures, rents and services, and an acre of land in Woodway furlong.

If either die without issue, their share goes to the survivor, and if both die without issue then both properties go to daughter Margaret. If she should then die without issue, it is to be sold, and half the proceeds to go to Houghton church to pray for souls of testator, his friends and all Christians, and the other half to be spent on highways where there is most need.

To wife Marion an acre of land in Sewell field, and if "she do troble or vex Richard or Robert my sonnys in this my last will in any thyng to them bequeathed" she is to forfeit any bequest to her.

Exors. John Wallys and sons Richard and Robert. Witn. master William Fossey, vicar of Houghton, John Eme the younger, Mathew Pedder.

94.
Johan Harper of Bydenham, widow. 26 July, pr. 14 Aug. 1521. (2: 88d)
Burial in churchyard of St. James in Bydenham; for mortuary as customary; to the high altar for tithes forgotten 12d.; to Our Lady altar a cloth of diaper; to Our Lady light 20d.; to the bells 4 bushels of barley; to St. John's light 12d.; to St. James' light 2 lb. of wax; to St. Nicholas light 8d.; to sister Emma Kyng a bed; to Robert Wright a bullock, to each god-child in the parish a sheep; to the children of William Harper, John Harper and John Emery a sheep to each; to church of Lincoln 4d.; to Thomas Mowse her two houses in the parish "the sayd Thomas shall make a drynkyng for the space of xx yerys every yere *dirige* and masse dispending vjs."; to the wife of John Emery a pot and a pan; to John Pestell 4 bushels of barley; to William Harper 6s. 8d.; to John Amere 6s. 8d.; to the making if the sepulchre 6s. 8d.; to the friars of Bedford 10s.; to the church of Mulshoo 6s. 8d.; to sir Thomas Harper and sir William Harper 13s. 4d.. Residue to Thomas Mowse my cousin.

Exors. brother John Wright, William Harper, Thomas Mowse; overseer John Faldo. Witn. sir John Billynges, John Harper, John Emery, John Awnsty, John Pestell.

95.
Alys Cooke of Eyton (Bray). 7 Aug., pr. 23 Sep. 1521. (2: 89)
Burial in the churchyard of Our Lady of Eyton; to mother church of Lincoln 2d.; to the high altar for tithes and oblations forgotten 12d.; to the rood light 8d.; to the sepulchre light 4d.; to St. Nicholas light 4d.; to the Holy Trinity light 12d.; to the three small lights 6d.; to every small light 1d.; to maintaining the torches 6d.; to Eyton church 10s.; "To the sowle prest or brotherhed prest if the parissh have oon" 10s.; to the highway 6s. 8d..

"I will that an yerely mynd be kept for my sowle and all Cristen sowlys to the sum yerely iiij s.. The name of the grownd that shall continew and kepe this mynd is called Patrikkes with mede and lond that longith thereto".

To son Richard Cooke "for his part of Patrikkes and so he is well content therewith" 26s. 8d.; to daughter Agnes 20 quarters of barley, 10 this year and 10 next year; to Richard Cooke an ox bullock. To daughter Agnes 40s. in money, a cow, a red heifer, four sheep, the best brass pot, the best pan, half testator's napery ware, a cauldron, a coverlet, a bolster, 2 pillows, 2 coffers, 5 platters, a basin, a chafing-dish, four saucers, a candlestick. To son John Cooke a horse, a cow, four sheep, 6 quarters of barley, a coverlet, a blanket, 3 pairs of sheets, a little cauldron, a brass pot of two gallons.

To "my mother Woorsley" half a quarter of wheat and half a quarter of malt; to son Thomas Cooke 26s. 8d. and the house he dwells in, for a reasonable price, the money arising to be distributed among his other brothers equally according to his father's will.

To Agnes Cooke her son's daughter a cow; to servant John a quarter of barley and a sheep; to brother's son Thomas Cooke half a quarter of barley; to the friars of Dunstable a quarter of barley; to John Peddar a sheet; to Richard and William the sons of Thomas Cooke two quarters of barley, and to Richard a sheet and to William two sheets; to Elizabeth daughter to Thomas Cooke a pair of sheets; to Agnes daughter to Thomas Cooke one sheet; to Jane daughter to Thomas Cooke two pairs of sheets.

Residue to son William Cooke, who is also to be executor. Supervisor Thomas Cooke, taking for his labour what executor thinks best. Witn. sir William Samson vicar of Eyton, sir Thomas Thomlynson, Richard Broke, William Draper.

96.
Thomas Knyght of Bedford, mercer. 14 Apr., pr. 31 May 1522. (2: 90d)

Burial in the churchyard on the north side of St. Powlys church by wife Elizabeth; to the high altar of the same church for tithes forgotten 20d.; to mother church of Lincoln 4d.; to convent of Newenham and to the Grey Friars of Bedford to each 10s. for a trental of masses for testator's soul; to an honest priest £5 6s. 8d. to say mass for one year at St. George's altar in St. Powlys church; to repair the long causeway beyond Stafford bridge 10s.; to repair Bedford bridge 13s. 4d.; to repair the long bridge beyond Turvey 10s.; for mending the highways round Bedford 13s. 4d.; to every poor person living in Bedford 2d.; to everyone of the "bedemen" in Bedford a shirt of canvas; to friar William Knyght 3s. 4d. "when he shall syng his first masse".

To testator's brother Richard Knyght his best gown, best doublet, best shirt, best hose and 20s. in money; to John Knyght smith and to Thomas his son a quarter of malt, to be divided between them; to his eldest daughter Johan all lands and tenements in Cayshoo/Keyshoe, and if she die without male heirs, the property is to be divided equally between Ame and Gynne testator's daughters; to daughters Ame and Gynne equally between them testator's tenements in Shepischepyng, and two tenements in the Well Street, and if either Ame or Gynne die without male heirs, her part to go to daughter Johan. If all daughters die without male heirs, then all property in Bedford and Keyshoo to be sold and the money used for an honest priest to say masses for "me and all my good frends in Powlys church by the space of ij yere". From the remainder of the money, 20s. is to be given yearly to poor people living in Bedford for as long as the money lasts.

To eldest daughter Johan half of everything in the shop, the other half to be divided between daughters Ame and Gyn; to daughter Ame £10 and to Gynne her sister £8, the money to be given them when they reach the age of 20. If any daughter should die before the age of 20, her bequests are to be divided between the surviving sisters, and if all die then the "ware and money" to be "spent in prayers and other good meritorious dedes for the wealth of my sowle" and the souls of his friends and all Christians.

Residue to his father and mother, to have "in governaunce to help my childerne when they shall have nede".

Exors. father Thomas Knyght, and Richard Knyght, each to have 13s. 4d.. Overseer sir John Bikleswade "I will that he have xiijs. iiij.". Witn. Nicholas Hogys, William Rige.
Probate granted to Thomas Knyght.

97.
Alexander Crawley/Crowley in the parish of St. John the Baptist in Bedford. 4 Dec., pr. 12 Dec. 1523. (2: 92)

To be buried in the church of St. John the Baptist before St. Katerin's altar; to the high altar for tithes forgotten 2s.; to mother church of Lincoln 4d.; for his "layer" [flagstone] in the church 6s. 8d.; to a good honest priest to sing for his soul for half a year in the same church 4 marks; to the friars of Bedford 10s. to sing a trental and 10s. to repair their house; to the prior and convent of Newenham and to the prior and convent of Chixsand 6s. 8d. each to pray for his soul; to Jane Lacy, after the death of testator's wife Margery, 3 silver spoons, a silver salt and a featherbed and what belongs to it; to her sister Agnes Lacy 3 silver spoons and a silver goblet.

To wife Margery for life the house testator lives in with 4 acres of land, two in Bedford field, one in Karyngton field and one in Kempston field. After her death the property goes to Henry Lacy for his lifetime, and then to Jane and Agnes Lacy his children by testator's daughter.

To friar Crawley 10s.; to every god-child 4d..

Residue to wife Margery. Exors. wife Margery and Thomas Knyght the draper, he to have 6s. for his labour. Overseer son-in-law Henry Lacy. Witn. sir John Kyng parish priest, John Duffyn, John Wilkynson.

98.
Thomas Bottisford in Wynfeld in Chalgrave parish. May, pr. 12 Dec. 1523. (2: 92d)

Burial in the churchyard of Chalgrave; for mortuary as the manner of the town; to mother church of Lincoln 2d.; to the high altar of Chalgrave a bushel of wheat; to the lights in the parish church half a quarter of barley; to the bells and to the torches 2 bushels of barley; to wife Johan for life, the tenement testator dwells in with appurtenances in Wynfeld, and after her death to son Henry and his male children, or

"if he hath none I will that it shall remayn and cum agayn to the name";
to wife Johan also the cottage in Tebworth with ten acres of land, and
then to son John, he to pay her 8s. a year as long as she lives.

Exors. wife Johan and son sir Thomas, to whom the residue, to dispose part for testator's soul, and part as they think best. Overseer sir
John Barsott the curate. Witn. "thes men" [*unfinished*]

99.
John By of Colmorth. 27 Feb. 1524/5, pr. 8 Apr. 1525. (2: 93)
Burial in the churchyard of Saint Denes in Colmorth; to the high altar
for tithes forgotten 12d.; to the mother church of Lincoln 4d.; to
Colmorth church 2s.; to a priest for 3 masses of Scala Celi 15d.; to
Revennysden church 6s. 8d.; to Thomas Pecok 33s. 4d.; to Robert
Bulmer 6s. 8d.; to wife Johan during her life, his house and land "with
closyng" and appurtenances as long as she remains unmarried. When
she dies or remarries, the house is to be sold, and Robert Bulmer is to
buy it for the price of £15 6s. 8d., having 3 years to pay. After the sale
a priest is to celebrate mass for testator and friends for three quarters
of a year. To John Peryn 3s. 4d.; to mending Lemannys bridge 6s. 8d.;
to Colmorth church 2 wax tapers of 4 lb. each.

Residue "to the disposicion of myn executors". Exors. Thomas Pecok
and testator's wife. Supervisor Robert Bulmer. Witn. sir Richard Ford,
Richard Pecok, Robert Bulmer, "she to make no wast of the wood".

100.
John Peke of parish of St. Powlys in Bedford. 12 July, pr. 19 July 1524.
(2: 93d)
Burial in churchyard of St. Powlys in Bedford; to high altar for tithes
forgotten 20d.; to mother church of Lincoln 4d.; to sir Alexander
Symson, parish priest 12d.; to sons Thomas, Henry and Richard Peke
40s. each; to daughter Johan 26s. 8d.; to wife Margery for life testator's
house, and after her death it is to be sold "to the performance of this
my will to the most advauntage" and then 40s. to an honest priest "to
be song in Powlys church".

Residue to wife Margery. Exors. wife Margery and Thomas Knyght
smith. Overseer John Baker.   Witn. sir Alexander parish priest; sir
Thomas Py, John Gydyng.

101.
William Cooke of Todyngton. 1518, pr. 8 May 1518. (2: 94)
Burial in church of Todyngton; for mortuary his best beast; to church
of Lincoln 4d.; to Todyngton church 20s.; to the candlestick before Our
Lady 8d.; to the church of Latbere [Lathbury, Bucks.] 13s. 4d..

To wife Elizabeth his house in Todyngton and his house in Heryng

[Herne] with their appurtenances for 12 years, she keeping them in repair. At the end of the 12 years the property is to go to his daughter Agnes and the heirs of her body.

To daughter Johan and the heirs of her body his house in Latbere with appurts. with 12 acres of land and meadow and two closes in the township of Latbere and Gothiris [Gayhurst, Bucks.] after the death of testator's mother. Should mother die before Johan comes to lawful age, then testator's brother Thomas is to look after the land until she comes of age.

If either child die without issue of their bodies, their lands to go to the survivor; if both should die without issue the lands in Todyngton and Latbere to go to testator's brother Thomas and his heirs, who are then to give £10 to Todyngton Church to buy two silver candlesticks for the high altar. Brother Thomas will also be required to give £10 for testator's soul for the Latbere house, and in that house testator's great table, his lead, cupboard and great coffer are to remain as "standers" (fixtures) of the house.

Wife Elizabeth is to keep an annual obit in the church of Todyngton with the whole choir, and she is to distribute 3s. 4d. to poor people for the 12 years, and to hire a priest to sing for testator for a whole year in Todyngton church "as shortely as she can".

To brother Thomas his best gown, his worsted jacket, his camlet doublet, his best shirt, and Thomas is to have two trentals sung for testator. Thomas is to look after all the lands after the 12 years on behalf of the children until they are of lawful age or until they marry. The children are "to be at the rule and governaunce of my brother Thomas as he thynketh best".

Residue to wife. Exors. wife Elizabeth and brother Thomas. Witn. sir Thomas Milward, sir John Bager, sir George Popele.

102.
Richard Sternall. 21 Febr., pr. 5 Mar. 1518/9. (2: 95d)
Burial in the churchyard of St. John the Baptist of Eversoll; for mortuary as custom of the town; to church of Lincoln 2d.; to Our Lady 2d.; to the rood 2d.; to St. Sith 2d.; to the Trinity 2d.; to St. Nicholas 2d.; to Our Blessed Lady of Wobourne 2d.; to daughter Elyn 6s. 8d..

To wife for life, house and land in Eversoll, and after her death to son John Sternell. Residue to wife Isabell to use for souls of testator and all Christians.

Executrix wife Isabell. Witn. sir John Slow, Herry Draper, Thomas Plommer.

103.
Thomas Bray, Chawley end in Cadyngton parish. 10 July, pr. 13 July 1521. (2: 96)

Burial in churchyard of All Hallows of Cadyngton; to the high altar of Cadyngton 20d. "in recompence of my tithis and offerynges eny tyme withdrawen or negligently forgotten in dischargyng of my sowle"; to mother church of Lincoln 4d.; to rood light 8d.; to Our Lady light 8d.; to all the other small lights in the church a pound of wax to be divided among them; to the repair of the said church a quarter of malt; to each god–child 4d..

To John Maydwell his servant a quarter of malt; to Alis Bradwyn a red heifer; to William Deane 6s. 8d. "toward his mariage"; to Alys Deane 6s. 8d. "toward her marriage"; to Agnes the wife of Andrew Bray, 2 half-acres of wheat in Rismare field.

Elizabeth his wife is to have a trental of masses said in the parish church of Cadyngton for souls of testator, his father and mother, and all Christians, during the year after his death.

To wife Elizabeth for life, all his lands, tenements, rents and services in the towns and fields of Chawley, Cadyngton and Luton, in the counties of Beds. and Herts.. After her death property is to go to Andrew Bray and Agnes his wife and the heirs of Andrew for ever. If Andrew should die without issue, which God forbid, then the property is to go to Thomas Bray of the Bury, and to his heirs for ever. Instructions to his feoffees to hold his property to these uses.

Residue to wife Elizabeth. Executrix wife Elizabeth. Overseer Thomas Bray of the Bury. Witn. sir Thomas Elson vicar, William Albright, Thomas Pett.

104.
Cuthbert Cutlatt of Eyton (Bray). 4 July, pr. 13 July 1521. (2: 97)

To be buried in churchyard of the parish church of Our Lady; to mother church of Lincoln 4d.; to the high altar of Eyton for tithes and oblations forgotten 3s. 4d.; to the upkeep of the sepulchre light 12d.; to the Holy Trinity light 16d.; to the rood light in the "soler or loft" 12d.; to St. Nicholas light 8d.; to three other small lights 6d.; to the repair of the bells in the steeple 8d.; to maintaining the torches 8d.; to St. Thomas' light a taper of a pound of wax; to St. Loys' light "a pound of wax redy made in a tapyr"; to St. Erasmus bishop and martyr 1d.; to St. Sunday's light a taper of a pound of wax; to an honest priest £6 "for his wages or salary" to sing for souls of testator and all Christians for a whole year, to be paid quarterly or at the half year; to removing the high altar in the chancel of Eyton 6s. 8d. "when it shall happen to be removed made and don"; to son-in-law Richard Bukmaster 20s. sterling.

To wife Alys for life, all purchased lands and tenements and all lands and tenements in Eyton or Toternow "namyd by divers parcellys in my new dede of feoffement with medows lesis pasturys toftis closys rentes and services as they are more playnly rehersed and namyd in the dede of feoffment". After her death the property is to go to son John Cutlatt and the heirs of his body, or if he should die without issue, to Marion Condliff, Elizabeth Stringer and Alys Bukmaster testator's daughters and their heirs, equally divided between them.

Should the daughters also die without issue, then the property is to go to Thomas Cutlatt, son of Henry Cutlatt testator's deceased brother, and to the heirs of his body in fee simple for ever, to hold of the chief lords of the fees by due and customary services.

The feoffees, named in his deed of feoffment as Cutbert Jenkyn, Henry George, Richard Bukmaster, Edmund and Hugh Alen, shall stand enfeoffed in the said property "unto the behoff and use of this my sayd will to be fulfilled and to the use of all the sayd remaynders aboverehersed" that is, to wife for life, then to son John, then to daughters, then to heirs of Thomas Cutlatt.

Executrix wife Alice, to whom the residue. Supervisor William Condliff "takyng for his labour as the discrecion of my wife will thynk best". Witn. sir William Samson vicar of Eyton, John Cutlatt the elder, John Smyth, Richard Broke, Richard and William Cooke.

105.
William Offode of Henlow. 2 Apr., pr. 27 Jul. 1521. (2: 98d)
Burial in the churchyard of Our Blessed Lady in Henlow; for principal after the custom of the country; to the high altar a bushel of barley for forgotten tithes; to the mother church of Lincoln 1d.; to the brotherhood of Our Lady in Henlow 6s. 8d. to be paid at 10d. a quarter to the priest until it is all paid; to the Crutched Friars of London 16d. for four masses of Scala Celi, one each for the souls of testator's father, mother, first wife and himself.

To Bredstret bridge 2 loads of stones to be laid at his own cost and charge; to wife Elizabeth six quarters of barley owed to testator by John Edward the younger. To John son of William Waren an ox.

To wife Elizabeth testator's tenement with appurtenances until son William is 18 years old, when he is to have it for his own. Should he die before then Elizabeth is to have it, and if Elizabeth should die before William is 18, then William is to have the tenement. If wife and son William both die, the property is to go to testator's daughter Ame and her children.

Executrix wife Elizabeth to whom the residue. Overseer sir Richard Malcot vicar of the same town. Witn. sir Robert Bisshop parish priest of the same town, Thomas Bret supervisor.

106.
William Warlow of Aspley. 6 July, pr. 27 July 1521. (2: 99)

Burial in churchyard of St. Botolff in Aspley; for mortuary as customary; to high altar half a quarter of barley; to St. Botolf's lane 2 bushels of barley; to son William the crop on the ground.

Executors are testator's natural sons Thomas Warlow, Nicholas Warlow and William Warlow, who are to sell the house in which testator dwells to pay his debts and to have 2 trentals sung in the parish church of Aspley by an honest priest. Residue to the three sons named above to be equally divided between them "with the cownsell and after the cownsellys of Thomas Harding and Thomas Stratton". Supervisor Thomas Stratton. Witn. William Pell parson of Aspley, John Brakley.

107.
Rawff Smyth of Litlyngton. 12 Aug., pr. 23 Nov. 1520. (2: 100)

Burial within the parish church "afore Our lady of Pitie"; to mother church of Lincoln 4d.; to the high altar for tithes forgotten 8d..

To wife Alys for life, testator's copyhold house in Litlyngton with reversion to son Richard.

To the monastery of Barkyns 20s. to pray for his soul.

Executrix wife Alys, to whom the residue. Witn. sir Peter Dent his ghostly father, John Semys.

108.
Thomas Hopkyns alias Serle of Millo in the parish of Dunton. 31 Oct., pr. 22 Nov. 1521. (2: 100d)

Burial in churchyard of Our Lady of Dunton; to the mother church of Lincoln 6d.; to the high altar of Dunton for tithes negligently forgotten 20d.; to the gilding of Our Blessed Lady in the chancel of Dunton 13s. 4d.; to the sepulchre light 3s. 4d.; to the rood light 3s. 4d.; to the bells 3s. 4d.; to the torches 3s. 4d.; to William Barford and his wife 13s. 4d.; to Gerard Carinton and his wife 13s. 4d.; to Thomas Beton a quarter of barley; "to the makying of the Palme cross in the church yard of Dunton" 3s. 4d.; to the friars of Bedford 10s.; to the Black Friars in Cambridge 3s. 4d.; to each god-child a bushel of barley.

Wife Alys to hire a priest for £5 13s. 4d. to celebrate for one year mass and other divine service for souls of testator and his friends in the church of Dunton.

To wife Alys for her lifetime, the house testator dwells in called Kirwyns, with all appurts., and all moveable goods, and she is to keep the house in repair. After her death his executors are to have the house (keeping it in repair and paying 8s. for an annual obit and an annual trental) until Gerard Hopkyns, son of Nicholas Hopkyn, reaches the age of 22. Then the property is to go to Gerard Hopkyn and his heirs male, and he is to keep it in repair and pay for an obit costing 8s. for souls of testator, his wife, his father and mother and his friends.

If the obit is not kept or if the property is not in repair, then it is to go to Robert Hopkyns and his heirs male under the same conditions, and if Robert fail then it goes successively to Richard Hopkyns and his heirs male, then to Rawff Hopkins and his heirs male, and then to John Hopkyns and his heirs male. If all these fail to keep up the repairs and the annual obit then his executors "with cownsell of the vicar of Dunton with the most part of the parissh" shall sell the property and bestow the money in Dunton church where there is most need. And "who so cum by the foresayd hows" is to keep the obit of 8s. a year.

Exors. wife Alys, William Burford, Gerard Karyngton, John Clay. Witn. sir John Lamb priest, William Mychell, Robert Rostoll.

109.
Thomas Osbourne of Markyate. 3 Dec., pr. 7 Dec. 1521. (2: 101d)

Burial in churchyard of Cadyngton; to mother church of Lincoln 2d.; to the high altar of Cadyngton church 12d.; to Our Lady light 4d.; to the rood light 4d.; to the bells and torches 8d.; for a trental of masses in the parish church of Cadyngton 10s..

To wife Johan for life the house he bought from Thomas Clovyer and Elizabeth his wife. To son Thomas all other houses and lands in Cadyngton, Stodham and Flamsted, both copyhold and freehold. To wife Joan half his beasts and sheep; to son Thomas and daughter Alys the other half of his beasts and sheep to be "indifferently devydid" between them; to wife Johan 3 horses; to son Thomas 2 horses, to daughter Alys a quarter of wheat and 6s. 8d.; to son Thomas a quarter of wheat, 6s. 8d., and an acre of wheat "an halff uppon the grownd"; to John Osborne his brother's son 2 sheep.

Executrix wife Johan to whom residue. Supervisor Geffray Basseley he to have 3s. 4d. for his labour. Witn. sir Thomas Elneston vicar, William Dane clerk, Nicholas Tayllour, William Osmond, Thomas Blowright.

110.
John Petitt of Dunstable. 26 Nov., pr. 7 Dec. 1521. (2: 102d)

Burial in churchyard of St. Peter's; for mortuary best good as customary; to the high altar in the Priory church 4d. for tithes and oblations forgotten; to church of Lincoln 2d.; to making the "roff" (roof) in the parish church 20d.; to the friars 20d..

To wife Johan for life his house and lands in Toternow, and after her death to testator's daughter Mawde. To the torches 4d..

Residue to wife Johan. Exors. John Holdorne who is to have 6s. 8d.

for his work, and wife Johan. Witn. sir William Thippes, Thomas Buttler.
Probate granted to John Holdorne.

111.
Elizabeth Wynch of Luton, widow. 8 Nov., pr. 7 Dec. 1521. (2: 103)
    Burial in church of Luton, next to the body of husband John Durant; to high altar of Luton 6s. 8d. for tithes forgotten; to mother church of Lincoln 4d.; to each god-child 20d.; to keep a perpetual light to St. Sith in Luton church, the annual rent of an acre of land in Blakwalle field on Kingishill; to repair the church a quarter of malt; to a priest to sing for testator and her friends for a year 9 marks; to Agnes Wynch daughter of Thomas Wynch 3s. 4d.; to John Smyth a pair of sheets, a towel, 2 brass pots, a blanket; to Elizabeth Petit testator's russet gown.
    To the Awlmeshows in Luton her best red covering; to Christian Ordway her best violet gown; to Mawde Adam her next violet gown; to Thomas Petid a quarter of malt; to every child of Thomas Perrot 6s. 8d.; to every child of William Welsh 6s. 8d.; to Thomas Broke's wife of Todyngton a kirtle; to Thomas Leycroft a quarter of malt; to Robert Wynch a silver spoon; to Elizabeth Elder a silver spoon; to the fraternity of the Blessed Trinity in Luton 7s. 6d.; to repairing a highway called The Red Lane 6s. 8d.; to repairing other highways "where most nede is" 20s.; to Robert Adam a quarter of malt; to Margaret Carter a quarter of malt and the best basin; to Elizabeth Stopisley a quarter of malt and the second basin; to repair the candlesticks at the brotherhood altar 13s. 4d.; to Thomas Broke a quarter of malt; to Emme Yong a quarter of malt; to Johan Yong a pewter platter; to Johan Ordway a pewter platter; to Thomas Wynch testator's amber beads; to goddaughter Elizabeth Welsh a chafer with feet; to Thomas Perotte's wife a chafer; to Thomas Perott the featherbed testator lies on and her table; to William Welsh her other featherbed and her coffer.
    To Thomas Perott all her houses in Luton and all lands and meadows, paying for them £24, and he and his heirs are bound to keep a yearly obit perpetually in the church of Luton with the whole choir, both priests and clerks, to pray for souls of testator and her husband John Durant, and to pay for this at least 5s.; also to Thomas Perott her "closyng" called Hevyns in the parish of Flamsted, paying for it £10 and "performyng the premissis as concernyng the kepyng of my perpetuall obit".
    To William Welsh all her part of the tilth at Stoppisley for the term of her indenture.
    Exors. Thomas Perott and William Welsh, each to have 6s. 8d. for their work, and they to dispose of the residue for the health of her soul. Overseer Master Doctor Sheffeld, to have 3s. 4d. for his labour. Witn.

Master Doctor Sheffeld vicar of Luton, Thomas Hows notary, sir John Hunter priest, Thomas Marten smith, William Child of the same town.

112.
Thomas Atpownd of Maldon. 15 Nov. 1521, pr. 11 Jan. 1521/2. (2: 104d)
    Burial within the church of Our Blessed Lady at Malden; to the high altar for tithes and oblations forgotten 6d.; to the mother church of Lincoln 4d.; for his mortuary "my best good"; to All Souls light 12d.; to the bells 20d.; to the torches 8d.; an honest priest "to syng for me, my father and mother, my grandsire and grandmother, and all Cristen sowlys" for a whole year in Maldon church, having for his labour what is customary.
    To wife Margaret all household stuff and all cattle, and £6 13s. 4d. reserved from the sale of the renement in Maldon where testator lives.
    Residue to wife Margaret. Exors. wife Margaret, William Welle of Milbrok; William Lenton the elder of Malden. Witn. William Lenton parish clerk of Malden; sir Thomas Whalley priest; Robert Davy, William Harper.

113.
John Strynger. 31 Dec. 1521, pr. 8 Jan. 1521/2. (2: 105)
Testament   Burial in the churchyard of Alhalows in Houghton (Conquest); to the high altar for tithes forgotten a bushel of barley; to the mother church of Lincoln 1d.; to the rood light 2d.; to the tabernacle of All Hallows 2d.; to Our Lady light 2d.; to the Twelve Apostles light 1d.; to St. Anne and St. Thomas 2d.; to St. Martyn and St. Nicholas 2d.; to St. Margaret and St. Mary Mawdlen and St. Katerin 1d.
    To John my son a quarter of malt and half a quarter of wheat; to testator's four daughters 4 nobles.
    Residue to wife Elizabeth. Exors. wife Elizabeth and John Eme the elder. Witn. John Barbour, Thomas Hardyng, William Harrygate.
Will   He will to Elizabeth his wife all his house and lands in Houghton for 20 years, and then the property is to go to testator's son John, and should John die without heirs of his body, then to daughter Alys, and then (failing heirs of her body) in succession to daughters Johan, Agnes and Margaret, and if these all die without issue then to the youngest son of William Stringer, and in default of heirs of his body to his eldest brother and his heirs, in default to the next of testator's blood.

114.
William Church of Patenham in the parish of Stephynton. 1 Oct. 1521, pr. 25 Jan. 1521/2. (2: 106)

Burial in the chapel of St. Peter, under licence of the vicar of Stephynton; to the vicar of Stephynton his best beast as customary; to the high altar of Stephynton 12d.; to the high altar of St. Peter 12d.; to the mother church of Lincoln 4d.; to repair Stafford bridge half a quarter of barley; to every child of Robert Stroston a sheep; to each child of John Tollers a sheep; to testator's son William Church a cow; to Elysabeth Toller a cow; to Alys Strocton a cow; to an honest priest 4 marks to sing for souls of testator, his friends and all Christians for half a year.

To wife Agnes Church during her life all testator's lands and tenements in Stephynton, Patenham and Careleton, and on her death to son John Church and his heirs for ever. Residue to executors.

Exors. wife Agnes Church and son John Church. Supervisors: John Toller, Robert Strotton, William Church. Witn. Robert Gardiner, William Morys, Richard Heyward.

115.
Agnes Johnson of Chixsand. 21 Nov. 1521, probate not recorded. (2: 107)

Burial in the church "of the Priory of Chixsand byfore the roode byside my husbond"; for principal "as it shall require"; to the high altar 3s. 4d. for tithes and oblations forgotten; to the mother church of Lincoln 4d., to the prior of Chixsand 26s. 8d. at testator's burial day; to the subprior 2s. on the same day; to every canon there who is a priest 12d.; to every novice 6d.; to the nuns and sisters there 20s. equally divided among them; to the parson of Campton on testator's burial day 6s. 8d.; to sir Hugh Massy 12d.; to sir John Woodward 12d.; to every other priest at my burial 4d.; to every clerk 2d. "providid alway that I have made this gift more larger at my buriall day by cawse I will that myn executors shall kepe no moneth day for me".

To Richard Abolton and his wife 40s. in money and testator's second gown; to Kateryn the daughter of Richard Abolton a girdle with a buckle that is not turned; to William Vaughan 6s. 8d.; and to his wife testator's best kirtle and best cap; to Edward Johnson 6s. 8d. and to his wife 3s. 4d. and to his son Humfrey 2 sheep; to Mathew ap David 6s. 8d.; to Evan 6s. 8d.; to William Mathew 20s. at the age of 21 years; to every child of Thomas Warner 2 sheep; to the rood light of Campton 3s. 4d.; to the friars of Bedford 10s. for a trental; to Dane (Dom) John Johnson 6s. 8d.; to Dame Isabel Lamkyn 3s. 4d..

To Alys Flynders testator's best gown, best girdle, wedding ring and a cow; to Humfrey Flynders 5 marks in money, 10 sheep, a cow, a featherbed, a mattress, 4 pairs of sheets, a bolster, 2 pillows, 2 coverlets, 2 brass pots, a kettle, a pan, a chafer of a pottle, half a dozen pewter vessels, a silver ring, half a dozen silver spoons with knops, 2 bell candle-

Drawn by J.P.Neale

Engraved by A.Cruse

3. Chicksands Priory, a Gilbertine house founded about the year 1150. In the late sixteenth century Chicksands became the home of the Osborne family, who remained there until this century. Agnes Johnson of Chicksands made her will in November 1521 (no. 115) and asked for burial in the priory church.   *J. P. Neale, 1829*

sticks and a chafing dish; to Margery Flynders 5 marks in money, a gold ring, a blue enamelled harnessed girdle; half a dozen silver spoons, testator's best beads, a featherbed, 2 pairs of sheets, a bolster, 2 pillows, a bed of arras with flowers, a tester with blue curtains, a posnet, a basin, 2 bell candlesticks, a chafing dish, a chafer of a gallon, a cow, a maser and a brass pot; to Mary Flynders 5 marks in money, a harnessed girdle with a turned buckle, a pair of jet beads, a gold ring, two silver rings, half a dozen silver spoons, a featherbed, 2 pairs of sheets, a bolster, 2 pillows, her best brass pot, 2 bell candlesticks, a brass pan, a chafing dish, a laten basin of 2 gallons, a brewing lead, a covering of tapestry work, a folding table, a chair and a cow.

To every god-child 2 sheep; to Agnes Ecton a gown. "The resideu of my goodes not bequeathed my dettes and . . ." [unfinished]

116.
Mydesent Broke of Tillisworth. 15 Jan. 1521/2, no note of probate. (2: 108d)
Burial in the churchyard of All Hallows of Tillisworth; to church of Lincoln 2d.; to the high altar 2 bushels of barley; to the Trinity light and to Our Lady light 2 bushels of barley; to mending the torches one bushel of barley; to repair the steeple half an acre of land at Acurbusshes which is to be sown; to Our Lady of Todyngton in the rood loft 2 bushels of barley.

To daughter Elizabeth, testator's house and land "to se that my bodie be brought on erth", and Elizabeth is to pay 10s. for 30 masses to be said in Tillisworth church at the discretion of testator's ghostly father; to daughter Margaret her best brass pot, her aumbry, her great trough. To son Richard Broke her second brass pot, a mattress, a bolster, a pair of blankets; to Johan Broke a brass pot; to Medysent Broke a little brass pot; to Alys Carter her best coffer; to Thomas Carter her second best coffer; to William Carter and his son Thomas the next crops of her lands and leys.

Residue to William Carter, his wife and his children, to pray for testator's soul. Exors. Thomas Picke and William Carter. Witn. sir Robert Low vicar, Elys Wyld, Richard Sawnder, William Houkyns.

117.
John Samson. 12 Mar. 1521/2, pr. 13 Apr. 1522. (2: 109d)
Burial in the churchyard of St. Nicholas of Wilden; to the high altar 12d.; to the rood loft 8d.; to the bells 12d.; to the torches 12d.; to the church of Lincoln 4d.; to a priest 20s. for 2 trentals "my sowle to be prayd for and for ther sowlys that the good' cam of and all cristen sowlys and the foresayd Masse to be sayd in the church of Wilden"; to the friars of Bedford 12d..

To son Richard a quarter of malt; to daughter Agnes 40s. to be paid within 2 years of testator's death, a young red heifer of 2 years old and a ewe; to Johan a pan price 7s., a coffer of two bushels price 20d., a pair of sheets with a coverlet, a great spit price 6s., and a brass pot price 2s. 8d..

To wife Katerin for her life all testator's land and two tenements in Wilden, and after her death to his son William or his assigns. If William should die before coming of age, the land is to go to Johan Samson, and if she die before coming of age then to Margery Samson or her assigns. Whoever shall have Burres is to keep a yearly *dirige* for the souls of William Hutley and Joan his wife, John Samson, Elinor, Margery, Alice and Katerin testator's wife, with all his children, and for all Christian souls.

To daughter Joan an ewe "pucces"; to daughter Margery a ewe "puccs"; to each god-child a bushel of barley; to servant Thomas Quarell a bushel of barley.

Executrix wife Katerin; supervisor Henry Smyth, and he "to give my wiff good cownsell and to se this my last will and testament fulfilled and he to have xs. for his labour". Witn. sir John Knollys curate of Wilden, Henry Smyth, Thomas Wilshere.

118.
William Lane of Bydenham. 6 May, pr. 24 May 1522. (2: 110d)
Burial in the parish churchyard of Bydenham; for mortuary as customary; to church of Lincoln 2d.; to the high altar for privy tithes forgotten 4d..

To wife Agnes for the term of her life testator's house and all lands in Bydenham, reversion to his son Richard. Residue to wife Agnes "and Richard my sonne after her".

Executrix wife Agnes. Witn. sir John Billyngges, John Faldo, John Wright, Thomas Malcot, John Amery.

119.
John Patenham of the parish of St. Powlys in Bedford. 6 Feb. 1521/2. pr. 24 May 1522. (2: 111)
To be buried in Our Lady chapel in "Powlys church next unto my sete"; to the high altar for tithes forgotten 3s. 4d.; to the mother church of Lincoln 4d.; four marks of good money to "A prest that can help a qweer shall syng for my sowle in Powlys church".

Testator's crops and cattle are to be sold "at the best advise of myn executors". To son Henry £10 to be paid within a year of testator's death "and he to be good to his moder uppon my blessyng"; to son Richard £6 13s. 4d.; to son William £6 13s. 4d. and 5 pairs of sheets, "and he to be good to his moder"; to daughter Elizabeth £6 13s. 4d. and

5 pairs of sheets "and if she be rulyd after her moder or my gossipp John Baker".

To son John Pateman and his heirs, all lands and tenements in the town and fields of Bottisford, and should he die without heirs, the property is to go to the next of the blood. To same John 40s., to be paid within one year, and of this he is to have 20s. "to bryng hym to Bottisforth".

To wife Agnes the place where testator dwells with all appurtenances for as long as she remains single. On her death it is to go to son Richard and his heirs.

To wife Agnes for life the tenement in Fisshrow, two shops in the Bocherow and one shop in the Spicery Row, and on her death this tenement and 3 shops are to go to son Henry and his heirs. If Henry should die without heirs, then to son Richard and his heirs, in default to daughter Alice for life, then to son William and his heirs, in default to daughter Elizabeth and her heirs. If she die without heirs then the property is to go "to the Chamber of Bedford for evermore", and they are to pay the 15th penny for poor people "so oft tyme as it shall cum", and the Mayor and his brethren are to keep the property in repair.

Wife Agnes is to sell the tenement in Shepischepyng "to bryng me on earth and to pay my dettes". Residue to wife Agnes.

Exors. wife Agnes, Simond West, Robert Stewkley gentleman, and each to have 6s. 8d. for his labour. Overseer sir William Gascoyn, and he to have 6s. 8d.. Witn. sir Alexander the parish priest, John Baker.

120.
Elen Percevall of Arlesey. 10 Jan. 1521/2, pr. 21 June 1522. (2: 112)

Burial in the churchyard of Arlesey; to mother church of Lincoln 2d.; to the high altar 2d.; to Our Lady of Grace 2d.; to the torches 2d.; to the sepulchre light 2d.; to the rood light 2d.

To son Robert Scot when he comes to lawful age, testator's house and land, and out of these he is to pay son Richard 33s. 4d. and to son Henry 33s. 4d. "and either of them to be other heyrys". To son Robert a cow, when he comes of age.

Her executors are to have "the rule of my hows and londes" until the children come of age, that is to say 15 years of age. Executors are to use the house and land to the best profit, and are to keep the house in repair. The rest of the income arising "to be done for me my husbond yerely as long as they have it in ther hands". Executors are to sell her copyhold for the best price possible, to pay debts.

"I will that Travell shall have Richard my sonne and a cow, to bryng hym upp as he doth his owne". "Also I will that Harrison shall have Harry my sonne and a cow and a bullok". Residue to be divided between her three children.

Exors. Willyam Hennyng, Henry Harrison, each to have 3s. 4d..
Overseer John Travell he to have 3s. 4d.. Witn. Edmond Emere,
Thomas Karver, Thomas Slow.

121.
John Smyth of Willishamsted. St. Margaret V. & M. 20 July, pr. 16
Aug. 1522. (2: 113)
    Burial in churchyard of Willishamsted; for his mortuary as is lawful;
to the high altar for tithes forgotten 20d.; to cathedral church of Lincoln
2d.; to the sepulchre light 20d.; to the bells 12d.; to the torches 12d..
    Wife Joan is to have during her life an acre of land in "every feld
tilled redy to her hand" and is to have her living for the term of her life.
To daughter Alys a cow, two couple of sheep.
    To son Richard testator's "copies" copyholdings, lands, meadows and
pasture that he has taken of my lady of Elneston and of my lord of
Cotton, for the remainder of the terms. Residue to son Richard.
    Exors. son Richard, John Calnell. Witn. sir Richard Purcer vicar,
Richard Fordymell, Thomas Edward.

122.
Robert Caryngton of Dunton. 27 Nov., pr. 20 Dec. 1521. (2: 114)
    Burial in churchyard of Dunton; to high altar for tithes and oblations
forgotten 12d., and "I will therbe a trentall done for my sowle"; to
mother church of Lincoln 4d.; to the sepulchre light 20s.; to the painting of Our Lady in the chancel 3s. 4d.; to the painting of Our Lady of
Pity 3s. 4d.; to the maintaining of the rood light 12d.; to the torches
12d.; to the bells 2s..
    To son Gerard the farm where testator lives "duryng my yerys that I
have taken with the lord". To son Gerard also 6 horses, 2 oxen, 2 steers,
all ploughs and plough gear and carts and cart gear "as I use them", 30
quarters of barley "to maintain the farm withal", his great brass pot, a
brass pan, two beds "with honest reparell accordyng to them", 20 ewes,
3 beasts and his coffer.
    To daughter Agnes 10 quarters of malt, 5 delivered this year and 5
next year, and 6 ewes and a bullock.
    To daughter Alys 10 quarters of malt in like manner, 6 ewes and a bullock.
    To daughter Isabel 6 quarters of malt within three years, 4 ewes and
a bullock.
    To daughter Margery [sic] 6 quarters of malt when she is 12 years old,
2 ewes and a bullock.
    To daughter Margaret the same as he has given to Maryon.
    To his mother 2 quarters of malt.
    To brother Richard 3 quarters of barley, and all debts between them
are freely forgiven.

To god-child sir Thomas Caryngton 20s.; to testator's sister Anys 3 quarters of malt; to sister Isabell 3 quarters of malt; to brother Gerard 2 quarters of barley; to every servant testator has one bushel of barley; to every poor body in Dunton having no ploughland a peck of wheat and a peck of malt next Christmas.

Residue to son Gerard to be used for testator's soul. Exor. son Gerard. Supervisors Thomas Serle and Gerard, testator's brother. If any of his children should die before the age of 12 years, their bequests are to go to the survivors, their burial being allowed out of the same.

Witn. Thomas Caryngton priest, John Serle, John Smyth, Thomas Graunt.

123.

sir Randall Grevys, parish priest of Shitlyngton. 1521, pr. 22 Mar. 1521/2. (2: 115d)

Burial in parish church of All Hallows "afore the sowth doore behynd the piller"; to the parson of the same church testator's best good in the name of mortuary as use and custom requires; to the mother church of Lincoln 4d..

To the fraternity of the Name of Jesus 3s.; to the parson of Nether Gravenhurst testator's furred tippet; to Robert Camber of Hexton his best cloth jacket, his second doublet, a shirt and a night cap; to every god-child in Shitlyngton and Over Gravenhurst 12d.; to Johan Eve a chair and testator's best hat; to Bartholomew Eve his worst worsted jacket; to Gayton his second hat; to Henry Cranwell of Hexton his second cap and his best night cap; to Richard Eve his worst pair of slippers, a pair of "dry shoys" (shoes); and a night cap; to the butcher's wife of Aspley a kerchief; to Johan Eve 2 napkins for the table, a towel, a pillowbeer; to Richard Eve a shirt; to Robert Bellow a shirt and a cap; to Johan Eve the younger a salt cellar and a psalter; to Johan Eve the elder a gown; to sir Thomas Tetlow [blank]; to the brotherhood priest "Sermones discipulorum et postilla maior" and a leather bottle.

Exors. Mathew Hulson and William Cowch each to have 6s. 8d. for his labour; supervisor Thomas West, who is to have for his work a coffer with a strong lock and a pitchfork.

Witn. Richard Eve, Thomas Clerk.

124.

William Thommys of Wodell. 12 Mar. 1521/2, pr. 29 Mar. 1522. (2: 116)

Burial in the churchyard of All Hallows of Odell; to mother church of Lincoln 4d.; for mortuary as custom of town; to the high altar 4 bushels of barley; to the sepulchre a bushel of barley; to the rood loft 12d.; to the bells 2 bushels of barley; to the torches 2 bushels of barley.

To son Thomas a bare cart, a couple of oxen, 6 quarters of barley, a cow, a heifer, a couple of sheep and two mares. To daughter Alys a cow, a bullock, 3 quarters of barley, a quarter of malt, half a quarter of wheat, a mattress, a coverlet, a bolster and a coffer. To daughter Agnes a cow, a heifer, two couple of sheep, 3 quarters of barley, a quarter of malt, half a quarter of wheat, a mattress, a coverlet, a bolster and a coffer. To daughter Grace a cow, a heifer, two couple of sheep, 3 quarters of barley, a quarter of malt, half a quarter of wheat, a mattress, a coverlet, a bolster and a coffer. To son Robert a bullock, 2 quarters of barley and 2 theaves. To son Richard a heifer, 2 quarters of barley and 2 sheep.

Residue to wife Elizabeth and son Thomas. Exors. wife Elizabeth and son Thomas. Witn. sir Marten Hurst parish priest, Henry Wellys, Walter Tanner.

125.

Henry Bisshopp of Kempston. 11 Mar. 1521/2, pr. 29 Mar. 1522. (2: 116d)

Burial in the churchyard of All Hallows of Kempston; for mortuary as custom of town; to mother church of Lincoln 2d.; to high altar for tithes forgotten 4d.; to the light of Our Lady of Pity 4d.; to the torches 4d.; to the bells 4d..

To wife Margaret for life, his house and land in Kempston, she to keep it in repair, and after her death the property to go to Robert Bisshopp testator's son and to his heirs and assigns.

To son Robert a bay horse, a mare, 6 ewes, 6 lambs, 2 acres of pease land sown with pease, one ley in a furlong called Bancroft and another acre in Ertyng; an acre in Lawlond furlong.

To daughter Agnes 4 sheep, 3 lambs and a weaned calf.

Residue to wife Margaret to use for testator's soul.

Exors. Edward Lenton and son Robert Bysshopp. Witn. sir Robert Alen, John Barbour, Bartholomew Boughton.

126.

John Smyth of Nether Stondon in parish of Shitlyngton. 1 Mar. 1522 [sic], pr. 5 Apr. 1522. (2: 117d)

Burial in churchyard of All Hallows of Shitlyngton; for mortuary as customary; to mother church of Lincoln 2d.; to the high altar for tithes forgotten 12d.; to a priest for a quarter's wages 30s.; to the fraternity of the Name in Shitlyngton 3s. 4d.; to mending the highway 3s. 4d.; to the upkeep of the bells 6d.; to the upkeep of the torches 6d..

To Thomas Smyth 2 quarters of malt; to John Halle a quarter of malt and a sheep.

To wife Elizabeth testator's house and land.

Exors. wife Elizabeth and brother Mathew Smyth, who is to have 3s.
4d.. Witn. sir Robert Sqwyer, Mathew Colmun, Thomas Childerhows.

127.
Gerard Caryngton of Dunton. 24 Dec. 1521, pr. 30 Jan. 1521/2. (2: 118)
Burial in the churchyard of Dunton; to the high altar for tithes and
oblations forgotten 20d.; to the sepulchre light 20d.; to the painting of
Our Lady in the chancel 3s.; to the painting of Our Lady of Pity 3s.; to
the rood light 12d.; to the torches 12d.; to the maintaining of the bells
6s. 8d.; to the making of the Palm Cross in Dunton churchyard 10s. for
testator's father and for himself. His executors are to pay to the making of this cross the 6s. 8d. that John Slow bequeathed to it.

To sister Agnes 5 quarters of malt, the best milch bullock, 6 ewes; to
sister Isabel 5 quarters of malt, the next best milch bullock, 6 ewes; to
sister Marion 10 quarters of malt when she is 12 years old, 10 ewes and
a milch bullock; to sister Margaret the same legacy as to Marion; to testator's uncle Gerard and to John Clay 8 quarters of barley; to his uncles
Richard and William 6 quarters of barley; to his "Grandsire and
Grandam" 6 quarters of barley and a quarter of wheat.

To god-child Gerard Serle 2 ewes; to god-child William Caryngton 2
ewes; to god-child John Blewet 2 ewes; to John Cook alias Bestavisid 2
quarters of barley; to aunt Agnes 3 quarters of barley; to his uncle John
4 quarters of barley; to Cicele Serle 3 quarters of barley; to his uncle
Thomas of "Browme childern" 3 quarters of barley.

John Clay is to have Margaret testator's sister in keeping till she is 12
years old, and for this he is to have 5 marks and the increase of her
stock.

His uncle Gerard Caryngton is to have his sister Marion in keeping
till she is 12 years old, and for this he is to have 4 marks and the
increase of her stock.

If Margaret and Marion should not be honestly kept, then two "indifferent men" are to see them kept the said years with the profits belonging to them. If any of testator's sisters should die before they are 12
years old, their bequests, after paying burial expenses, are to go to the
survivors. If they should all die before they are 12 years old, then their
bequests are to be sold "with the consent of ij indifferent men", and a
priest is to sing in Dunton church for as long as the proceeds last.

To his sisters all the household stuff that was the testator's father's
and mother's and his own.

To Robert Mody 3 quarters of barley; to Edward and Thomas
Caryngton 2 quarters of barley; to Thomas Beton 2 quarters of barley;
to Thomas Cook of Langford 2 quarters of barley; to "every poore
bodie" in Dunton who has no ploughland, one bushel of malt; to the
vicar and churchwardens of Dunton 4 milch bullocks price 4 marks and

4 quarters of barley, to be delivered next Michaelmas, for an obit worth 10s. to be kept once a year in Dunton church for the souls of his father, mother and himself. If the obit is not kept, then the bequest is to go to the prioress and convent of "Holwell in London" to keep the obit at Holwell.

To a priest to sing for his soul for a year £6. Residue to his sisters.

Exors. his uncle Thomas of Brome, his uncle Gerard. Supervisor his uncle John Serle. Witn. sir John Lamb, sir Edmond Grenall/Grevall, Thomas Beton, Richard Caryngton.

128.
Nicholas Carter of Kempston. 24 June, pr. 6 July 1528. (2: 119d)

Burial in churchyard of Kempston; mortuary after the custom of the town; to the high altar for tithes forgotten 4d.; to the mother church of Lincoln 2d.; to the sepulchre light 4d.; to the bells 4d.; to the torches 2d..

The house in which testator dwells is to be sold by his feoffees, that is to say by Mr. Rainold Gray esq., William Smyth and John Newold, and part of the money arising is to be used for a priest to sing for a quarter of a year in Kempston church.

Residue to be divided evenly between his two sons John Carter and Bartholomew Carter.

Exors. William Gogyon, Thomas Ronall. Witn. Robert Alen, Rainold Gray, William Smyth, John Newold, Roger Dove, John Radwell, Thomas Cromwell.

Executors refused to act. Letters of administration granted to Reginald Gray, Robert Alen and John Carter.

129.
Richard West of Bedford. 3 Dec. 1525, no note of probate. (2: 120)

Burial in parish churchyard of St. Powlys; to mother church of Lincoln 2d..

Testator's house in Stephynton to be sold by Master Robert Stewkley gentleman, who if he wishes may buy it before any other. Proceeds to pay debts and to pay for a trental to be sung in St. Powlys church for souls of testator and all Christians.

To brother-in-law Robert Gilbert his best gown furred with fox. Residue to wife Agnes.

Exors. wife Agnes, and Master Stewkley, who is to have 3s. 4d. for his work. Witn. Thomas Rokisborough alias Lutar, Peter Mak, Robert Gilbert notary.

130.
John Alyn/Alen of Litlyngton. 13 June, pr. 21 June 1520. (2: 121)

Burial in the churchyard of All Hallows of Litlyngton; to the high altar for tithes forgotten 6d.; to mother church of Lincoln 4d.; to the rood light a lb. of wax; to "Our Lady on the Stok" 20d.; to Our Lady of Pity a lb. of wax; to St. John Baptist half a pound of wax; to certain other saints in the church a quarter of a lb. of wax to each; to the bells and to the torches 12d..

To his wife and to Johan his daughter all brass and pewter that was testator's, to be divided between them; to daughter Johan a complete bed; to son John 10 marks of money; to son Thomas 40s.; to testator's two daughters 5 marks each, and if any child die, then their money is to go to his wife, part of which is "to be disposid for my sowle"; to each of his two daughters 2 silver spoons; to son Thomas one silver spoon; to John Clerk 2 couple of ewes and lambs.

To wife Johan for life all his lands and tenements, and after her death to son John. Should John die without heirs, the property is to pass to son Thomas, and if Thomas die without heirs it is to be divided between the two daughters, and if they die without heirs then it is to be sold, and from the proceeds a priest is to sing for testator and his friends for a year, and the remainder of the money used for other deeds of charity. Residue to wife Johan.

Exors. Raff Smyth, wife Johan. Overseer testator's brother Thomas Alyn. Witn. sir Peter Dent vicar of the same church, Thomas Archar, Thomas Julyan.

131.
Richard Goodrich of Luton. 18 Mar. 1518/9, pr. date aforesaid. (2: 122)

Burial in the churchyard of Our Lady in Luton; to the high altar 12d.; to the torches 12d.; a priest is to sing a trental for testator and his wife Johan in Luton church.

To son William testator's place in Abbottis Walden to him and his assigns for ever, provided that they keep a yearly obit for him and his friends in the church of Walden for the next 20 years.

To son John and his assigns for ever testator's place in Luton, all wheat in the barn and 2 acres growing in the field at Walden. To every child of son John 12d.; to John Whight of Hichyn 4 bushels of malt. Residue to son John to dispose of for the health of testator's soul.

Exors. son John and John Grene. Witn. Thomas Tymmys chaplain, Richard Amyot, John Kyng.

132.
William Thomson of Turvey. 13 Oct. 15—, pr. 19 Nov. 1519. (2: 122d)

Burial in the churchyard of Turvey; for mortuary as custom of the town; to the high altar for tithes forgotten 12d.; to the bells 6d.; to the torches 6d.; to the bridge 8d.; to the Trinity light 8d..

To son John 20s.; to son Thomas 20s.; to testator's wife the house testator bought from Robert Harryson as long as she remains single. If she remarries, then the property passes to testator's daughter Elene and her children, and should Elene die without heirs, then "the child that my wiff goth with" is to have it, and if that child die without heirs then the house is to be sold and the money "done for my sowle" and for all Christian souls. Residue to wife.

Exors. wife, John Odell, Walter Skevyngton. Witn. sir Edward Croft testator's ghostly father, John Odell, Walter Skevyngton.

133.
David Jonys of Hawns. 28 Jan. 1513/4, pr. 18 Mar. 1515/6. (2: 123)
Burial in the chapel of Our Lady in Hawns church; to the high altar for tithes forgotten 8d.; to the church of Lincoln 4d..

To wife Alice all tenements and lands which testator has purchased in the town and fields of Hawns (except one acre of land at the Wyndemylnne lane end, which testator has given to found a lamp before Our Lady in the same church) on condition that the said Alice finds a priest to sing for souls of testator, his father and mother, and all Christians "for the space of a yere in my lyf tyme and a nother tyme immedyatly after my dethe". If she does not fulfill these conditions, she is to have the property for her life only, and after her death it is to be sold and the money disposed of for souls of testator "in goode dedys of charyte". If she does fulfil the conditions then she is to have the property in fee simple for ever.

To wife Alyce for 6 years after testator's death the house in which he lives with all appurtenances, which testator bought from Simon Fytz. She is to contribute 3s. 4d. in Lent every year on Good Friday under the oversight of the churchwardens, each of whom is to have 4d. of the 3s. 4d. for his labours. At the end of the 6 years the house is to go to Alyce Burges and her heirs for ever. If she should die without issue, the house is to be sold, and of the money £5 is to go to John Burges, 40s. to Antonye Burges, and the rest is to be "bestowed in good dedys of charytie for my soul and for the soules of them that hyt came of". If John Burges is able to buy the house, he may have it cheaper by £5 than any other man, and this in addition to his bequest.

To John Burges, immediately after testator's death, all lands and tenements in Strotton in Bykylswade.

Exors. wife Alyce, sir Oliver Ewe parson of Campton, Robert Alec citizen and goldsmith of London, Thomas Maple of Hawnes. Supervisor Richard Halam mayor of Bedford. Witn. sir John Whalley priest, Richard Harpynghame, Richard Weralle.
Probate granted to Alice Johnnys and sir Oliver Ewe, reserving powers of the other executors.

134.
Thomas Pake of Stephynton. 27 June 1530, no note of probate. (2: 124)
   Burial in the churchyard of Our Blessed Lady of Stephynton; to
mother church of Lincoln 4d.; to the high altar 3s. 4d.; to the rood loft
a lb. of wax; to the 2 tapers of the sepulchre 2 lb. of wax; "The tapers
in Our Lady chapell to be reparid agayn and to burne still ther"; to the
torches 2 lb. of wax; to the bells 12d..
   To wife Joan all the goods she brought to testator which are left, also
6s. 8d., 2 kine, and "a blak and a red huid cow". To son Thomas Pake
the best brass pot and a spruce coffer. To cousin Richard West a calf
of this year's weaning. To cousin Margery West a brass pan with other
"trash"; to Margaret West a coffer with a "virgine" barrel, 2 bee hives
and testator's best cow. To son-in-law Simon West 2 bee hives and a
cow. To John Barbour a bee hive. To testator's wife another bee hive.
Residue to Thomas Pake and cousin Margare West, they to dispose
them as they please for the health of souls of testator and of all
Christians.
   Exors. son Thomas Pake and cousin Robert Pake. Supervisor sir
Thomas Botolff vicar of Stephynton, he to have 3s. 4d. for his labour.
Witn. sir William Gybon clerk, John Walgrave, Edmund Walgrave,
George With'.

135.
Thomas Fesauntt of Coupull. Friday after the feast of St. Barnabas the
Apostle, 14 June, pr. 19 June 1510. (2: 125)
   Burial in churchyard of All Hallows of Coupull; for mortuary his best
beast; to the high altar 2s.; to repair the church 2 sheep; to the bells
12d.; to the sepulchre light 12d.; for a trental 10s..
   To every child of his brothers and sisters a sheep; to every god-child
a bushel of barley; to Margaret daughter of testator's brother John a
ewe and a lamb and a bullock.
   To wife Alice all the household stuff she brought with her the time he
married her and all her cattle, as much as is left. After legacies and debts
paid the residue to go to wife and son Thomas, evenly divided between
them.
   To wife Alice, the house testator lives in with appurtenances, for the
term of her life, while she remains single. If she should marry then son
Thomas is to have it, and she is to have the house testator bought from
Goldeney for the tern of her life. Son Thomas is to enter "the said
howse" after testator's death, and he and his mother are to keep an obit
of 2s. for 20 winters for testator and his friends.
   If son Thomas should die without heirs of his body, the tenements are
to be sold and distributed in the church and town of Coupull "in almes
dedes" where it shall be thought most needful.

Exors. wife Alice, son Thomas, brother William. Overseer Master Robert Spencer. Witn. sir Thomas Bamford vicar, Master Robert Spencer, Thomas Paswater.
Probate granted to Alice and Thomas Fesand, reserving power of William Fesand.

136.
William Hensman of the parish of St. Giles of Toturnho. 2 Apr., pr. 19 July 1510. (2: 125d)
Testament (in Latin) Burial in the churchyard of St. Giles of Toturnho; to fabric of the church of Lincoln 2d.; to the high altar of Toternow 2 measures of malt; to three small lights 1½ measures of malt; to four principal lights of the said church 2 measures of malt; to the torches 2 measures of malt.

To daughter Helen his best brass pot, a pair of jet beads the gaudes of silver, one heifer; to each of testator's five younger children half a quarter of barley. Residue divided between wife Johan and son Symond. Exors. wife Johan and son Symond. Supervisor Thomas Tayler of Eyton. Witn. Thomas Horton, John Asshwell.
Will Son Symond and wife Johan to have the tenement called Cowpers and all lands and meadows belonging to it in the towns and fields of Toternow and Eyton, as long as Johan remains unmarried. If she remarries, then the property goes to Symond and his heirs for ever.

To John Hensman testator's second son and his heirs an acre of land on Otehill. To son Cristofer an acre of land of which half an acre abuts on Taggyshedelong, one rood lies by Cartersway and another rood is a headland on Cokkysthorn Hill. To son Edmond an acre of land at Burlettes Busshe. To daughter Helen half an acre "that buttithe into Welhede Way". Wife Johan is to have the said 2½ acres for 4 years after testator's death for her own use, and after that time they go as above-written to Christopher, Edmond and Helen and their heirs.

To the keepers of Our Lady light half an acre of land on Schortte Neme next John Grasbroke's headland, to keep the light of Our Lady. To wife Johan an acre of arable land at Welhedmyll to her and her heirs for ever.

137.
John Milward of Kardyngton. Thursday before the 2nd Sunday in Lent 1 Mar. 1508/9, pr. 12 Sep. 1510. (2: 126)
Burial in churchyard of Kardyngton; for principal his best beast as custom of the law; to the high altar for tithes forgotten 12d..

To son Thomas Milward the messuage testator bought with 3 roods of land in the Croft and 10 acres 1 rood "yn divers feldes of Kardyngton as itt lyethe". To son John the place where testator dwells with 11 acres of land as it lies in the field.

To son Thomas for life the "easement" use of the forge with all the "tole longyng therto". To wife Margaret for her life all other houses and goods. Residue to wife Margaret.

Exors. wife Margaret and son Thomas. Witn. sir John Huchynson vicar there, Thomas Paswater, John Mylward.

138.
Richard Smyth of Luton. 22 Aug., pr. 8 Sep. 1510. (2: 126d)
(*Latin*) Burial in churchyard of St. Mary of Luton; for mortuary as is lawful; to high altar for tithes forgotten 12d.; to sepulchre light 12d.; to the repair of the church 2s.; to the brotherhood of the Holy Trinity of the said church 6s. 8d. for the souls of testator's father and mother Robert Smyth and Elizabeth his wife; to mother church of Lincoln 4d.; to the brotherhood of the Holy Trinity at Luton 3s. 4d..

To son William and the heirs of his body testator's tenement in the South End, and he is to keep the day of testator's anniversary in the said church with full choir for ever. If William should die without issue, the testator's daughter Joan Perot is to have the tenement to her and her heirs for ever, and she is to keep the anniversary. Should Joan die without issue, then the property is to be sold for the best price and the proceeds disposed of for the souls of the testator and his friends. Residue to son William and daughter Joan equally between them. Exors. son William and John Perot junior the daughter's spouse. Witn. sir William Godfrey, Thomas Bruys, John Dier, Richard Heren.

139.
Thomas Pharow (*in margin* "Thos. Farow de Pertenhall"). 11 Apr., pr. 15 Apr. 1511. (2: 127)
Burial in the churchyard of SS. Peter and Paul of Per'nale; to the high altar for forgotten tithes 12d.; to mother church of Lincoln 4d.; to "the werke off the roode lofte" 6s. 8d.; to the bells of Merys Asbye (Mears Ashby, Northants.) 3s. 4d.; to the bells of Per'nale 12d.; to the torches 12d.; to the sepulchre of Browton 7 hoggerels.

To testator's father John Pharow of Asby 13s. 4d.; to testator's brother Robert Pharow his best gown and a pan; to his children when they come of age, his two tenements in Asby, and if the children should die before they come of age, testator's wife is to have the tenements for her lifetime, then they are to be sold and "don for me and hyr and all Crysten sowlys". To Em Newton two couple of sheep. Residue to wife Mare and his children.

Exors. wife Mare and brother Robert Pharow. Supervisor William Stanton who is to have for his labour 2 sheep. Witn. sir Bertylnew

Archebold, William Lynford, John Pecoke, William Ramston, Robert Lynford.

140.
William Reve of Pernale (Pertenhall). St. Ambrose's day 4 Apr., pr. 15 Apr. 1511. (2: 127)
Burial in the churchyard of SS. Peter and Paul in Pernale; for his principal as custom of the town; to mother church of Lincoln 2d.; to the high altar for tithes forgotten 6d.; to the torches 12d.; to the bells 6d..
To Margett testator's wife all moveable goods.
His house with its appurtenances is to be sold to pay his debts, and wife Margett is to have 20s. of the money received on condition that she gives 6s. 8d. to each of his children when they come to the age of 14 years. If any of them should die before reaching this age, his part is to be "dysposyd to the werke off the church and to por' pepull". The rest of the money from the house, if there is any left when debts have been paid, is to go to Pertenall church for testator's soul and for "the sowles that ytt come off".
Exors. William Stanton and John Grene, to have 3s. 4d. each for their labour and costs. Supervisor sir Bartilmow Archebold to see will fulfilled within a year. Witn. John Schepard, Thomas Chandeler, William Shepard.

141.
Anne Bilcoke. 14 July. pr. 26 July 1511. (2: 128)
Latin Burial in churchyard of All Saints of Howghton Conquest; for mortuary her best beast to the rector of the church as customary; to mother church of Lincoln 2d..
To testator's son John the house where she lives with its lands and appurtenances, and all the lands she has lately obtained through her husband.
Exors. sons Richard Bilcoke and John Bilcoke. Witn. William Bylcoke, John Bylcoke, Thomas Egilston.
Probate granted to John Bilcoke, rserving power of Richard Bilcoke.

142.
Robart Dermere of Dunstaple. 1515, pr. 4 July 1515. (2: 129)
Burial in the parish church of Dunstaple; to mother church of Lincoln 2d.; to the high altar for the upkeep of the lights 12d.; to the high altar of the Priory Church 8d.; to the brotherhood altar a quarter of malt; to the friars of Dunstable half a quarter of malt.
To son William a house called the Cross Key with a close at Sowthys and all the land. To daughter Joane five marks to be paid at the time of her marriage the money to come from the rent of the house

bequeathed above to William. To son Simon the house that stands in the midst of the street against the Frerys gate with a barn and a slaughter house in Halwyke lane. To son Symon a "tenture" close in the West End with an acre of land pertaining to the same. To daughter Elizabeth 40s. from the rent of the house bequeathed to Symon. To son John 3 tenements with 2 gardens in the North End, two called Slowse and the other Sulgrave. To daughter Agnes 40s. at the time of her marriage to be paid out of the same 3 tenements.

To wife Margete for life a house called Doggettes Howse with its two tenements and afterwards it is "to remayne amonges my childerne". To Marget also all moveable goods, and she is to have a trental done for testator in the parish church of Dunstaple. Also "she shall honestly bury me and kepe my monethes mynd and every yerys so long as she keepys Doggetes Howse and the tenements of the same".

If any of the sons should die, his bequest goes to the survivors, and if all the sons die, his daughters are to inherit in the same way. If all his children should die, the property is to be sold by his executors and the proceeds are to be disposed of for the souls of testator and all his friends, who are to be prayed for in the parish church of Dunstaple and in the Priory church of the friars.

Testator's father-in-law William Grene to have the keeping of son William, with the deeds of the house and land limited to the said William.

Robert Thomsone to have the keeping of son Symonde with the deeds of the house and lands limited to Symonde.

Nicholas Purvey shall have the deeds of the three houses bequeathed to John, and testator's wife is to have the rent from them and the keeping of the boy until he comes of age. Nicholas is to have the oversight of the child and is to repair the house, and he is to have for his work 10s. of the rent.

Exors. William Grene, Robert Thomson, each to have 6s. 8d. for his work. Overseer Nicholas Purvey to have 6s. 8d.. Witn. sir John Sarson, Richard Miller, William Bruce.

143.
Bawdwyn Smyth of Sutton, husbandman. 24 Jan. 1483/4, pr. 30 Apr. 1484. (2: 130)

Burial in the churchyard of Sutton; for mortuary as customary; to mother church of Lincoln 4d.; to the bells 12d.; to the torches 12d.; to the high altar for tithes forgotten 20d.; for a trental to be sung for his soul 10s..

To testator's wife 3 kine, 4 horses, a cart, a plough and plough gear, and 20 nobles "in money and money worth".

To testator's son Thomas Smyth and his heirs his messuage with all lands, meads and pasture in Sutton, and if Thomas should die without heirs, as God forbid, the property is to go to the next of testator's blood and kindred and their heirs. In default of such issue the property is to be sold and the money bestowed in charitable deeds for testator's soul and for all Christian souls.

Residue to son Thomas Smyth. Executor son Thomas Smyth. Witn. John Andrew of Sutton, Henry Whitside, Henry Rutter of Potton.

144.
Richard Lucas of Shefford. 8 June, pr. 23 June 1515. (2: 131)

Burial in churchyard of Camylton; for principal as required; to the high altar of Camylton for tithes forgotten 12d.; to the church of Lincoln 4d.; to the bells of Camylton 12d.; to the chapel of Shefford 12d..

To wife Christyan for her life the house testator dwells in, she paying testator's brother Thomas £4 6s. 8d., and after her death it is to go the the heirs "lawfully be goten be twene the seid Crystyan and me". Should these heirs die without issue, the house is to go to testator's brother Robert and his heirs. Residue to wife Cristyan.

Exors. wife Cristyan and William Kynswyke, he to have 12d. for his labour. Witn. John Dunsey, John Hyll, George Whytt, Thomas Warner. Given at Shefford.

145.
John Cotton of Brom in the parish of Southivell/Southell. 28 June, pr. 10 July 1515. (2: 131d)

Burial in the churchyard of Sowthill; for his mortuary his best beast; to the church of Lincoln 6d.; to the high altar of Sowthell 2s..

To son Richard a messuage called David Johns and the pightle next to it. To son William an acre of land at 20 Akyrs. To son Richard a piece of land in Gese Hery' and 5 roods at Gosteland.

To wife Chrystyanne testator's tenement in Brome as long as she remains single, and 4 acres 1 rood of land "belongynge unto the same for evermore to give or to sell". To wife also all household goods except those she chooses to divide among testator's children. If she marry again, testator's children by his wife shall have the said tenement, one after another and to their issue, in entail. If all the children of his wife and himself die without issue, then the tenement goes to son Richard and his heirs.

To wife also one cow. To his two elder sons one beehive. To Matthew Arnold another beehive. To son William all testator's horse carts and cart gear and his plough and plough gear, and he is to till for wife 4 acres of land for 3 years. To the "hyle" (aisle) 20s. if the parish make it, or else the money to go to the "moste needes of the church". To son

Richard the copyhold testator has from the abbot of Wardon. To son William a pair of sheets and a blanket. To the friars of Dunstable a quarter of barley. To Robert Hunt's children a quarter of barley.

Testator's crop is to be divided thus: his wife is to have half a quarter, and the two eldest sons are to have 2 "strike" between them and so to divide all the crops.

Exors. wife Crystyan and Hewe Harrowden/Harrowoden, to whom the residue. Witn. John Maynard, Richard Barbur.

146.
John Eynsam/Aynsam of Shitlyngtonn. 23 July 1515, no note of probate. (2: 132)

Burial in the churchyard of All Hallows of Shitlyngtonn.

To wife Alice £10, 4½ acres of barley, and all household goods.

To testator's two children, and to the third "that my wyfe is withe, when it hath the baptysm" 20 marks between the three of them. If any of the three should die, the one is to be other's heir, and so from first to last, up to the age of 20 years. If all three should die, the said value "is to be donne for me and theyme and our freyndes".

To his father 5 marks, to the intent that he shall receive the house that testator dwells in to the use of his children, for cost and charge that testator has done thereupon, and so that every child shall be the other's heir.

To servant Thomas Barklet 40d.; to servant John Sternyll 40d.; to servant George 5s.; to Thomas Mychaell 20d..

To the high altar 20d.; to St. Margarete 2s.; to the mother church of Lincoln 4d.; to every light that is "customably kept" 4d.; to the four almshouses "howsis of almys" in Shitlyngton 2s. 4d. each "to a permanens within the howsis for the tyme it may indure".

To his father his best gown. He forgives the debts between his godfather Thomas Boziat and himself and leaves to Thomas Boziat his lined doublet and his best russet coat.

To every child of his brother's 4d.; to every god-child 4d.; to the three houses of friars, that is Bedford, Hychynn and Dunstable a trental; a priest is to sing in Shitlyngton church for half a year; to the brotherhood of the Name of Jesus 40d..

Exors. brother Mathew Aynsam and John Feld of Shitlyngton, to whom the residue to use for his soul. Witn. Thomas Robyns, John Her', John Clark, William Awnncell.

147.
William Knyght of Karyngton. 8 Mar. 1527/8, pr. 4 Apr. 1528. (2: 133)

Burial in the churchyard of Our Lady of Cardyngton; to the cathedral church of Lincoln 2d.; to the high altar for tithes forgotten 12d.;

for mortuary as is the custom; to the King's highway as far as testator's ground extends 6s. 8d.; to the bells of Cardyngton 16d..

To Thomas son of John Knyght testator's brother 20s. to be delivered to him when he comes to the age of 18 years. If he should die before this age then it is to go to a priest to sing for souls of testator, his wife and all Christians.

To wife Christian during her life the house where testator dwells, and after her death it is to go to his son John, on condition that he gives a priest 20s. to sing for souls of testator, his wife and all Christians. Residue to wife Christian to do with as she wishes.

Exors. wife Christian and son John. Witn. sir John Mathew, William Prees, Simond Dunston.

148.

Robert Rey. 11 June 1527, pr. 4 Apr. 1528. (2: 133d)

Body to be buried in Christian burial "where my departure shalbe"; to mother church of Lincoln 12d.; to the high altar of the parish church of St. Peter de Dunstable in Bedford for tithes forgotten 12d.; for a solemn *dirige* with requiem mass in the said church of St. Peter 10s..

To son Robert a cow price 10s. and 20s. in money; to daughter Grace a cow price 10s. and 20s. in money; to Our Lady light in the conventual church of Cawdwell 2s..

Residue to wife Johan with the intent that she shall see testator's natural mother sufficiently kept. The surplus of goods she is to bestow as she shall think "most meritoriows for my sowle and the sowle of my sayd wiff with our frends".

Exors. wife Joan and master Robert Stewkley, he to have 10s. for his labours. Witn. Master John Bikleswade prior of Cawldwell, Master Hanslapp, Thomas Marston, Robert Baker, Robert Johnson.

149.

John Momford alias Barbour of Hardwik in Kempston. 28 Feb. 1527/8, pr. 4 Apr. 1528. (2: 134)

Burial in churchyard of All Hallows of Kempston; for mortuary after the custom of the town; to mother church of Lincoln 4d.; to the high altar for tithes forgotten 20d.; to the light of Our Lady of Pity 20d.; to the sepulchre 20d.; to the torches 2s.; to the bells 2s.; to sir John Billyng priest, a trental of masses to be sung within the parish church of Alhalows of Kempston for souls of testator and all Christians; to the convent of Elnestow a quarter of barley; to Wotton church 3s. 4d.; to repairing Hardwik bridge 3s. 4d..

To Johan wife of William Malcott a heifer of one year and a sheep; to Margaret Barbour testator's son's daughter a cow, a bullock one year old; the best brass pot, a sheep, a mattress, a coverlet and a pair of

sheets; to god-daughter Joan Hich' a one year old calf; to god-son
Augustyin Hich' a sheep; to each god-child a sheep; to son's daughter
Elyn Barbour a two year old heifer; to Elyn the wife of old John Hich'
a cow.

To wife Margaret for life, all his free lands with their appurtenances
in the fields of Elnestow and Kempston, and also a house in the East
End called a copy with its "commodities". After her death this to go to
testator's son Thomas with all its profits "to do with it at her pleasur
and at the pleasur of God". Residue to wife Margaret and son Thomas
Barbour, to be divided between them by the oversight of John Hich' the
elder and John Newold. Exors. wife Margaret and son Thomas. Witn.
sir Robert Alen priest, sir John Billyng priest, John Newold, John Hech'
John Browne.

150.
John Coole of Riseley. 16 Jan. 1527/8. pr. 4 Apr. 1528. (2: 134d)

Burial in parish churchyard of Riseley; to high altar for tithes forgotten 6d.; to the bells 2d.; to the torches 2d.; to the sepulchre of Our
Lord 2d.; to the mother church of Lincoln 2d..

To wife Isabell for life testator's house, and after her death to Kateryn
testator's daughter and her heirs. Should she die without issue "as God
forbede" then it is to go to John Wite for his life, and after that it is to
be sold "and done for them that it cam of". He leaves also an acre of
land in Wilwat hill abutting on Cole's land at the south end and abutting north the other end on the headland in Wyllysworth Hill.

Residue to wife Isabell, William Wrotham and John White who is to
help wife Isabell, to dispose of for health of souls of testator and his
benefactors, and the same three are to be his executors. Witn. sir Henry
Queene vicar and John Peter.

151.
John Tymmys of Luton. 10 May 1527, pr. 4 Apr. 1528. (2: 135)

Burial in Luton churchyard; to high altar of Luton 8d.; to the high
altar of Walden church 6d.; to church of Lincoln 6d.; to the low rood
at Kynges Walden 12d.; to St. Katerin's light in Walden church 12d.; to
the torches of Luton church 8d.. To the church of Luton "a book cal-
lid a processionall in print". After testator's death son John to pay 20s.
for 2 trentals to be sung in Luton church.

To wife Johan all moveable goods; to son John Tymmys all lands and
tenements in Kynges Walden, and he is to pay to wife Johan for the
term of her life 13s. 4d. annually from one of the tenements, and 7s. 4d.
from the other. To each unmarried god–child 4d..

Residue to son John. Executor son John. "Also I revoke all other sin-
guler willys or disposicions made by me oon tyme afore this present day

and it is my Will and last mynd that this shall stond in strenth and take effect and non other". Supervisor sir Thomas Tymys and "he to have for his labour and to pray for me xx.s.". Given at Luton. Witnesses Master Roger Bawdwyn curate of Luton, Thomas Bruce, John Day. *Probate granted to son John Tymmys reserving power of Joan the widow, although Joan was not named as an executor in this text.*

152.
Richard Swift of Roxton, weaver. 26 Mar., pr. 4 Apr. 1528. (2: 135d)
Burial in churchyard of Roxton; for principal as customary; to mother church of Lincoln 4d.; to the high altar for tithes forgotten 12d.; to the bells 10d.; to the torches 10d.; to the sepulchre light 20d..

To wife Johan testator's house beyond the way that Richard Clement dwells in and four acres of land and the yard to the barn, as long as she lives single and without a husband, and keeps the house in repair. Should she marry, testator's son and executor Thomas Swift or his assigns shall give her 3s. 4d. a year for life. After death of wife testator's son Thomas Swyft to have the property to find a priest to pray for soul of testator, his wife and his friends for half a year.

To son Thomas Swift testator's counter, settle, the pan that hangs on the furnace, all the gear belonging to the shop, his best gown, his best doublet, all the timber squared and able to be squared and all ready money "to bryng her honestly to erth".

To John Stepheyns sometime testator's apprentice, the gown furred with white lamb. To the friars of Huntingdon the best brass pot.

Residue to wife Johan and son Thomas to be equally divided between them by the oversight of Robert Chessham. Exor. son Thomas Swyft. Witn. sir Thomas Stoughton parish priest, John Mux, Henry Fissher.

153.
Alexander Kirk of Amthull. Testament 11 Mar. 1527/8, will 27 Mar. 1528, pr. 21 Apr. 1528. (2: 136d)
Testament Burial in the parish church of Amthull; for mortuary as customary; to the high altar of parish church 20d.; to Our Lady of Lincoln 4d.; to repairing the bells of the parish church 20s.; to All Souls light 20d.; to the lights before the rood, Our Lady and St. Andrew 3s. 4d.; to Amthull church 40s. to be bestowed on things thought most expedient for the parish "by the chefe and hedmen"; towards mending the wall over the chancel door 20s.; to the churches of Milbrok and Houghton Conquest 3s. 4d. each; to the church of Malden 20d.; to repair Hasilwood Lane 3s. 4d..

To son William Kirk and his assigns the rents of testator's meads in Malden and Flitwick, to distribute this rent every week yearly in Amthull or elsewhere where there is most need, 5d. weekly for ever.

From the same rent the son shall spend 4s. for a yearly obit in Amthull church for souls of testator, his wife and all Christians.

To testator's son the prior of Belvere 4 marks, to son Henry of Newenham 13s. 4d. a year for life; to Amy Kirk testator's son's daughter 10 kine towards her marriage, and if she should die before her marriage then the said 10 kine are to be distributed between the rest of the son's children. To his son's children all the stuff in testator's tenement called The Bell to be equally divided between them. To Master Alexander Wethirwik, testator's sister's son and vicar of Molton, 40s.; to Isabell Brill 3s. 4d..

Exors. Alexander Wetherwik, son William Kirk "to dispose for me in such manner as may be most pleasur to God and helth of my sowle". Supervisors my lord the prior of Newenham and my son the prior of Belvere. Witn. Master William Cartwright, John Dalton clerk, Robert Huet, John Davy, Christopher Jurden, William Stephyn, Hew Pavy, John Cooke, John Woodcok.

Will Will of Alexander Kirk of Ampthull concerning his lands and tenements in towns and fields of Tyngriff, Stepyngley, Milbrok, Ampthull, Wotton Pyllyng and Houghton Conquest.

Son William and his male heirs to have all above property for the term of his life, and after his death William's eldest son William and his male heirs to have property in Tyngriff, Stepyngley and Milbrok, in default of heirs to Edward the second son of testator's son William.

Son William's second son Edward and his male heirs to have the property in Ampthull, and in default of male heirs then to son William's youngest son William.

Son William's youngest son William and his male heirs to have the property in Wotton Pillinge and Houghton Conquest, and in default of male heirs then to the issue of testator's son William.

In default of male issue of said son William, the property is to be sold "by the discrecions of myn exequutors and supervisors" and the money is to be distributed "in meritoriows and charitable dedes as to poore people, mendyng of high ways and otherwise" as shall be thought most expedient for the health of souls of testator, his wife, his father and mother and all Christians.

If son William Kirk "depart unto God" before any of his sons reach the age of 21 years, then the rents of the property assigned to them is to be received by some honest man appointed by the lord prior of Newenham, by testator's son the prior of Belvere and by his nephew Alexander Wetherwik, and he is to deliver the money so received to the prior of Newenham to be used for the son's children, provided always that if Elizabeth Kirk the son's wife survives her husband, then she is to have all the lands and tenements in Tyngriff for the term of her life.

Witn. Master William Cartwright, sir John Dalton, Robert Huet,

John Davy, Christopher Jurdayn, William Stevyn, Hew Pavy, John Cook, John Woodstok and the said Alexander Kirk.
Sealed the Friday next before Passion Sunday (27 Mar. 1528).

154.
Alys Johnnys of Hawns. 20 Mar. 1527/8, pr. 21 Apr. 1528. (2: 137d)
   Burial in the church of Hawns; her best beast for principal; to mother church of Lincoln 4d.; to the high altar of Hawns for tithes forgotten 8d.; to Our Lady light 2 lb. of wax; to the rood light 1 lb. of wax; to St. Sunday's light 1 lb. of wax; to All Hallows light 1 lb. of wax; to the sepulchre light 2 lb. of wax; to the bells 12d.; to the torches 8d..
   To Johan Samys of Hychyn a gown, a kirtle of violet, 20s. in money. To god-daughter Alys Ardren a silver goblet and half a dozen silver spoons "after the decesse of her father and mother". To Agnes Stepyngley a coverlet, 2 pairs of sheets, 2 pewter dishes, 2 pewter plates, a new brass pot.
   To William Ardren and Margaret his wife, testator's daughter, and the heirs of their bodies all lands and tenements in Hawns, Houghton and Cardyngton, and if they have no surviving issue, the property is to be sold and disposed in Hawns church for souls of testator, her husband David Johnys and all Christians. Residue to William Ardren of Hawns.
   Executor William Ardren. Witn. Thomas Baxter her curate the vicar of Hawns, William Viner the bailiff of Hawns, Thomas Boughton of the same.

155.
John Golston of Stageden. 29 Jan. 1522/3, no date of probate. (2: 138)
   Burial in church of St. Leonard of Stageden; to the church 6s. 8d. for his burial; for his principal his best beast; to the high altar for tithes forgotten 2s.; to the light of the crucifix 20d.; to the fabric 20d.; to the torches a quarter of malt; to a priest 4 marks to celebrate in the parish church of Stageden for souls of testator and his parents for half a year.
   To son Lionel 40s.; to each of his sons 40s.; residue to wife Thomasina and Nicholas Cok. Executors wife Thomasina and said Nicholas Cooke, he to have for his labours 3s..
   He wills to his wife all his land in Bedfordshire for the space of one year; to son Thomas his corn chest and the evidence coffer with other standards "that was given to the place".
Executors refused to act and Thomasina the widow was granted letters of administration.

156.
John Gray. 4 Apr. 1527, pr. 29 Apr. 1528. (2: 138b)
   To be buried in the churchyard of Our Lady Church of Eton (Socon);

for mortuary as customary; to the high altar 12d.; to church of Lincoln 4d.; to Master Halam 20d.; to Our Lady light of Eton 12d.; to Newenham Abbey 20d.; to the friars of Huntingdon 20d.; to sir Edmund Beket and sir William Walwyn 8d. "for their labours to say 2 masses"; to Busshmed Abbey 20d.; to St. Neots Abbey 20d.; to the chapel of Hale Weston 20d. to be paid within a year after testator's death.

To wife Margaret for her life testator's house and lands, on condition that she will keep John "my sonne and hers", and after her death the property goes to son William, and he is to keep John "or els to be at the discrecion of my feoffers to kepe my son withall, the terme of his liff". If son William should die before John, then house and lands are to descend to William's heirs after death of John, and if William has no heirs the property is to be sold and the money "disposed for my sowle in the church of Eton".

To every living god-child 4d.. Residue to wife Margaret.

Executors wife Margaret and son William. Supervisor brother William Gray. Witn. sir Edmond Beket priest, John Courtman, Edmond Pikbone, Hugh Caysford (or Taysford), John Hamond.

157.
William Alen of Careleton. 12 Feb. 1527/8, pr. 11 May 1528. (2: 139)

Burial in "the holy church of Our Lady Careleton" before the rood; for mortuary his best good; to Our Lady of Lincoln 8d.; to the high altar 12d.; to the painting and gilding of the tablernacle of Our Lady in Careleton 3s. 4d.; to the rood loft 3s. 4d..

To sons Richard, John and Robert 40s. each to be given them by wife Johan "when she may best and when she shall perceyve ther most nede".

To wife Johan for life the house where testator lives with all the lands, pastures and commodities belonging to it in the fields of Carleton and Chelyngton. After her death the property goes in tail male to Thomas Alen testator's eldest son and to his heirs, in default of issue to son Robert and his heirs, in default of issue to son John and his heirs. Failing any heirs the property is to be sold and the proceeds used for the health of the souls of testator, his wife and all "that we be bownd to loke uppon" and of all Christians.

To wife Johan the farm held from "my Master and my lady Lucy" for the remainder of the years in the lease, and if she does not live for the full term, then son Thomas to have it for the remaining years.

To son Richard and his heirs and assigns the house bought from Thomas Serat "with my peny".

Residue to wife Johan. Exors. wife Johan and eldest son Thomas. Supervisor Robert "By the Re" "that it may be done to the pleasur of God and to my sowles most pleasur". Witn. sir William Parre curate,

Richard Grene, William Hyd, William By the Re, Alexander [?]Cree.
Probate granted to wife reserving the power of Thomas Alen.

158.
Thomas Stoughton of Chauesterne, husbandman. 31 Mar., pr. 3 Aug. 1528. (2: 140)
Burial in Roxton parish church in the space before Our Lady of Pity; for principal as customary; to mother church of Lincoln 4d.; to the high altar for tithes forgotten 12d.; to the church of Roxton 13s. 4d.; to repairing Stoughton bridge 6s. 8d.; to wife Johan 2 beasts, a bullock and all household stuff.
To wife Johan his messuage with all lands, meadows, pastures and appurtenances until Michaelmas come twelvemonth, and after that date his executors are to provide her with a messuage to the value of 6s. 8d. a year for the term of her life.
Testator's feoffees, Robert Chessham and Richard Tynghey, are empowered to fulfill his will, which is that the property is to be sold within a year by his executors with the oversight of sir Edward Hunt vicar of the said parish, and from the proceeds and honest priest is to be employed to pray for souls of testator, his friends and all Christians in Roxton church "so long as the money will extend".
Executors Thomas Scott of Eton, Robert Chessham of Roxton, and each to have 6s. 8d. for his labour. Overseer sir Edward Hunt vicar of Roxton who is to have 10s.. Witn. sir Thomas Stoughton parish priest, Robert Hasshwell, Richard Tyngay, Thomas Tyngay.

159.
Robert Wales of Syth Houghton. 23 July 1527, pr. 3 Aug. ?1527. (2: 140d)
Burial in the churchyard of All Hallows of Houghton; to the mother church of Lincoln 8d.; to the high altar 6s. 4d.; to the rood 16d.; to every one of Our Lady's lights 12d.; to every "gathered" light 2d.; to be bestowed "at my buryyng" 16s. 8d.; to poor people 3s. 6d.; "To the ryngers and them that bere me to church" 18d..
To each of his sister Wales' children 4d.; to the said Elizabeth Wales 3s. 4d.; to Robert her youngest son 3s. 4d.; to each of the said 5 children 2 sheep; to Thomas Barbour's wife a sheep and testator's wool; to Richard Wild's wife a sheep; to John Smyth 3s. 4d. that he claims for wages; to testator's sister, his wife, 3s. 4d.; to sir John 20d.; to be bestowed at testator's yeartide by his executors 10s.; to his brother Jamys a certain land containing 3 half acres with testator's whole crop, and for this he is to pay 3s. 4d. to a priest to pray for testator and his friends, and is also to give 3s. 4d. each to the mending of Cokkes lane and Lalise lane.

To mending the church highway between the Green and the church 3s 4d.; to Podill street 3s. 4d.; to his brother Jamys his best coat "and he to bestow therfore for me and my frendes in dedes of Charitie xxd." and to the same Jamys 5 sheets "he to bestow therfore in dedes of charitie xxd."; to John Croker the parish clerk testator's best sleeveless coat. Thomas Hardyng is forgiven one half of a bargain of 6 quarters of malt at 9s. a quarter, and the rest of the money (27s.) in Thomas' hands to be bestowed in deeds of charity for testator and his friends. To the maintenance of the parish church 10 bushels of malt; to be bestowed among poor people 2 bushels of malt; to be used in deeds of charity the other 12 bushels "that remaynyth" as thought best by John Barbour, Thomas Hardyng and James Walys. Residue to Thomas Hardyng to use for testator's soul. Executor Thomas Hardyng who is to have 20d.. Supervisor James Walys, to have 20d. for his labour. Witn. sir John Walter, James Walys, Margery Barber, Katherine Wild.

160.
Stephen Hamerton of Sandy. 20 Sep. 1518, pr. 29 Jan. 1518/9. (2: 141)
Burial in parish church of Sandy "at the oversight of my executors if it fortune me to depart ther or nygh the sayd parissh church where it shall please them".

To the church of Lincoln 4d.; to the high altar of the said church of St. Swythune for tithes forgotten 4s.; to the high altar of St. Batholomew of London for tithes forgotten 3s. 4d.; to the high altar of St. Sepulchre in London for tithes forgotten 20d.; a trental of masses to be said for his soul and all Christian souls "in the day of my buryall or shortly after when they se tyme convenient".

To wife Ann for her life ten acres of land which lies to testator in mortgage for £5 as appears by deed, if Thomas Aldrith does not redeem them again according to the said deed. After Anne's death the property goes to testator's heirs for ever, or in default of heirs it is to be sold and the money distributed in masses and other deeds of charity for souls of testator, Anne his wife and all their good friends.

To wife Anne all household stuff; to aunt Isabell a cow; to each godchild one ewe sheep; to Thomas Burgoyne parson of Sandy 10s. to see his will performed. Residue to go to his wife and his sons William and Peter, to be divided into three parts "indifferently" by the advice of executors. If either of his children should die, the survivor is to have that part, and if they both die their parts "to remayne to his wiff". Wife Anne to have the children's shares as long as she finds them "in all thynges necessary for them", with the increase of the same, and she is to give them each their parts when they support themselves.

Exors. wife and Master Thomas Burgoyne clerk.

No witnesses are recorded. Note that the testator signed and sealed his testament.

161.
Richard Rudy of Carleton. 7 Jan., pr. 29 Jan. 1518/9. (2: 142)
Burial in churchyard of St. Mary of Carleton; for his principal his best good; to mother church of Lincoln 2d.; to Carleton church 2s.; to Our Lady a sheep; to the bells a sheep; to the torches 6d.; to the sepulchre 6d.; to Harrold bridge a bushel of barley; to son Robert a cow, a bullock, 6 quarters of barley; to son John 20s.; to son Robert 2 sheep; to the friars of Bedford 12d..
He wills that William Rudy his son is to have the farm where testator lives for the term of years specified in his indentures. If William should sell his years, then son Robert is to have 40s.. Residue to son William to use for testator's soul.
Exors. son William and William Michell. Supervisor Richard Grene. Witn. Thomas Bonam his ghostly father, Richard Edward, William Hynd.

162.
James Franklen of Shefford. 25 Jan., pr. 27 Mar. 1527/8. (2: 143)
Burial in churchyard of Campton, for principal as "it shall require"; to the high altar of Campton 12d.; to mother church of Lincoln 4d.; to the bells of Campton 12d.; to the bridge toward Clifton 3s. 4d.; to the bridge toward Hardwik 3s. 4d.; to the friars of Dunstable 10s. to sing a trental; to the high altar of Clifton 12d..
To wife Margaret his house in Shefford for the term of her life, if she remains unmarried, and for 7 years if she remarries. After her death the house is to go to Agnes, testator's daughter, and her issue, or if Agnes die without issue, the house is to be sold and the money used for souls of testator, his father and mother and wife, and "for Humfey's sowle".
To daughter Agnes £5 to her marriage; to brother's daughter Joan 40s., a mattress, a bolster, a pair of sheets, a coverlet. To brother's daughter Anne 40s., a mattress, a bolster, a pillow, a pair of sheets, a coverlet. To each of them brass and pewter "at my wivis mynd".
Residue to wife. Executrix his wife. Supervisor Thomas Strynger of Langford, who is to have 6s. 8d. for his labour. Witn. sir John Woodward, George Flynders, William Amps, Robert Webster.

163.
Simond Stratton of Houghton Conquest. 1527, pr. 17 Mar. 1527/8. (2: 143d)
To be buried in the parish church in the space before the rood; for his mortuary "after the lawdable cutome of the towne"; to the high altar

for tithes forgotten 12d.; to the mother church of Lincoln 4d.; to a priest to sing for testator for a year £5 6s. 8d.; to Houghton Conquest church 40s. to be disposed by his executors for the maintenance of the church.

One sheep each to the lights of the Sepulchre, Sweet Jesus, the Trinity, All Hallows, Our Lady, and St. Katerin. To the maintenance of the bells half a quarter of malt. To the churches of Wotton, Westonnyng, Flitwik and Harlyngton, half a quarter of malt each.

To Robert Sturmy a quarter of malt; to every poor man in Houghton Conquest half a bushel of malt; to every god-child a bushel of malt.

To wife Agnes the house called Whites at the Town's End, 2 kine, 4 pairs of sheets, a brass pot, a brass pan, half a dozen pewter [blank], 2 candlesticks, and to have each year for the term of her life 3 quarters of corn, wheat or malt "as she likith best" to be delivered to her by his executors.

To son Roger a tenement in Chapell End in Houghton, he paying his mother 6s. 8d. for the term of her life; to him also both testator's copy-holdings "copies" lying in the fields of Houghton Conquest, one called Potters, the other Harvys Pond; also the rest of his household stuff, his cart and cart gear, plough and plough gear, all other "stuff to husbandry" and the rest of the farm where testator dwells. Roger and his heirs or assigns are to keep an obit each year "while the world endurith" for testator, his wife and all Christian souls to the value of 6s. 8d..

To son Thomas a tenement at the Church Stile in Houghton and his mother's tenement called Wights after her death, and 2 copyholdings in Chapell End, one held by John Cooper and the other by Thomas Tayllour, paying the lord of the manor his rent.

To son Roger and the heirs of his body testator's last purchase in Chapell End with all appurtenances, lately held by John Punter. If Roger should die without issue, then it is to go to son Thomas and his heirs, and if Thomas die without heirs it is to be sold, and half the proceeds are "to be done for me and my wiff and all Cristen sowlys" and the other half goes to Houghton Church "to help and enlarge the fore-sayd obit if nede require", otherwise it is to be disposed as the church-wardens think best to the profit of the church.

The residue to son Roger. Executors son Roger and William Slow the elder who is to have 6s. 8d. for his labour. Overseer John Mylnar who is to have 3s. 4d. for his labour. Witn. sir Richard Graunt curate, Henry Alen, William Dey, John Bilcok, Robert Sturmy.

164.
Thomas Lucy of Roxton. 17 Dec. 1527, pr. 17 Mar. 1527/8. (2: 145)

Burial in the churchyard of Roxton between the cross and the chancel door; to the high altar of Roxton for tithes forgotten 8d.; to the mother church of Lincoln 1d.; to the torches 8d.; to the bells 8d.; for his principal as customary; to the sepulchre light 8d.. Testator's best brass pan, "a fissyng start" and all timber and tools are to be sold and "done" for testator and his wife by his executors under the supervision of Robert Chessham.

To the children of Henry Child, Thomas Child and Robert Cooper all testator's sheep to be equally divided between them under the supervision of Robert Chessham; to Alice Child his settle standing in the hall; to Agnes Cowper his great ark; to Thomas Child his best gown; to Robert Cooper his best coat; to Agnes Cooper his second gown; to Richard Hond his best brass pot and best brass pan.

His executors are to have said for him 5 masses on the day of his burial, and as soon as they can they are to have 5 masses said by the friars of Bedford.

"Also I will that where Thomas Swift and Thomas Sexton were and be enfeoffid and state to them delivered accordyng to the use of me the sayd Thomas Lucy and of myn heyrys shall stand seasid in full strength to the use of Thomas Hunt and of his heyrys and assignes accordyng to my promesse and sale to the sayd Thomas Hunt aforemade".

Residue to wife Katerin for the term of her life, and then to be equally divided between Thomas Child and Robert Cooper by Robert Chessham. Exors. Thomas Child, Robert Cooper. Overseer Robert Chessham. Witn. sir Thomas Stoughton parish priest, Thomas Hunt, Robert Asshwell, Thomas Wiff, William Dawntre.

165.
Thomas Cley/Clay of Beston in the parish of Sondy. 19 May, pr. 20 July 1528. (2: 145d)

Burial in the churchyard of Sandy; for mortuary his best beast according to custom; to the high altar for tithes forgotten 12d.; to the sepulchre light 6d.; to the rood light 6d.; to the upkeep of the bells 12d.; he bequeaths one pound of wax towards making a taper to burn on holy days at the "sacryng" or consecration time of high mass; to mother church of Lincoln 4d.; to Northivell church a quarter of barley; to Old Wardon church 2 bushels of barley; to Barkford church 2 bushels of barley; to Temmysford church 2 bushels of barley; to each god-child one bushel of barley; to his brothers John and William and to his sister Alen a quarter of barley each; a priest is to sing a service in Sandy church for half a quarter for souls of testator and of all Christians; to the gilding of the sepulchre in Sandy 6s. 8d.; to John Lawman of Sandy his violet gown; to wife one ewe and a lamb.

To wife Alys for life the house where testator dwells, with all land, meadow, pastures and appurtenances in Beston, on condition that she remains unmarried. After her death or marriage the property is to be sold by his executors and supervisor "to the most and best advauntage that they conveniently may" and the money is to be disposed for the wealth of souls of his friends and of all Christians. Half is to be used for a priest to sing in Sandy church "for the sowlys above rehersed"; 40s. of the other half is to go to the abbot and convent of the monastery of Our Blessed Lady of Wardon for a trental of masses, placebo, *dirige*, lauds and commendations, and the rest is to be disposed in deeds of charity.

His executors and supervisor may sell the reversion of her estate during the lifetime of his wife. If his executors and supervisor are not all living when the time comes for making the sale, then the responsibility rests with the survivor or survivors.

To his wife 4 horses, 3 colts, 4 oxen, all his beasts, 30 sheep, all his stuff of household and husbandry, 12 acres of barley that is being tilled; all his peas and oats and all wheat and rye now growing; all fallen timber, the rest of his barley and all sawn board. Residue to his brother John Clay and John Bromsall the younger.

Exors. brother John Clay and John Bromsall the younger, each to have 6s. 8d.. Supervisor John Colbek, he to have 20s. for his pain and labour. Witn. John Bromsale the elder, Richard Hawkyn.

"And in case that the foresayd Alys my wiff after my decease have not her parfayte remembraunce but that she continew ony space or tyme in such like case as she is at the present day, then I will that myn exequutors and my supervisor have the disposicion and distribucion of all the foresayd corne catall and other moveable goods to th'entent that she during her liff shall and may be honestly kept with the same, and in case she fortune to dy, havyng not her parfayte mynd to make a will and to dispose her forsayd goodes, then I will my sayd exequutors by th'advise of my said supervisor all the foresayd goodes which at the tyme of her sayd decease shall remayne unspent shall all the same dispose for the helth and profit of our sowlys as shall seme them best". Witness Thomas Aldrige.

166.
Richard Colyer/Colyer a parishioner and inhabitant of Blownham. 1 Nov. 1526, no probate. (2: 147)

Burial in churchyard of Blownham; mortuary after custom of the parish; to high altar for tithes forgotten 2s.; to mother church of Lincoln 2d.; to the upkeep of the church 6s. 8d.; to the upkeep of the bells 8d.; to the maintenance of the sepulchre light 8d.; to the torches 8d..

"Also, to th'entent I may be prayd for, I give to the mayntenance of the brotherhed kept in the honor of the Trinite within the parissh of Blownham so much money as shalby v good mylch ky other havyng calvis or els beyng with calff, the which ky I wil be letten for ijs. viijd. a cow yerely and so from yere to yere to continew to the emolument and profit of the sayd brotherhed, and if any casuallty of deth or any other mysfortune channce or happyn to any of the sayd v keen I will then the tutors of the brotherhod for the tyme beyng shalby agayn so many as shalbe nedeful to fulfill the nowmber agayn so the nombre of ky may ever remayn and be kept".

To the painting of banner poles 2s.; to buy a banner cloth 10s.; to mending the "slakkes" (holes or bogs) between Barford amd Blownham 12d.; to the mending of Lincoln Cross at Blownham town's end towards Barford 8d..

To testator's wife a house with four acres and one rood of arable land and one acre of mead in the town and fields of Blownham, sometime called Festens, for the term of her life if she remains unmarried.
The rest of the page is blank.

167.
John Perott of Luton, 3 May, pr. 27 May 1525. (2: 148)
Burial in Luton church "angenst my seete ther as I sitt"; to the high altar 2s.; to the church of Lincoln 4d.; to the rood light 6d.; to every other light in the church 2d.; to the friars of Dunstable 12d.; to Lynbury chapel a quarter of malt; to the brotherhood of the Trinity a quarter of malt.

To his wife during her life the house where testator dwells, and one acre 3 roods of land on Stopisley Hill, one acre in Bayly feld, and three acres in Sewell field. After her death land is to go to Thomas Perott his son, and for it he is to keep a yearly *dirige* and mass for testator's soul in Luton church for the space of 20 years. Shortly after death of wife Thomas is to have a stone laid price 53s. 4d..

To son Roger Perott testator's place at Biscott with its appurtenances, to hold to him and his assigns, he paying testator's wife 20s. yearly during her life. He is also to keep a yearly *dirige* and mass in Luton church for 10 years after death of testator and his wife.

To son William Perott and his heirs for ever testator's place at Lynbury with all its lands.

To each of his children's children a bushel of malt; to each god-child a bushel of malt; to every child of John Perott of Biscott a bushel of malt. Residue to wife Margaret to pay debts and to his executors to use for soul of testator.

Exors. wife Margaret and sons Roger and Thomas. Roger and Thomas are each to have 6s. 8d. for their work. Witn. Master Roger Bawdwyn, Thomas Steppyng, John Ordway, William Wellys.

168.
William Gere the elder of Sharnebrok. 22 Dec. 1519, pr. 18 Jan. 1519/20. (2: 149)

To be buried in the parish church of St. Peter of Sharnebrok "givyng therefore unto the sayd church" 6s. 8d.; his mortuary as custom requires; to Our Lady light 12d.; to the sepulchre light 12d.; to the rood light 12d.; to the Trinity light 12d.; to the torches 2s.; to the bells 3s. 4d.; to Suldropp church 3s. 4d.; to Thurly church 3s. 4d.; to Mylton church 3s. 4d.; to Bletnesho church 3s. 4d.; to the rood loft in Suldropp church 3s. 4d.; to the painting of the Holy Trinity in Sharnebrok church 6s. 8d.; to the rood of the same 10s.; to buying a new cope 10s..

If the parishioners of Sharnebrok begin the brotherhood of the Trinity, they are to have 20s. for it, otherwise not.

To repairing the way about Sharnebrok where most needs to be done 10s.; to Chenyhogges bridge 3s. 4d.; to repairing Melton town 10s. "if they will mak it byfore Michaelmas" otherwise not; to each god-child a ewe and a hoggerel; to John Gere son of William Gere a ewe; to John Gere son of John Gere a ewe; to John West a ewe; to Elizabeth Udsall 2 sheep; to Margaret Oldershew 2 sheep; to son John 4 horses and testator's cart.

To wife and son, equally divided between them, all testator's corn and grain, the tilth of the land and all other household stuff.

An honest priest is to sing for souls of testator, his wife, children, father and mother in Sharnebrok parish church for 2 years after his death.

To wife Margaret for life the tenement where testator dwells with a little orchard in Calfulende, reversion to son John and the heirs of his body.

To son John and the heirs of his body all testator's other tenements, lands, meadows, leases and pasture in Sharnebrok. Should John die without issue before Margaret, testator's wife, then this property goes to Margaret for the term of her life, then to be sold and used "for me, my wiff, my childerne, my father, my mother and all Cristen sowlys". Should John survive the wife and then die without heirs, the property is to be sold and used as described above.

To Felmersham church 20d.; to brother Thomas 3 sheep; to William son of testator's brother Thomas 3 sheep; to parish church of Odell 3s. 4d.; to the vicar of Sharnebrok and his successors an acre of testator's best land in Sharnebrok on condition that he keeps testator's obit yearly with placebo, *dirige*, requiem mass, with a "solempne pele rong" for souls of testator and all Christians.

Residue to wife and son jointly together "so long as they can accorde and agre to gither, she kepyng her self sole, and when and what tyme they can not agre, or discorde, I will she have deliverd unto her xx li. or els asmoch other goodes and catallis concernyng the sum of the said xx li.".

Exors. sir William Lenton vicar of Sharnebrok, sir William Grene parson of Suldropp, son John Gere. Witn. Richard Newman, John Odam, Richard Fissher.

169.
John Cranwell of Flitwik. 8 Mar., pr. 17 Mar. 1519/20. (2: 151)
Burial in the churchyard of St. Peter in Flitwik; for mortuary his best beast; to the high altar 8d.; to Flitwik church 20s.; to the welfare of the town a "stok" of 8s.; to wife Kateryn during her life, his tenement and all that belongs to it, and on her death this goes to son Thomas; to son Richard 20s. and 2 kine. Residue to wife Kateryn and on her death to son Thomas. Exors. wife Kateryn and son Thomas. Witn. William Barne, Thomas Acotton, Thomas Lord.
Probate granted to Thomas Cranwell reserving power of widow.

170.
William Smyth [*margin* Smyth alias Cooper] of the parish of St. Powlys in Bedford. 24 Feb. 1519/20, pr. 30 Mar. 1520. (2: 151d)
Burial in the churchyard of St. Powlys; to high altar for tithes forgotten 3s. 4d.; to mother church of Lincoln 12d.; for a trental 20s. "the day of my buryall to be done if it may be for the welth of my sowle" and his executors are to give the priests, clerks and poor people 33s. 4d. on the same day, with more if need be; for a trental on his month's day 10s. and to priests, clerks and poor people on his month's day 10s.; to sir John Asshwell the prior of Newnam his bay gelding; to sir John Salpho cellarer of the said house 20s.; to every canon who is a priest 20d.; to every novice 12d.; and they of their charity to sing a *dirige* and mass for his soul; to Our Lady's mass bell in the same house 12d. to have my "sowle knyll rong at my departyng"; to the ringers 8d.; to the image in Newneham called the White Lady, one of his best kine to find a light before the said image.
To Thomas Borne testator's wife's son 6s. 8d. and testator's indenture with the years to come of a close that testator has from the abbot and convent of Warden lying by the High Field, paying yearly what testator has paid for it; to Elizabeth Walker 10s.; to Richard Saybroke her father all the testator's sheep which he has in his keeping, and the increase of them to be distributed among his children that are left alive; to the reparation of Powlys steeple 20s.; to the reparation of the bridge 3s. 4d.; to Harrold bridge 3s. 4d.; to godson Robert Fissher a sheep and 12d. in money; to every godchild a sheep or 12d. in money; to Symond, testator's brother's eldest son, a red coffer; to godson Harry Walker a red coffer; to the son of William Bernys his best coffer; to Elizabeth his maiden a black coffer. Residue to wife Elizabeth to do for his soul as he would for her.

Exors. wife Elizabeth and John Baker, who is to have for his labour 13s. 4d.. Overseer sir John Asshwell prior of Newenham. Witn. sir Alisawnder the parish priest, Rawffe Mosse, John Gayton.

171.
Walter Parell [*margin* Parcell] of Bolnehurst. 19 Mar. 1519/20, pr. 30 Apr. 1520. (2: 152d)
Burial in parish church of St. Dunstone "byfore the roode agenst my seet end"; to the high altar for tithes forgotten 6s. 8d.; to the painting of St. Dunstone 6s. 8d.; to the painting of the sepulchre 6s. 8d.; to the torches 6s. 8d.; to the bells 6s. 8d.; "For breking of my grownd for my grave" 6s. 8d.; to mother church of Lincoln 12d.; to Bolnehurst church testator's house in Sowthend, after his wife's death, making the church-wardens feoffees of the same "to thentent that they shall kepe a lamp light every holyday from the begynnyng of Matens unto Cumplayn be all done".

To Johan Parell his son [*sic*] towards her marriage one cow, beside her wages; to Agnes Markham "if she be lovyng to my wiff, when she shalbe maryyd, she shalhave to the valor of liijs. iiijd.; if she be not lovyng to my wiff then she shall take ij honest men and reward her as she hath deservid and better"; to every one of his godchildren a ewe and a lamb; to every servant in his house a ewe and a lamb; to buying a bell to Much Stoughton church 20s.; to the church of Litill Stoughton 6s. 8d.; to Busshmede 6s. 8d.; to Colmorth 6s. 8d.; to Wilden 6s. 8d.; to Raynoll 6s. 8d.; to Ravennysden 6s. 8d.; to Thurly 6s. 8d.; to Riseley 6s. 8d.; to Bletnesho 6s. 8d.; to Kayshoo 6s. 8d.; to Pertenhall 6s. 8d.; to Swannyshed 6s. 8d..

A priest is to sing for testator for 2 years in the said church of St. Dunstone. Residue to be at the disposal of his executors. Exors. Edmond Parell his brother, wife Agnes, John Hayn his son. Witn. Thomas Cressey curate, Thomas Alcok, Richard Borough.

172.
sir John Stokis, clerk, rector of Wymyngton. 26 Apr., pr. 12 May 1520. (2: 153d)
Burial in the parish church of Wemyngton; to mother church of Lincoln 12d.; to the repairing of the church 20s. "in a stok"; to the friars of Bedford and to the Black Friars of Northamton 10s. each for a trental for the souls of testator, his father and mother and all Christians; to sir William Eliott parson of Farndeissh 20s.; to sir William Stokys vicar of Thyndyn [Finedon, Northants.] testator's whole bed that he now lies in, with all its belongings.

Exor. sir William Stokys. Residue to be disposed of by his executor "as by his discrecion shall thynk most best, as I have shewd my mynd

4. Brass of sir John Stokys, rector of Wymington, who died in 1520. From his
will (no. 172) it would seem that he died in Finedon, where his brother was
vicar. *Thomas Fisher.*

unto hym". Witn. John Abotton, Robert Tesdale, Henry Broke and many others of the town of Thynden.

[*After the year date of the making of the will the manuscript adds "and the x th yere of the raigne of Kyng Henry the viij th" which would make the year of making 1518. Presumably 1520 is correct.*]

173.
William Wodell of Marston. 20 May 1520, pr. 12 May 1520 [*sic*] (2: 154)

Burial in the churchyard of the parish church of Our Lady of Marston; for mortuary as custom of the town; to mother church of Lincoln 2d.; to the high altar 2 bushels of barley; to Our Lady in the chancel 2 bushels of barley; to the sepulture light a bushel of barley; to All Hallows light a bushel of barley; to the bells a bushel of barley; to St. Anne a bushel of barley; to St. Laurence chapel 2 bushels of barley; to the Trinity chapel 2 bushels of barley; to West End lane 2 bushels of barley; to a priest to sing half a trental 5s..

To John Lynwood a doublet; to William Lynwood his tawny coat; to Richard Lynwood a lamb; to Richard Britten his violet coat; to Alison Slow a bushel of wheat.

To eldest son John Odell a great pot, a great pan, a sheet that was his mother's, a laten basin, a tin basin, 2 pillowberes, a coffer, 2 pairs of sheets, a pair of blankets, a coverlet, 2 platters and a candlestick. To testator's mother half a quarter of wheat.

To wife Johan his house and land with appurtenances, until his son comes to lawful age, on condition that she keeps for testator a yearly anniversary to the value of 3s. 4d.. If the said John should die without issue of his body, then Harry, testator's youngest son, is to inherit the house and lands, with all the other legacies made to John, provided that whichever of them enjoys the property shall keep the anniversary as aforesaid. Should John and Harry both die without issue then the property goes to the parish church of Our Lady at Marston, and the churchwardens are to keep the "yeretid" of 3s. 4d. as aforesaid. Residue to wife Johan to pay debts and funeral expenses and to succour his children.

Exors. wife Johan Whodell and John Cornell. Win. sir William Cokkes curate, Richard Briten, Nicholas Stanbrige.

174.
John White of Rigemond. 6 Dec. 1519, pr. 19 July 1520. (2: 155d)

To be buried in the church of Seggenho; for mortuary his best beast; to cathedral church of Lincoln 2d.; to the high altar of Segnow for tithes forgotten 8d.; to the light of Our Blessed Lady in Segnow 2 laten candlesticks with 2 wax tapers upon them; to maintain the said light a cow; to every altar in Segnow except the high altar and Our Lady altar 12d.;

to the bells 12d.; to the said church a torch; to eldest daughter Alice some "convenient goodes" to the value of 40s..

The testator bequeathed for a trental of masses for souls of self, his father, his mother and all his friends 10s. to the Grey Friars of Bedford and 10s. to the friars of Dunstable, a second 10s. to the friars of Dunstable, and 10s. to a "convenable" priest in Segnow church. In addition a "convenable" priest is to have 4 marks to say mass in Segnow church for half a year with the same intention. To every god-child 4d..

He bequeathed to Master William Marshall of Edlesborough, gentleman and to his assigns, all his houses, lands and closes which he has by copy of court roll in the lordships of Brokborough, Rigemond, Norwood and Crawley, or elsewhere adjoining, after the custom of the manor.

Of the residue half is to go to his wife, and the other half to be "at the disposicion of my sayd right wellbeloved and singular good Master William Marshall, to th'entent that if Elizabeth my yongist doughter be gidid and maryyd after his discrecion and councell then that he shall reward her as it shall please hym towardes her sayd mariage, and if the said Elizabeth marye contrary to his counseyll, then I will he shall dispose the same half of my sayd goodes as he shall thynk best for my sowle and all my frends sowlys".

Exors. William Marshall and testator's wife. "I bequeth to the sayd William for his labour and payn, as well for that that he hath of his goodnes takyn for me byfore this tyme afore, I must desire hym to tak hereafter xx s.".

Witn. sir John Marcam vicar of Segnow, William At Slow, William Tilcok, John Ploughright, Roger Mathew.

175.

Thomas Frount (Frownt *margin*) of Riseley. 3 July 1520, pr. "day, month and year aforesaid" probably as no. 174, 19 July 1520. (2: 156d)

Burial in the churchyard of Riseley; to the high altar for tithes forgotten 20d.; to the bells 16d.; to the torches 12d.; to the sepulchre of Our Lord 16d.; to the mother church of Lincoln 8d..

To his wife, both his places in Riseley until his children are of lawful age, and if they live until that time, then son Robert is to have the place lying next Hard. If Robert die, it goes to Thomas, and if Thomas die it goes to William, and if William die the place next Hard is to be sold, and done for the souls of testator and his friends.

As for his place next to Thomas Fissher, when his sons Thomas and William come of age they are to have half of that place with its appurtenances, his wife having the other half for the term of her life. After her death, if the children are dead (as God forbid) then it is to be sold and the money used for the souls of testator and his wife and all his friends.

To Thomas, Robert and William a weaning calf each "at my departyng" and testator's wife is to bring them up to the most profit with the
increase till the children are of age to guide them themselves. Residue
to wife Alis and to Thomas Woodward on behalf of his wife. Exors. wife
Alis and Thomas Woodward. Overseer sir Henry Queene vicar of
Riseley. Witn. sir William Woodward, William Pentlow, Thomas
Fissher.

176.
Elizabeth Hunt, widow, of Roxton. 7 Mar. 1519/20, pr. 17 Aug. 1520.
(2: 157d)
Burial in the churchyard of Roxton "at the chauncell end by my
sonne"; for principal as custom is; to mother church of Lincoln 4d.; to
the high altar for tithes forgotten 12d.; to the bells 12d.; to sir Thomas
the parish priest 12d.; to sir John Tayllar 6s. 8d. yearly for 6 years.
To Edward Hunt her bed with all that belongs to it and a mattress;
to Roger Hunt her silver piece; to Gregory Hunt the cover of the same
piece; to Edward Hunt half a garnish vessel, a charger, her great pot,
her great pan, her second basin, 2 spits and 2 of her biggest covers; to
Roger and Gregory Hunt her 2 covers standing in her chamber; to
Edward Hunt two candlesticks and the hangings of her hall; to Thomas
Hunt a featherbed and a coverlet; to each god-child 4d..
To Edward Hunt her brazen mortar and stone mortar; to sir John
Tayllour a basin, a towel, a flaxen sheet; to Christian Fissher a mattress;
to Edward, Roger and Gregory Hunt, 2 cushions each, a greater and a
smaller; to Gregory Hunt her green coverlet; to daughter Mary Hunt
late the wife of Roger Hunt all her moveable goods, not previously
bequeathed, in the manor of Chalstorne.
To sir John Tayllour the priest, for his payment, testator's sheep, with
the increase. Her best girdle and her silver salt are to be sold, and the
money used for the payment to sir John Tayllour. The greatest brass pot
at Chalstorne, after the death of testator's daughter Mary, is to be left
to the use of Thomas Hunt. To Thomas Hunt testator's second chafer
at Roxton.
The tenement called Joys at the west end of Chalstorne next William
Fage on the east side, with all appurtenances, is to be maintained and
kept in repair to keep an obit in Roxton church for testator's husband
and for herself and their friends "as it is playnly expressid in his last
will". When any wood is sold from this tenement, the money is to be
used for repairing the tenement, or else spent for the health of their
souls, as her husband charged her, and she charges her executors.
Exors: daughter Mary Hunt, Thomas Hunt, Roger Hunt, to whom
the residue "to dispose it at theyr myndes". Witn. John Mighton,
Thomas Francis, sir John Tayllour, Richard Fitzhugh.

All the goods left to Roger, Gregory and Edward Hunt are to remain in the custody of testator's daughter, their mother, "unto such tyme as they be of age and discrecion to receve hit", and if any of them should die before this, his share to be divided between the remaining two.

177.
Thomas Underwood of Henlow. 3 Aug., pr. 15 Sep. 1520. (2: 158d)
Burial in the churchyard; mortuary his best good after the custom of the country; to the high altar for offerings and tithings forgotten a bushel of barley; to the brotherhood of Our Lady in the same church 2 bushels of barley; to Our Lady of Lincoln 1d..
To son John and his heirs for ever, a three rood "stich" of land on the Ra furlong; to Thomas Underwood, son of John Underwood, and his heirs for ever half an acre of land at Dogdich; to John Underwood the younger and his heirs for ever, half an acre of land in Clifton field and an acre of mead in Northmede; to son John Underwood and his heirs for ever half an acre of land on Lows land.
To daughter Agnes Edward for her lifetime half an acre of land lying in the croft against testator's place, and on her death it is to go to testator's son Richard Underwood and his
heirs for ever.
To son Richard Underwood all testator's house and land, with all the mead pertaining to it, except the above bequests. His executors are to lay a grave stone on his father's grave in the churchyard of Henlow.
Exors. sons Richard and John, to whom the residue, to dispose of for testator's soul. Witn. sir Hugh priest of Henlow; William Jacob, William Offode. Written at Henlow.

178.
John Lodyngton the elder of Eton (Socon). 3 Oct., pr. 11 Oct. 1520. (2: 159d)
Burial in the churchyard of Our Blessed Lady of Eton; for mortuary as customary; to the high altar for tithes forgotten 12d.; to the mother church of Lincoln 4d.
Wife Elizabeth to have testator's head place with 9 acres of land at the end of the said place for the term of her life, "and that ther shall no man cary nor recary within the sayd place". After her death testator's son John is to have the 9 acres "to kepe myn obit withall", and after John's death the land goes to his son Thomas, and he is to keep the obit "like as his father did byfore, and so to remayn from oon child to another". In default of issue, the land is to be sold "and done for them that it come of".
Wife and son John to dispose of £4 for the wealth of testator's soul.

Exors. wife Elizabeth and son John, to whom the residue. Witn. John Bakster, Jamys Greneleff, John Man.

[*Note: there is now no folio 160, and so the text runs on from f. 159d to f. 161.*]

179.
Thomas Hich' the elder of the parish of St. Poulys in Bedford. 17 Sep., pr. 28 Oct. 1520. (2: 161d)
Burial in the churchyard of St. Powlys, on the south side next to testator's wives (or wife's) and his children. To the high altar for tithes forgotten 12d.; to the mother church of Lincoln 4d.; to a good honest priest 4 marks in good money to sing for testator's soul in Powlys church for half a year.

To daughter Agnes a brass pot, a pan, half a dozen pewter, 4 saucers, a salt cellar, a mattress, a bolster, a coverlet, 2 pillows, 4 pair of sheets, a table cloth, a towel, 2 candlesticks, a coffer, a pair of coral beads that was her mother's, and £3 6s. 8d. in money, when she comes to the age of 20 years. To daughter Johan a brass pot, a pan, hald a dozen pewter, 2 candlesticks, a mattress, a bolster, a coverlet, 2 pair of sheets, a table cloth, a towel, a coffer and £3 6s. 8d. in money, when she comes to the age of 20 years. If either daughter die before the other, then each is to be the other's heir, and if both die, their bequests are to go to testator's son William Hitch'.

To son John Abyngton 20s. in money, a mattress, a pair of sheets, a coverlet and a bolster. To daughter Elizabeth Thody 20s. in money. To son Thomas Hich' 20s. in money and testator's little house in the Fishmarket.

To son William Hich' the place that testator dwells in and a close in the parish of Kempston. Wife Johan is to have her dwelling in the said house as long as she remains unmarried "if she please and that they can agree together if she can be so contented". All remaining household stuff as pots, pans, pewter, woollen and linen, with all other moveables, is to be evenly divided between wife Johan and son William, and half testator's stock of money. If she please to tarry, then she is to be a partner in all buying and selling done by testator's son, and the money of both of them is to be used together. If son William should die without issue, the place and close are to be sold and the money distributed between testator's surviving children. If William has issue, then the place and close to go to them.

Exors. son William and wife Johan, to whom the residue, to be equally divided between them. Overseer Thomas Hich'. Witn. sir John Bikleswade, sir Alexander the parish priest, Thomas Knyght, Rawff Mosse, John Baker.

[*Note: on a separate sheet of paper sewn to this page there is a further statement about the probate, dated 13 Feb. 1520/1, saying that the wife Johan declined to act and so son William Hich' was empowered to act as sole executor.*]

180.
Thomas Harper of Bydenham. 17 Nov., pr. 1 Dec. 1520. (2: 162d)
Burial in the churchyard of St. Jamys of Bydenham; for mortuary as customary; to church of Lincoln 4d.; to Our Lady light 2 bushels of barley; to the high altar for privy tithes forgotten 20d.; to the bells 12d..

To wife Johan for life testator's three houses. With two of them she can do what she will. However, after her death John Amere is to have the house testator purchased from John Tyrett, and he is to pay for it. Residue to wife Johan.

Exors. brother John Wright and William Harper. Overseer John Amere. Witn. sir John Billynges, John Faldo, Thomas Mowce, John Awstyn.

181.
John Pett of Cadyngton. 6 Nov. 1520, no note of probate. (2: 163)
Burial in the churchyard of Cadyngton, to the high altar 20d.; to the mother church of Lincoln 4d.; to the six lights in the church 12d..

To brother Thomas Pett all testator's houses and land in Cadyngton, to order and guide testator's two sons Thomas and John until son Thomas is of lawful age. Should son Thomas die without issue, then property to go to son John, and if he also should die without issue, then it goes to testator's brother Thomas and the heirs of his body, according to the will of testator's father. Residue to brother Thomas.

Exors. Thomas Bray and Andrew Bray, each to have 6s. 8d. for his labour. Witn. sir Thomas Elnestone vicar, William Deane clerk, William Pett.

182.
Henry Tilly of Henlow. 1 Sep., pr. 4 Dec. 1520. (2: 163d)
Burial in churchyard of Henlow; for his mortuary the best good as custom of the town; to the high altar 2 bushels of barley; to the bells 2 bushels of barley; to the guild priest of Our Lady in the said church of Henlow 28s. 4d. to sing a quarter service especially for testator and his friends and generally for the brethren and "susturne" of the same guild. If there is no brotherhood priest, then another honest priest is to perform the said quarter service.

To each of the children of testator's son Thomas Tilly the outside of a coat of canvas.

To wife Johan for the term of her life, testator's place, and after her death this is to go to testator's son William Tilly. If they both agree to sell the place, then testator's son Thomas Tilly is to buy it "byfore any other, payyng as moch as another man will". Should William die without issue before the place is sold, then it is to be sold to hire a priest to pray for testator and his friends as long as the money lasts.

Exors. wife Johan and son William Tilly, to whom the residue. Supervisor: son Thomas Tilly. Given at Henlow. Witn. John Underwood, William March, sir Robert Bisshopp.

Probate granted to William Tilly, reserving the power of the other executor.

183.
William Morcott of Turvey. 1520, pr. 20 Dec. 1520. (2: 164)
Burial in the churchyard of All Hallows in Turvey; for principal as customary; to the high altar for tithes forgotten 20d.; to the bells 20d.; to Turvey bridge 20d.; to the rood of Brayfield 20d..

To daughter Elizabeth a brass pot, a pan, a mattress, a pair of sheets, and a coverlet. To daughter Agnes a mattress, a coverlet, a coffer and 2 sheep, and if either die before marriage, then the other sister to have her stuff.

To wife for life testator's tenement in Brige End in which he dwells and also another house in Turvey High Street. After her death testator's son John, his eldest child, is to have the Brigg End tenement, and second son Edmond is to have the other tenement in Turvey High Street. If either of them die without heirs, his tenement to go to the survivor. If they both die "as God forbede" then the two tenements to go to testator's daughters Elizabeth and Agnes and their heirs for ever, Elizabeth, the eldest daughter, having the one in Brig Street and Agnes the other in the High Street. Should all die, testator's executors are to sell the tenements and use the proceeds for charitable deeds and works of mercy. Residue to executors to use for souls of testator, his father and mother and all Christians.

Exors. wife Johan, John Hodell. Witn. Walter Skevyngton, John Page, John Chandler.

184.
Richard Ball of Turvey. n.d., pr. 20 Dec. 1520. (2: 165)
Burial in churchyard of All Hallows Turvey; for his principal as customary; to mother church of Lincoln 2d.; to the high altar 6d.; to the rood 4d.; to the bells 8d.; to Our Lady of Pity, 2d.; to St. Katerin 3d.; to the bridge 2d..

To daughter Edeth 40s., and if she should die the money is to be used for souls of testator and all his good friends. To sister Agnes 2 sheep; to sister Johan 2 sheep. Residue to wife Johan.

Exors. testator's father and his wife. A trentall is to be sung for testator's soul in Turvey church and five masses of the Five Wounds sung for his soul. Witn. John Balle, Johan Ball.

185.

John Hynde of Bletnesho. 26 Dec. 1520, pr. 12 Jan. 1520/1. (2: 165d)

Burial in the churchyard of the parish church of Bletnesho; for mortuary as customary; to the mother church of Lincoln 1d.; to the high altar for tithes forgotten 2 measures of barley; to the light burning before the image of the Crucifix 2 measures of barley; to the friars of Bedford 2 measures of barley to pray for souls of testator and all the faithful departed; to the bells 2 measures of barley; to the torches one measure of barley.

To son Robert and the heirs of his body all testator's lands, tenements, meads and pastures with their appurtenances in the towns and fields of Bletnesho, Sharnebrok, Felmersham and Thurly, on condition that Robert pays to testator's wife Elizabeth 10s. a year during her natural life. Residue to be equally divided between wife Elizabeth and son Robert.

Exors. wife Elizabeth and son Robert. Witn. sir John Ryell, Robert Naksey, Robert Halle.

186.

Thomas Bromsalle the elder of Beston. 24 Dec. 1520, pr. 12 Jan. 1520/1. (2: 166)

To be buried in the churchyard of Sandy; for his mortuary his best horse.

To son Thomas and his heirs male testator's house and all his lands and tenements in the town and fields of Bestone, except Cristian's orchard, on condition that he gives testator's wife Johan 26s. 8d. "of lawfull money of Ingland" yearly during her lifetime, that is 13s. 4d. at Lady Day and 13s. 4d. at Michaelmas. He is also to give her "howse rome, mete and drynk, and an honest chamber with all thyng necessary for her duryng her liff". He is also to have testator's daughter Annys dwelling with him for the term of her life, if she so wishes, and he is to give her meat, drink and necessary clothing. When Annys is no longer able to work, then he shall still give her meat, drink and clothing as before, or else 13s. 4d. yearly during her life. To son Thomas 3 half-acres of land in the fields of Calcott.

To wife Johan his house in Gretford with all its lands and pastures together with Cristyan's orchard in Beston until son John attains age of 20, when all this property is to go to him and his heirs male. Should wife die before John reaches age of 20 years then son Thomas to receive profits of this property on behalf of John until latter reaches age of 20.

Should John die without issue before he is 20 years old then wife Johan to have the property for her life, and after her death it is to go to son Thomas and his heirs for ever, he giving for the same 40s. each to testator's daughters Cicely and Johan, and if either die, then the other sister to take her share. Thomas is also to give 20s. to testator's daughter Alys and £5 in charitable deeds of alms, as he shall think most needful, for the souls of testator, his father and mother and his friends.

To daughters Cicely and Johan 40s. each; to the high altar of Sandy 12d.; to the high altar of Northivell 12d.; to the church of Lincoln 4d.; to the torches of Biston and Grytford 2s.; to St. Katerin's light in Sandy 8d.; to the sepulchre light there 12d.; to Biston bridge 3s. 4d.; to Gritford bridge 3s. 4d.; to the lane between John Carter and testator 3s. 4d.; to the lane by Thomas Clay 3s. 4d.; to son Thomas 2 oxen at Dunton; to son John 2 steers; to daughters Cicely and Johan 6 sheep each; to daughter Agnes 3 sheep; to every godchild 4d.; to each of the sons of testator's brother 20d.; to Thomas Briten and his son 12d. each. Residue to wife Johan.

Exors. wife Johan and son Thomas. Supervisor brother John. Witn. sir Thomas Pek, Thomas Aldrich, Stephen Rayll.

187.
Johan Eyer of Bydenham. 26 Nov., pr. 7 Dec. 1520. (2: 167)

To be buried in churchyard of St. Jamys in Bydenham; for mortuary as customary; to church of Lincoln 4d.; to the bells 12d.; to Johan Row the house in Newport Pannell; to each of testator's two daughters a gown and a kirtle. Residue "to be done for me and my husbond".

Exor. son Sextus. Overseer: Richard Samson. Witn. John Billynges, Edmond Fox.

188.
John Man (*margin* Manne) of Eton (Socon). 8 Jan., pr. 26 Jan. 1520/1. (2: 167d)

Burial in the churchyard of Eton; to the high altar 5d.; to the mother church of Lincoln 2d..

To daughter Elizabeth a mattress, 2 pillows, 2 pillowberes, a bolster, a coverlet, 2 pairs of sheets, a pot, a posnet, a pan, a skillet, a saucer, a platter, 2 pewter dishes, 2 candlesticks, a tablecloth, a towel and a coffer.

To wife Elen all the rest of his moveables and also testator's two tenements for her life. After her death the tenement in Eton goes to testator's son sir John, and the tenement in Wiboston to daughter Elizabeth with all its land except an acre of land at Bathley Cross, which testator gives to keep a yearly obit for himself. Testator's wife is to have the acre for her life, to keep his obit, and on her death the churchwardens of

Eton are to "have the ordryng of it and to kepe myn obit". If daughter should die without issue, then the tenement in Wiboston is to be sold "and done for my frends' sowlys and myn".

Executrix wife, who is to pay 5s. "to the necessities of Eton church". Witn. James Stephynson vicar of Eton, sir Robert Yarway, Robert Hatley.

189.

Thomas Colyer (*margin* Collier) dwelling in the parish of Blownham. 1520, pr. 26 Jan. 1520/1. (2: 168)

Burial in churchyard of St. Edmond King and Martyr at Blownham; for his principal his best beast; to the high altar 8d.; to the mother church of Lincoln 4d.; to the sepulchre light 8d.; to the bells 8d.; to the causeway against Geoffrey Osbourne 8d.; to the "plank" in Bedford way 8d.; to buy a canopy for the high altar 3s. 4d.; to Ronull church 3s. 4d.; to Barford church 20d..

To son Richard Collier the house where testator lives with its land and 6 acres of bought land, and he is to keep a priest for half a year to sing for the health of testator's soul.

To wife Alys for her life, half an acre of free land in the Middle Field that was William Mores, and after her death it is to be sold "to have a trentall for her and for me". To her also half an acre of mead "to do with what she will"; also a messuage with an acre of land that was once Chapmans in the North End "at her owne will to give or to sell".

To Alys Collier 6 sheep, a pot and a pan; to Alys Potter 4 sheep; to Anne Ward 6 sheep; to Christian Yerell 1 sheep; to Thomas Pulter 2 sheep; to William Wotton 1 sheep; to Richard Yerell 1 sheep; to Christian Holmys 1 sheep; to the brotherhood 2 sheep; to Thomas Bere 2 sheep; to Michael Bere 2 sheep; to William Bere 2 sheep; to Isabell Fissher 2 sheep. Residue to wife Alys.

Executrix wife Alys. Overseer son Richard Collier. Witn. sir Thomas Bruer parish priest, John Slade.

190.

Thomas Mylner (*margin* Myller) of Bletnesho. 17 Jan., pr. 5 Feb. 1520/1. (2: 168d)

Burial in the churchyard of Bletneshoo; to the high altar for tithes forgotten 3s. 4d.; to the bells 3s. 4d.; to the torches 3s. 4d.; to the rood loft 6s. 8d..

To son Thomas 13s. 4d.; to brother Simon testator's coat; to Thomas testator's servant 3s. 4d.; to Rawff Wise 3s. 4d.; to servant Margery a cow, a bullock and 6s. 8d.; to each godchild 4d.; to each of the children of my sons Robert and Thomas one sheep.

To wife Johan for her life all lands in Bletneshoo and Sharnebrok, and after her death all these are to be sold and "done for her and me and them that they come of". If either son Robert or son Thomas wish to buy the lands, one of them may have the property before other people provided that "they will do as an other man will, or els not". Residue to wife Johan.

Exors. wife Johan, sons Robert and Thomas. Supervisor sir William Lenton vicar of Sharnebrok who is to have 3s. 4d. for his labour. Witn. sir William Lenton, Richard Roger and Christopher Sutton.

191.
John Balle of Turvey. 9 Feb., pr. 19 Feb. 1520/1. (2: 169d)
Burial in the churchyard of All Hallows of Turvey; to the high altar for tithes forgotten 12d.; to the bells 5s.; to the sepulchre light 12d.; to the torches 12d.; to Our Lady light 12d.; to Turvey bridge 20d.; a priest to sing for souls of testator and all his good friends for half a year in Turvey church.

"Also I bequeath the house at Hillys that my father gave me (after the death of my father) to Margaret my wife, and after the death of my wife, to Richard Ballys child and [if] it be a man child when it come to a lawful age, and until it comes to a lawful age I will it be at the will of Margaret my wife, to do for my soul and her soul and all my good friends' souls; and if it fortune that Richard Ballys child be not a man child, then I will William Balle my son have it to him and his heirs male, and [if] he have none heirs male then I will it return to the heirs male of the Balles, and he that hath that house at Hillys shall have a house in the town called Camfeldes for to do yearly obit for my father and my mother and me and for all our good friends' souls for to endure for ever, and he that hath the house Hillys shall give to Thomas Balle my brother's son 40s. and if he live and if William Balle have not the house at Hillys then he shall have the house at Town that I dwell in to him and to his heirs and assigns, and [if] he have the house at Hillys, then I will that the house at Town be sold to William Balle if he be able to buy it, and[if] he be not, then I will William Skevynton buy it 40s. within the price, and the money of it to be disposed for my soul and all my good friends' souls".

To daughter Agnes Skevyngton £3 6s. 8d. and 10 sheep; to daughter Johan £6 13s. 4d., ten sheep, two kine and 2 calves; to son William Balle the best shod cart with its gear, 5 horses, and a plough with its gear.

Exors. wife Margaret, William Skevyngton, John Stephynson. Overseers testator's father William Balle and John Cooper the elder, each of them to have 40d. for their labour. Witn. Gilbert Laurence, John Lawrence, William Purre.

192.
Nicholas Wolmer dwelling in the parish of Our Blessed Lady of Elnestow. 3 Jan., pr. 19 Feb. 1520/1. (2: 170d)

Burial in the churchyard of Elnestow; to the high altar 12d.; to the mother church of Lincoln 4d.; to the middle light before the rood 3s. 4d.; to the rood in the "lane" in the church 20d.; to the torches in the same church 3s. 4d.; to the bells 3s. 4d.; to repairing Newneham Priory 10s.; to Cawdwell Convent 10s. for a trental of masses for my soul; to repairing the house of friars in Bedford 6s. 8d..

His executors are to sell his place in the parish of St. Peter, Bedford, and to give his wife Elizabeth £4 of lawful money "to her mariage".

To wife Elizabeth two messuages in Spital Croft Street in the town of Elnestow with 7 roods of land in the fields of Elnestow, till she is married, and if she marry then the property is to go to William testator's eldest son and his issue. He is to keep testator's yearly obit with *dirige* and mass, to the value of 2s.. If William die without issue, the property is to go to testator's younger son William and his heirs, or if he has no issue, to son Robert and his heirs. If their are no heirs, the property is to be sold and the money distributed in deeds of charity.

To testator's two youngest sons, William and Robert, his house beyond the bridge in Elnestow, provided that it be sold by his executors and the proceeds divided equally between William and Robert. If either of them should die then the survivor is to have his part and if both die, the money is to be "disposed for my soul".

To every one of testator's daughters a mattress, a bolster and a pair of sheets. To his four daughters to Julyan 40s., to Margaret 40s., to Katerin 26s. 8d., and to Johan 26s. 8d., making £6 13s. 4d. in all. If one die the others are to be her heirs, and if all die, the money is to be distributed in deeds of charity by his executors.

"If any of my sonnys or doughters trobill or vex my wiff or myn executors or cawse ony other to vex or troble, contrary to this my testament, I will that he or they shalbe therby excluded from all such thynges as I have bequeathed to them and such thynges as I have given them to be at the distribucion of myn executors to give among myn other children ther as they thynk best".

The rest of the money from the sale of testator's houses in Bedford to be used for a priest to sing for him in the parish church of Elnestow.

Residue to wife Elizabeth. Exors. brother John Wolmer and Richard Waynman, each to have 6s. 8d. for his labours. Witn. master William Whalley parish priest, Richard Wyrall, Laurence Lynold.

193.
John Whitchurch. Mar. 1520/1, pr. 16 Mar. 1520/1. (2: 171d)

"My bonys to be buryyd in the church yard of Alhalows of

Ravennysden". For principal his "best good"; to the mother church of Lincoln 2d.; to Ravennysden church 6s. 8d.; to the high altar 20d.. A priest is to sing in the church of Ravennysden for souls of testator and all Christians a year, and a trental to the friars of Bedford. To Barford bridge 3s. 4d..

To son William a cart, 2 old horses, a young horse, 2 kine, 6 sheep, 3 quarters of barley; to his son John the elder 40s.; to daughter Alys 40s.; to his son John the younger 40s. and a cow; to daughter Isabell 40s.; to Margaret 40s. "and that she goyth with all" 40s.. If any of them die, their bequest is to be given to the survivors, and if they all die, then it is to be done for souls of testator and all Christians.

When testator's wife Agnes remarries, the money is to be delivered to sir Adam Nik and to testator's son John the elder, to dispose to the profit of the children.

To William Danger a ewe and a lamb; to John Crane a ewe and a lamb.

To wife Agnes for her life testator's house, messuage and land in Ravennysden, and after her to son John the younger, and after him to son John the elder and his heirs.

Exors. wife Agnes and son John the elder. Sir Adam Nik to be supervisor. Witn. Richard Fricher, John Chaplen, John Baker.

194.
William Samson of Bydenham. 4 Mar., pr. 16 Mar. 1520/1. (2: 172d)
Burial in the parish churchyard of Saint Jamys in Bydenham; for mortuary as customary; to the high altar 4d.; to the bells 12d.; to St. Katerin's light 4d.; to Our Lady 4d.; to the church of Lincoln 4d..

To son Richard Samson testator's house and lands in Bydenham; to son William a brass pot of a gallon and a half, a pan of 7 gallons, a coverlet, a pair of flaxen sheets; to son Richard a great brass pot, a coverlet, a pair of flaxen sheets; to William Balle a little posnet; to John Ball a kettle of 2 gallons. Residue to be used for souls of testator and wife Ellyn.

Exor. son Richard Samson. Overseer sir John Billynges. Witn. sir John Billyng, John Faldo, William Samson, Johan Carter, John Chapman, Bartilmew Alyn, Thomas Long.

195.
Richard Atkynson of Potton, husbandman. 1 Mar., pr. 16 Mar. 1520/1. (2: 173)
Testament Burial in the churchyard of Potton; for principal and mortuary his best gown; to the high altar 10s.; to the sepulchre light 3s. 4d.; to repairing the torches 3s. 4d.; to repairing the bells 6d. 8d.; to Margaret Butler 3s. 4d.; to William Clay's eldest daughter 3s. 4d.; to

Thomas Clay's daughter 3s. 4d.; to Cokkes daughter 3s. 4d.; to William Sixforth and Robert his brother 26s. 8d. each, if it may be performed; to John Wright 4 marks, if it may be performed, testator's best russet gown and his doublet, jacket and hose; to Margaret Thomson a mattress, a coverlet, a blanket, a pair of sheets, a pot, 2 pans. Residue to son William. Executor son William. Witn. sir William Atkynson, Walter Woorlich, John Waren.

Will Touching the disposition of all his houses and lands in Potton, son William is to have all these "frely to hymselff" on condition that he takes 6s. 8d. yearly from testator's tenement in Horselow Street for an obit or anniversary to be kept for souls of testator and of Margaret and Alys his wives and of the aforesaid William. The overplus of the rent from this tenement with the close is to be given to the brotherhood of Potton annually for the maintenance of the same brotherhood. The brotherhood is to have testator's house in Church Street with the close, which Jamys Momford dwells in, for them to have it for ever, under such conditions as his executors shall think expedient.

196.
Robert Spenser (*margin* Spencer) of Coople. 20 Mar. 1520/1, no note of probate. (2: 174)

Burial in Our Lady chapel of Coople; for mortuary his best beast as customary; to each godchild a ewe sheep; to the friars of Bedford 20s. for a trental "to be sayd as shortly as goodly may after my decease".

Testator's feoffees are to allow his executors to take the rents of all the messuages, land, meadow and pasture in Southmyll in Blownham parish now occupied by testator's son Batell, and a messuage with land, mead and pasture in Honydon in Eton parish "only except and reservyd" until they may therewith pay testator's debts and perform the bequests listed below.

To the high altar for tithes forgotten 10s.; to the "necessaries" of Coople church 20s.; to mending the streets in the same town 10s.; to the "mortyfyyng" [obtaining a licence to hold property in mortmain] of the brotherhood in Blownham or to the covering in lead of the steeple there £5; to Southo church, towards a cross 6s. 8d.; to Sandy church 6s. 8d.; to the college of Northivell 6s. 8d.; to the four orders of friars, 3 in Cambridge and the 4th in Bedford 3s. 4d. each; to Blownham bells and torches 3s. 4d. each.

His executors are to pay master Mordant "such money as it shall please hym to demand of the arrearages for the Ward and Mariage of Hugh Hasilden".

His executors are to pay to Richard Monyngham the arrears due to him of the £40 that was bequeathed to Margery his wife by her father, and also the "halfdele" of her necessary wedding apparel of the "hadde" 20s..

His executors are to find an honest priest to say mass and other divine service in Coople church for five years for souls of testator, his ancestors and friends and those for whom he is bound to pray.

If testator's son John should die before his mother, which Almighty God forbid, a priest is to sing for souls of testator and his son and friends for another 5 years after his death.

To either of his son Dikon's sons 40s. to their schooling; to his daughter's marriage 5 marks; to Batellys daughter's marriage 5 marks; to either of his son John's daughters 5 marks "if they have any brother alyve tyme of ther maryage"; to Elizabeth Laurence 40s. to her marriage "if she wilbe rulyd and advisid by myn executors"; to Agnes Bays 10s.; to Robert Symond 20s. a year during his life; to the houses of Newenham, Elnestow and Cawdwell 10s. each to pray for his soul "as theyr devocion shall serve them".

His feoffees are to allow his daughter Alys to occupy the house she lives in, with the land and mead and pasture, for the term of her life, she paying the out-rents and keeping it in repair, provided always that "if her husbond be mysruled or disordryd that myn executors be discontentid with him" then this bequest to his daughter shall be void, and his feoffees are to allow his executors to take the profits of the property during the life of his daughter Alys and use them "accordyng to my mynd which they know truly as I putt them in trust".

His daughter Dikons is to have the rent of his house in Honeydon for the term of her life with its land, mead and pasture, she keeping it in repair and paying the out-rents.

His heirs and executors shall keep his obit yearly with the profit of his house and land that belonged to Agnes the wife of Thomas Reve.

To his daughter-in-law Anne during her life, the rent of all testator's wife's lands and tenements in Litle Brikhyll after his wife's death, with the remainder to testator's son John and his heirs.

After legacies and debts are paid, his wife is to have the issues and profits of all his lands and tenements during her life, and after her death they are to go to his son John Spenser and his heirs. Residue to his executors.

Exors. wife Anne, son John, Thomas Dikon, Robert Spenser, the two last to have 20s. each for their labour. Witn. sir Thomas Bamford vicar of Coople, Henry Mannfelt, Thomas Tooth.

197. [*This may have been added to this page of the volume later, for the end part is on a separate sheet of paper stitched to the bottom of the page.*] Anne Spencer, widow of Robert Spencer of Coople, gent. 14 Dec. 1524, no note of probate. (2: 175)

To be buried in the chapel of Our Lady in Coople church, "next unto my husbond"; to the high altar for tithes forgotten 20d.; to John Spenser the great brass pot and 2 spits; to Elizabeth his daughter and testator's god-daughter, testator's wedding ring, her bright brass pot and the two-eared pan; to John Spenser's daughter Rose a little pot broken of the "brynk" (rim), a pan of 3 gallons and a chafer with one handle; to Agnes Batell the great pot that is broken on the brink and testator's red girdle that was testator's aunt Adams.

To Robert Hasilden testator's daughter's son her best piece, a featherbed, a pair of sheets, a pair of blankets, a red coverlet and a bolster; to Thomas Hasilden his brother a piece of silver next the best, a featherbed, a red coverlet, a pair of sheets, a pair of blankets and a bolster; to Thomas Batell the little piece and a pair of sheets.

To each of her son Dikon's children, that is to say William, Richard, Robert, Nicholas, Frances and Elizabeth, 6s. 8d. to be paid "at convenient laysur"; to Thomas Spenser 6s. 8d..

For the salary of a priest for a year to sing for souls of her husband, herself and all their friends, 8 marks. John Hatley is to sing one half year and Thomas Yardy the other, where this is to be her executors shall choose.

To Elizabeth Spenser, her son's daughter, testator's best cow; to Rose her sister, the calf of the cow; to Elizabeth Dycon the other cow; to Palmer's daughter the other calf; to testator's daughter Alys all testator's sheep and the corn in the barn; to Batell one of her ricks; to Gaunt her old black gown; to Gaunt's daughter a yard of white blanket "to mak it a peticot"; to Johan Piers her kirtle last made; to Johan Frank a smock; to Thomas Dikons £5 of the money testator makes of her crop, if he makes no claim for the rent of Honyden since the death of testator's husband. Residue to son John to distribute in alms for her soul.

Exor. son John. Witn. sir Thomas Bamford, Richard Slade, Robert Newman, Robert Hasilden.

198.
John Joy the elder of Salphoo Bury in Ronall. 30 Mar., pr. 13 Apr. 1521. (2: 175d)
Burial in the churchyard of Ronnall; for his mortuary "my best and principall best which is an horse"; to the church of Lincoln 4d.; to the high altar for tithes forgotten 6s. 8d.; to the torches 6s. 8d.; to each god-child a ewe.

Eight marks "to be disposid immediatly as may be after my departyng" for testator's soul and for the souls of his wife Elizabeth and his son Edmond Joy in this manner: four marks to sir Brian to sing for half a year in the parish church of Ronhall; the rest, that is 6 marks [sic] to be given to some virtuous priest as it shall seem best to his sons Henry and George Joy, so that this priest "be disposed and apply and continew his study and lernyng at the Universitie of Cambrige" there to sing the other three quarters [*sic*] of the year for testator's soul and those listed above and all Christian souls.

To daughter Alys certain implements of household stuff in the loft over testator's chamber, which he has certified and shown to his sons Henry and George, to be given her at their pleasure and disposition, or to dispose otherwise.

Residue to son Henry to use for souls of testator, his wife and his son Edmond.

Exors. son Henry and John Ede. Overseer son George. Witn. George Joy, William Abbot, Richard Fynmor.

199.

John Cramfeld of Felmersham. 10 Apr., pr. 21 Apr. 1521. (2: 176)

Burial in Felmersham churchyard; to the mother church of Lincoln 4d.; to the high altar for tithes forgotten 2 bushels of barley; to the sepulchre 2 bushels of barley; to the bells 2 bushels of barley; to the torches 2 bushels of barley; to brother William Cramfeld half a quarter of barley; to children of William Cramfeld 2 bushels of barley each; to Morgan Amore 2 bushels of barley; to Margery Smyth 2 bushels of barley.

To wife Alys Cramfeld his messuage with its appurtenances for her life, and after her death to his daughter Elizabeth and her heirs and assigns; to daughter Johan a messuage called Gardes with an acre of land called Fokkispitt Slade next to the land of Sir John Mordant.

To John Amore a rood of land above Roksweek, next to Mr. Michael Fissher's land. Residue to wife Alys.

Executrix wife Alys. Overseer William Cramfeld. Witn. William Otway, John Serth, Henry Okeley.

200.

Robert Wyot of Eton (Socon). 5 Apr., pr. 23 Apr. 1521. (2: 177)

Burial within the church of Our Lady of Eton; to the high altar for tithes forgotten 6s. 8d.; to the mother church of Lincoln 6d.; to be given to "poore people" on the day of his burial "peny dole and halfpeny bred"; to the parish church of Eton 10 marks.

To son William testator's house and lands, and he is to pay 40s. a year to testator's wife, who is to have a chamber in the house "at her pleasur" during her natural life.

To a priest a year's service to pray for souls of testator and his father and grandfather; to the brotherhood of Corpus Christi 20s.; to every poor householder in Eton half a bushel of malt; to Thomas Fissher half a quarter of malt; to Richard Fissher 6s. 8d.; to Robert Kypes and

Robert Raynold a ewe and a lamb for each; to every godchild a sheep; to daughter Elizabeth 20 marks; to each of her children 5 marks; to mending the highway "agenst the Brotherhed and other places of the towne of Eton" 10s.. Residue to wife Margaret and son William.

Exors. wife Margaret and son William. Supervisor John Kypes. Witn. Thomas Scott, William Raynold, William Kyng.

201.
Margaret Parcell of Riseley, widow. 2 May, pr. 13 May 1521. (2: 177d)
Burial in the chapel of Our Lady in the parish church of Riseley; to the high altar 20d.; to the bells 12d.; to the torches 12d.; to the sepulchre 3s. 4d.; to the mother church of Lincoln 4d..

"I give to my doughter Johan Umfrey A velvet bonet which my Sonne Mullinsworth' bowt with a fruntelett of tawny saten

I give to my doughter Sibell Pemberton A nother Velvet bonet with my best fruntlet of crimyson velvet

I give to my doughter Cristian Parsell my best letis bonet with a fruntelett of Crymysyn velvet

I give to my doughter Anne Mullinsworth' my best girdill with bukkill and pendant of silver and doble gilt which my husbond gave me and I give my doughter Anne Mullinsworth my best bedes of Corall with pater nosters silver and gilt

Item I give to Sibill Parsell doughter to Thomas Parsell A silver salt with a Cover parsell gilt and vj sponys of silver and x li. or goodes to the valeu of x li. to be deliverd her at full age or such tyme as it shalbe thought necessary by the discrecion of myn executors and friends and Also I give to her a federbed with a good cownterpoynt and A payr of fustian blankettes A good bolster and iij payr of good flexyn shetes A good table cloth of flexen A towell and vj napkyns and my wedding corse girdill of colour crymysyn and bocle and pendant of silver and gilt and A payr of bedes of corall gawded with silver a spruce focer [coffer]

and I give to my doughter Cristyan Parcell all such bequests as her father late my husbond did give her

and also I geve to Ser Henry Queene vicar my tawny mantell and I will that he have xx s. to pray for me and for my husbond with all my benefactors as I have apoynt hym".

The bequests to Sibill Parcell to go to John and William Parcell if she die "er she cum to lawful age or discrecion". If John Percell die without issue his bequests to go to William Parcell, and if William die without issue, his bequests to be sold and used for the health of souls.

To John Parcell and William Parcell the residue of goods and chattels appointed by her husband and to be delivered by the hands and oversight of Sir John Saint John knight (to whom 10s.) and Master John Saint John his son and heir (to whom 6s. 8d.) and by John Mullinsworth of Helpstur gent. (to whom 6s. 8d.) her executors. Overseer sir Henry Queene.

All such debts and sums of money remaining in the hands of Richard Langley to be used by her executors to pay her debts and those of her husband, and for the souls of herself, her husband and all Christians, as is clear in a letter of attorney sealed by the testator to her executors.

Witn. John Groke, William Wrotham, Robert Fissher, Thomas Bocher, Robert Mason.

202.
William Conquest. 12 Aug. 1517, pr. 2 Jan. 1521/2. (2: 179)

To be buried in the church of Southhill in the space before the rood; for mortuary his best beast as is the custom; to the church of Lincoln 4d.; to the high altar of Southhill for tithes forgotten 3s. 4d.; to the church for his burial 6s. 8d..

To wife Elizabeth all the "plate and implements of howshold" that were hers before marriage; to little Alice his servant a featherbed and a coverlet, sheets and blankets, a pot, a pan, half a dozen pewter vessels, a cow and a bullock; to Edward Peke all other moveable goods, and he is to "bryng me honestly on erth" and to have a trental sung for testator's soul, if possible on the same day, or "if it cannot be done conveniently of the same day to be made on end on the morow".

To the master of Northivell College "myn old coupill of swan heyrys" and he is to have 2 trentals sung in the college for testator's soul "as hastly as can be folowyng".

To wife Elizabeth a couple of young "signettes".

Exors. brother Edmund who is to have a noble and a cygnet; Robert Stewkley to have a noble and a swan; Edward Peke to have a noble and a couple of swans. Supervisor William Hammylden to have 3s. 4d. and a swan.

William Hammylden and Robert Stewkley, the recoverers of testator's lands and tenements, are to enter on them and make an estate over to Edward Peke and to Edward Copley to the use of testator's last will "writ with myn owne hond the xx day of February" in the 8th year of King Henry VIII (1516/7).

Brownes place and land is to be sold, and 20 nobles of the proceeds are to be paid to the two daughters of John Bulmer, i.e. 8 marks to the elder daughter and 4 nobles to the younger daughter her sister. Of the rest sir William Lapage is to have 10s. to pray for testator, and 40s. is to be used to buy a stone "to ly uppon me". The remainder is to be spent at his executors' discretion "to bestow it in meritoriows dedes as they thynk best for my sowle helth".

Witn. Thomas Borage, Edward Copley, Thomas Melton, John Foster.
Probate granted to Edward Peke, the other two declining.

5. Brass of Richard Carlyll of Campton, who died in 1489, and of Joan his
wife, whose will (published in *BHRS* vol. 37) was proved in 1506. Joan is
shown wearing her beads, which hang from her waist. Women sometimes left
their beads to a favourite daughter, as does Joan Morcott of Turvey in 1521
(no. 203). *Thomas Fisher.*

203.

Johan Morcott, widow. [no place, but presumably of Turvey] 22 June, pr. 6 July 1521. (2: 181)

Burial in the churchyard of All Hallows: to the church of Lincoln 2d.; for mortuary after the custom of the town; to the high altar 12d.; to the bells 6d.; to the torches 6d.; to the bridge 6d..

To daughter Agnes a gown, 2 kirtles, testator's best girdle, her beads, 2 christening sheets, 4 pillow beres, 4 kerchers, her best cap, her "gadrid" gathered apron.

To Walter Skevyngton testator's tenement at Wellyngborough for the term of his life, and on his death to testator's daughter Agnes. Should Agnes die without heirs, then tenement to go to testator's youngest son Edmond and his heirs. If both die without heirs, then the property to go to eldest son John. If all children die without heirs, then it is to be sold by executors.

Residue to her executors, on condition that they sustain and maintain testator's children until they are of lawful age, and keep up her tenements on behalf of her children.

Exors. Walter Skevyngton, John Hodyll, Witn. John Cooper, Thomas Fraunces, John Stephynson.

204.

Thomas Canon. 3 Sep. 1525, pr. 6 Sep. (no year given) (2: 182)

Burial in churchyard of Our Blessed Lady in Cayshoo; for mortuary best beast; to the high altar for tithes forgotten 12d.; to mother church of Lincoln 2d.; to the bells 8d.; to the light of the "sepulture of Jhesu" 2 lb. of wax.

To eldest son Thomas Canon and heirs the house testator dwells in, with the 13 acres of land more or less, remaining to the house in Cayshoo field, and a close with a meadow plot of grass in Pertynhall field, after the death of testator and his wife. Should Thomas die without issue, then the property goes to second son John Canon the smith, and if John die without issue, then to testator's sons from heir to heir.

To John Canon testator's second son 4 acres of land.

To John Canon the third son, 4 acres of land, and of this 5 lands are under the Myll Hege, and 2 acres are in Elsgrene next to the land of William Alkyns.

To fourth son William Canon 4 acres of land.

These 12 acres are to be sold to son Thomas for 12 marks after death of testator and his wife, and the said 12 marks are to be paid to testator's three sons. Thomas is to pay rent to his brothers for 3 years until he has paid the 12 marks, and they are to agree to this under pain of their father's curse and of ——-[page torn]

Wife Alys Canon to have 20s. of the money if she has need.

To son John the younger 2 horses and a shod cart with its gear, if he is a good son to his mother, otherwise not.

To Agnes and Johan Canon his daughters an acre of land divided between them after the death of his wife. If they wish to sell this acre, then son Thomas shall have it before any other man, paying the same price. The residue to executrix.

Executrix wife Alys. Overseers son Thomas Canon and son John Canon the smith, who are to have 20d. each for their labours.

Witn. sir William Boydon vicar of Keyshoo, Gregory Day clerk, Thomas Malbe, Thomas French.

205.
Richard Mundes. 25 Oct., pr. 1 Dec. 1528. (2: 184)

Burial in the churchyard of Our Lady of Stotfold; to mother church of Lincoln 2d.; to the high altar a bushel of barley; to repairing the bells a bushel of barley; to the "tapers light" a bushel of barley; to the light of the torches a bushel of barley.

To wife Elizabeth all his crop, she to pay his debts and keep the house. To wife Isabell [*sic*] his house and half his land for 7 years, and longer, if testator's son Thomas and she can agree. If they do not agree, Thomas is to give her 13s. 4d. a year for life.

To son Thomas the other half of testator's land, and from this he is to give testator's son Richard one acre of barley for one year.

To son Robert one acre of barley.

To son Thomas and his heirs male testator's house and land after the period of 7 years mentioned above, and in default to son Richard and his heirs male, in default to son Robert and his heirs. If Robert die without issue, testator's "assignars" are to sell it and "bestow it to the honour of God and helth of our Sowlys".

To wife Isabell all moveables, except his horse and cart, which his son and mother are to share and "occupie to gether as long as they can agre". The son is in any case "to pay for halff woorkmanshipp and labours as he is reasonably required". Residue to wife Isabel. Executrix wife Isabel, but Jenkyn Sqwyer is to help her, she giving him 20d. for his labour. Supervisor Richard Lorymer.

Witn. Robert Pierson vicar, Thomas Slow, Johan Brown.

206.
John Reynold (Rainhold *margin*) of Farnedissh. n.d., pr. 21 Apr. 1526. (2: 185d)

Burial in the churchyard of Farnedissh; for principal his best beast as customary; to mother church of Lincoln 2d.; to the high altar half a quarter of barley; to the bells half a quarter of barley; to the torches 2 strikes of barley; to the sepulchre "yeld" half a quarter of barley; to the church of Farnedissh 12d.; to Welyngborough bridge 2 strikes of barley; to Harrold bridge 2 strikes of barley.

To wife Katerin testator's house, land and meadow within the bounds of Yrenchester for the term of her life, and then to testator's daughters Agnes and Ann for ever. Residue to wife Katerin, who is executrix. Witn. John Abbott, William Hunt, sir William Eliot parson, William Dyes of Wymyngton.

207.
John Collens (Colyns *margin*) of Eyton [Bray]. 29 Dec. 1528, pr. 25 May [year not given]. (2: 186)
Burial in churchyard of Eyton; to mother church of Lincoln 2d.; to the high altar 12d.; to the sepulchre light 4d.; to the Trinity light 4d.; to the rood light 4d.; to St. Nicholas light 4d.; to the three lights 4d.; to the bells 6d.; to the torches 6d.

To son Henry Collens a wort vat "yowt fat" to be a standard of the house.

Residue to wife Elizabeth Collens.

He wills that son Henry Collens and his heirs have all his lands for ever, and he is to pay wife Elizabeth 4s. 2d. each quarter day for the term of her life towards her keep. He is to "bring me on erthe" and keep testator's month day and twelvemonth mind, and he and his heirs are to keep a yearly *dirige* in the parish church of Eyton for souls of testator, his friends and all Christians for ever.

Exor. son Henry Collens. Witn. sir Thomas Conlynson vicar, Ralph Jenkes, Ralph Welles, John Bune, Richard Brokes.

208.
John Tape of Felmersham. 1 May, pr. 25 May 1528. (2: 186d)
Burial in churchyard of Our Lady of Felmersham; for principal as customary; to the high altar for tithes forgotten 12d.; to the sepulchre light a quarter of barley; to the torches half a quarter of barley; to the bells 3 bushels of barley; to Clarges Stret 20d.; to Stafforth bridge 3 bushels of barley; to the church of Mylton Harnes 3s. 4d..

To daughter Joan Leche the house where testator dwells, with appurtenances; to Robert Tappe's children 4d. each; to Luce Page's children 4d. each; to John Risley's children 4d. each; to all his godchildren 4d. each. Residue to wife Alice.

Exors wife Alice, son Robert Tappe, son-in-law Edmond Leche. Witn. sir Hugh Wynnard priest there, Richard Leche, John Hogham.

209.
John Marche of Milton Hernes. 3 May, pr. 25 May 1528. (2: 187)
Burial in the churchyard of All Hallows in Milton; for mortuary "my

best good as right will require"; to the high altar for tithes and offerings forgotten 6d.; to mother church of Lincoln 2d..

To daughter Cicile a tenement in Milton called Drowis for the term of her life, and on her death it is to go to testator's son Thomas; to Cicile also testator's wife's "furid frend"; to Joane Lankaster testator's wife's second kirtle; to Joan Randall, Cicile's daughter, a ewe and a lamb; to Grace Monk testator's servant 2 pewter dishes; to Thomas Osborne his blue coat; to William Bayntton his sleeveless tawny coat; to the friars of Bedford 2s.. Residue to son Thomas to dispose of for the health of testator's soul, and the souls of his friends and of all Christians.

Exor. son Thomas. Supervisor sir Richard Kyng vicar of Milton. Witn. sir Richard Kyng, William Harward the elder, John Linford, John Crowche, William Tynker.

210.
John Compton (Cownton *margin*) of Stageden. 9 May, pr. 25 May 1528. (2: 187d & 190)

Soul to Almighty God and body to be buried in the churchyard of St. Leonard of Stageden; for mortuary best beast after the custom of the town; to the painting of the rood 26s. 8d.; to the high altar for tithes forgotten 12d.; to the mother church of Lincoln 2d.; to repairing Bidynham bridge 2 trees; to the bells 3 bushels of barley; to the torches 3 bushels of barley; to the sepulchre light 2 bushels of barley.

To son John Compton 2 steers, 2 affers, 1 sheep; to wife during her life the house by the wayside, wood for her fire and 3 acres of land in every season; to Richard Teler a bullock; to son Gervais 2 oxen; to daughter Alice a bullock; to sir Robert Skynner 3s. 4d. to pray for souls of testator and of all his good friends. Residue to wife Joan.

Exors. wife Joan Compton and son Gervais Compton. Supervisor sir Robert Skynner. Witn. sir Robert Skynner, Thomas Teller, Thomas Osmond.

211.
William Ive of Tebworth in Chalgrave parish. 23 Sep., pr. 6 Oct. 1528. (2: 188)

Burial in churchyard of All Hallows of Chalgrave; for mortuary as customary; to church of Lincoln 4d.; to the high altar half a quarter of malt; to the sepulchre light 2 lb. of wax.

His heirs and executors to take 10s. a year from the rent of a house which testator's father bought of Richard Bottisford and use it to hire a priest to sing one trental every year in Chalgrave church for souls of testator, his father and mother, and all Christians.

To son Robert the house where testator lives after death of wife, also

6s. 8d. "in money and money worth"; to testator's two daughters Alys and Benet £3 6s. 8d. each; to his two sisters half a quarter of barley each. Residue to wife Alice and Thomas Hebbys of Wynkfeld.

Exors. wife Alys and Thomas Hebbys of Wynkfeld. Supervisor sir John Berford. Witn. John Osborne, Richard Sabyrton. Given at Tebworth.

212.
Henry Curwen of Todyngton. 27 Sep., pr. 5 Oct. 1528. (2: 188d)
Burial in churchyard of Todyngton; to the high altar for tithes forgotten 6d.; to mother church of Lincoln 4d.; for a trental to be sung for souls of self, friends and all Christians 5s..

To Richard Asshwell testator's sleeveless coat; to John Grene "my workyngday hose"; to his man William his fustian doublet; to Thomas Bocher his tawny jacket; to his shepherd his "frees" frieze coat; to the bells of Todyngton 12d..

To wife Anne the house where testator lives with the lands and pastures belonging to it and all his lands and pastures in England now and in the future. She is to have the profit of them for the term of her life, and if she "be constrayned by nede" she may sell part or all of the property. After her death testator's son George is to have the estate, and he is to give Elizabeth and Johan Curwen testator's daughters 40s. each "to ther mariage". Thomas Cooke is to have the "preferement" of such lands and pastures as wife "may conveniently forgo" at a price which they can agree. Residue to wife Anne.

Executrix wife Anne. Supervisor Thomas Cooke. Witn. sir William Burham curate, Thomas Cooke, Thomas Nightynggale, William Atkyns, William Spufford.

213.
Peter Leyceter of Stephynton. 31 Oct., pr. 9 Nov. 1528. (2: 189)
Burial "in what church or churchyard it shall please God and myn executors"; to the parson or vicar of the same church 12d. for tithes forgotten; to the curate of the same church 8d. to pray for testator; for a trental of masses for testator and his friends, by the advice of executors 10s..

To wife Margaret all moveable goods and implements which she now has, as "her apparell for her bodie", and all the goods that she brought with her at the time of her marriage; to her also testator's tenement with a watermill in West Hodford in the county of "Somort" to hold during her widow's estate after the custom of West Hodford.

To wife Margaret his two cottages in Stephynton that he now occupies, to have and to hold for her natural life, after the custom of the manor of Stephynton, she keeping them in repair.

After her death the remainder of his estate in the property is to be sold and divided into four parts, that is to say, one part each to sir George Leiceter priest, to George Leiceter "lettred", to Thomas Leiceter and to Agnes Leiceter testator's children. When the house or houses and the acre of land are sold, there is to be delivered into the hands of the churchwardens of Our Lady's church of Stephynton the sum of 10s. for an annual *dirige* and mass "on the morow", that is to say 4d. to the priest, 2d. to the clerk, 7d. in ale and 4d. in bread. After the death of wife the remainder of the other cottage, which testator bought from Thomas Darlyng, shall go to Agnes Barton for 20 years, if she live so long. After her death it is to be sold and the money divided into 4 parts as with the other cottage.

All moveable goods are to be divided into three parts, one to little George Leiceter testator's son, another part to his daughter Agnes Leiceter and the third part to son Thomas Leiceter.

To son George Leiceter the younger testator's little gold chain and silver salt; to daughter Agnes Leiceter 6 silver spoons and 2 small pieces of silver; to brother Laurence Leiceter priest, parson of Honysdon testator's gold signet, which he has in his keeping; to George Leiceter testator's gold ring engraved with roses and writing.

Testator's brother sir Laurence is to have the "rule and oversight of my sonne George Leiceter, with all his porcion of goodes, to be kept at lernyng for his profit and use" and after the death of the parson of Honydon sir George Leiceter is to have the custody of little George Leiceter with all his goods, and sir George Leiceter priest is to have the oversight and rule of Thomas Leiceter's portion of goods until he is 21 years old.

Wife Margaret is to have the rule and oversight of the third portion of goods to the use and profit of daughter Agnes Leiceter during her nonage, and after her nonage to have her portion delivered to her. After the death of wife, sir George Leiceter is to have the oversight of Agnes and all her goods.

Exors. wife Margaret Leiceter, sons George Leiceter priest and George Leiceter "lettred". Overseers sir Laurence Leiceter priest, brother Roger Leiceter, Thomas Moldesworth priest, and each to have 3s. 4d. for their labour. Witn. sir Robert Mody priest, William Cartwrite of Patenham, Thomas Nogare of Potton, William Laurence, Thomas Whalley. Note of sign manual and seal.
Probate granted to widow and to George Leiceter the clerk, reserving the power of George Leiceter junior.

214.
John Reynold the elder of Lytill Stoughton. 3 July, pr. 20 July 1528. (2: 190)

Burial in the churchyard of All Hallows in Lytill Stoughton; for mortuary his best beast or cow; to mother church of Lincoln 2d.; to the high altar for tithes forgotten 12d..

Testator's feoffees of his land and tenement called "Willhamcate" (except the barnyard} shall stand seized to the use of testator's son Robert and his heirs for ever. Instead of the barnyard Robert is to have an acre of land of which half an acre is in the Dynge and half an acre in the Church Field. He is to pay Bertilmers his brother—- xs. within 4 years.

As regards the residue, the feoffees are to stand seized to the use of John, testator's son, and his heirs, paying Bartilmewe his brother 30s. within 4 years.

To son Bartilomew a cow and a year old bullock. To daughter Elizabeth a cow, a three year old bullock, 3 quarters of barley, and two pairs of sheets at her marriage. To daughter Kateryn a coffer, 3 pairs of sheets, a milch cow, and a year old bullock at her marriage. To daughters Alice and Elyn a quarter of barley each. To daughter Agnes the best brass pot save one. Residue to son John.

Exors. son John, Robert Smyth, John Knyght, and each to have a rood of wheat for their labour. Witn. John Gurley parish priest, Henry Dene, William Halle, John Hill.

215.
Thomas Bretten of Temmysford. 4 Sep., pr. 9 Nov. 1528. (2: 191)

Burial in the churchyard of Temmysford; for mortuary his best good as customary in township of Temmysford; to church of Lincoln 1d.; to the high altar 6d.; to the Trinity altar 6d.; to the altar of St. Katerin 6d.; to the sepulchre light 8d.; to repairing the bells 6d..

To wife Katerin testator's house with appurtenances for the term of her life, on condition that she remains single and that she bestows 2s. for souls of testator, his father and mother and all Christians at the twelve month's day after the day of his burial, of which 4d. is for *dirige* and mass and the other 20d. for halfpenny bread to the poor people in the parish. This is to be done every year during wife's lifetime.

To repairing the causeway between the church and Lampat End 20d.; to the causeway at Lampat Bridge 20d.; for a trentall for souls of testator, his father and mother and all Christians, in the parish church 10s.. As regards his residue, the moveable goods are to be divided equally between his wife and daughter, and the other things are at the disposition of his executors.

Exors. his wife and John Spryng, and he is to be paid his costs and 3s. 4d. for his labours. Supervisor Master Thomas Sheffeld, gentleman, of Temysford. Witn. Robert Slade, John Everard, John Mylward.

216.
John Tayllor of Stephynton the elder. 28 Nov. 1528, pr. 22 Dec. [no year]. (2: 191d)

Burial in churchyard of Our Lady in Stephynton; for his mortuary as custom requires; to mother church of Lincoln 4d.; to the high altar 12d.; to Our Lady in Stephynton chapel a pound of wax; to the crucifix of the said church a lb. of wax; to the Trinity a lb. of wax; to the bells 8d.; to the torches 8d.; to the bridges of Bidenham, Turvey, Harrold and Stafford 6d. each.

To Johan Tawer testator's daughter a cow; to John Raineld half a quarter of malt; to godson John Tawer half an acre of land in Lovit croft.

A priest is to sing for one year for the souls of "sir John Fulk priest, Nicholas Tayllour and Agnes, John Tayllour and Agnes, and my wife, and for all Cristen sowlys" of which one half year is to be shortly after testator's death, the other half year after the death of testator's wife.

[*The page here has a torn edge*] Testator's house with lands, meadows and pastures——his wife so that one part be sold to fulfil the priest's service——first half year. The rest of the land, meadows and pastures———wife Agnes during her life, and after to be sold to fulfil the second half year. "If my wife lak or nede to sell an acre or——to help her selff."

Residue to wife Agnes. Exors. son-in-law William Tawer, who is to have 3s. 4d. for his work, and wife Agnes. Supervisor Nicholas Tayllour of Chelyngton to have 20d. for his labour. Witn. Geoffrey Lufday, George "Wt.", John Rainold.

217.
Robert Maynard of the parish of St. Peter's Marton in Bedford. 4 Dec. 15.., pr. 22 Dec. 1528. (2: 192)

Burial in the churchyard of St. Peter Marton; to mother church of Lincoln 2d.; to the high altar 4d..

Wife Elizabeth to have testator's house in Kempston, and if she sells it she is to have a trental of masses said for souls of testator and of all Christians. Residue to wife Elizabeth. Executrix wife Elizabeth. Witn. sir William Halam testator's curate, Thomas West, John Richardson.

218.
John Slade an inhabitant and parishioner of Blownham. 13 Dec. 1528, pr. 7 Jan. 1528/9. (2: 192d)

Burial in the churchyard of Blownham; for his mortuary his best good as customary; to the high altar 3s. 4d.; to mother church of Lincoln 2d..

To the parish church, testator's house abutting on the Knoll in Blownham with its meadow, land and appurtenances after the manner and custom of ancient demesne. This is to be sold by the parish after his death, and with the money "without ony alteryng or other colour of this my present will" a cope is to be bought price 20 marks "or more as the price of the hows will cum to" and given to the honour of God's service in the parish church.

To wife Agnes 13 acres of arable land and 2 acres of meadow which testator purchased in the fields of Blownham. She is to keep a yearly obit with mass and *dirige* in the parish church, and to have the Ave bell knolled "morow noone and evyn" as long as she lives. After her death these 13 acres of land are to go to the brotherhood of Blownham, and they are to keep the obit, with mass and *dirige* and the Ave bell. If the said obit is not duly kept nor the bell duly knolled then the 11 acres are to be divided equally between the poor [*sic*] of St. Neots and the Prior of Dunstable "to be prayd for perpetually", and the 3 acres [*sic*] to remain still to the brotherhood of Blownham to cause the bell to be knolled as aforesaid.

To the church of Barkford "all my play bookes and garmentes" with all the properties and other things belonging to the same.

To the prior of——3 dozen fine "cannas" [?hempen cloths] and a dozen coarse "cannas".

To wife Agnes "of my best shepe"————, all his household stuff, all his household implements, all linen and woollen yarn "my shopp except holely". To every godchild a ewe lamb. Residue to sir Richard Trigg parson of Barkford and Thomas Boston alias Farthyng of Blownham who are to be executors. Witn. sir William Bell clerk, Robert Spenser gent., Richard Ward.
Executors refused and widow Agnes Slade given letters of administration.

219.
[*This page much torn*]
Rainold Gray of Kempston esquire. 27 Jan. 1532/3 (25 Henry VIII), no note of probate. (2: 193d)

To be buried in the parish church of All Hallows in Kempston; "To the use of the church for my sepulchre" 6s. 8d.; to the sepulchre light 20d.; to the bells 12d.; to the torches 8d.; to the mother church of Lincoln 2d.; to the high altar for tithes forgotten 4d.; to every godson in Kempston 12d..

To wife Elizabeth testator's manor of Kempston "with all and singular" the appurtenances, for the term of her life, without impeachment of waste. After her death, the manor is to go to William Stokell and Anne his wife and the heirs of the body of Anne. For lack of such issue the manor is to go to the "right heyrys of me the same Rainold".

To wife Elizabeth the house where testator dwells, with its appurtenances, which he bought from John Carter, to hold to her and to her heirs for ever.

To testator's servant William Newold the younger, 40s. for the term of his life out of the same manor of Kempston "for occupyyng of the Baylyshipp" and doing his wife service after testator's death and keeping the woods there.

He wills that if William [Stokell] and Anne his wife, or any other person or persons——his or her procurement after testator's decease do vex——- in any wise Elizabeth Gray of and——-manor of Kempston or for any parcell thereof that——- – said gift of reversion to them—— the body of the said Anne —— lawfully begotten shall stand as void and of none effect, then the reversion of the said manor of Kempston with its appurtenances after the death of himself and his wife shall remain to——-Gray k—-.

Executrix wife Elizabeth Gray with Cromer—- -wyer. Witn.—— Newold—- Thomas——John——John——William—- – Edward—— John—- -.

ABP/R 3

220.
William Churche of Mylton Hernes. 21 Dec. 1528, pr. 7 Feb. 1528/9. (3: 1)

Burial in churchyard of Alhallows in Mylton; for his principal his best good; to high altar for default in tithing 4d.; to the painting of the image of Our Lady 12d.; to the bells 4d.; to the torches 4d.; to Alhallows light 4d..

To wife Jane his house with appurtenances for her life, then to testator's son John if Jane has not been compelled by necessity to sell it. To son John his cart and cart gear, plough and plough gear and a horse colt, two acres sown with barley, two acres sown with pease, a wheat land and one rye land. To daughter Johan a cow, and to every of testator's children two "howld" sheep.

Residue to wife Jane to pay debts and to dispose of for help and comfort of testator's soul, for comfort of her own body, and for the souls of their good friends.

Executrix wife Jane. Witn. sir Richard Kyng vicar of Mylton, William Herwer the elder, John Smythe the younger, William Smythe of the town.

221.
Joane Byworth of Reyslay. 8 Dec. 1528, pr. 1 Mar. 1528/9. (3: 1)

Her burial to be in the church of Reyslay by her husband; to the high altar for things forgotten 8d.; to the bells 6d.; to the torches 6d.; to the sepulchre 4d.; to the brotherhood of Marie Madlen 4d.; to mother church of Lincoln 2d..

To testator's cousin Robert her house in the West End of Ryeslay with all the land that she may lawfully give and sell, and her best brass pot; to cousin Elezabet her best basin; to her godson her best "pane Coverlet", her best candlestick and a pair of sheets; to cousin William Fyesse the second brass pot; to Annes Feysse her best coffer, her best girdle and her pewter basin; to John Feysse, Richard and Thomas, one sheep each and a lamb; to Gilbert Feysse a cow; to her god-daughter the daughter of Joan Bywortes testator's best pewter platter and a pewter dish.

Residue to Robert Feysse her cousin and her executor to dispose of for the health of her soul. Witn. sir Henry Queyn vicar of Reyslay, Thomas Feysse, William Harberd.

222.
William Wheyte of the county of Bedford. 7 Feb., pr. 1 Mar. 1528/9. (3: 1d)

Burial in Reyslay churchyard; to high altar for things forgotten 12d.; to the bells 8d.; to the torches 8d.; to the sepulchre 8d.; to mother church of Lincoln 2d.; to a priest to sing a trental for testator and his friends in Reyslay church 10s.; for a banner cloth for the church 13s. 4d..

To wife Margat testator's house for the term of her life and then to son William and his issue.

To daughter Ellen two beasts with a heifer. Her brother William is to give her 20s., and if the mother's house is sold because William dies childless, then Ellen is to have another 20s..

To son William as long as he can agree with his mother, testator's land with the occupying of his horse plough and "caste". If William die without issue the house is to be sold and the money used for the souls of "them that yt cameof".

Residue of the estate to executors to be used for benefit of wife.

Exors. Margat Wheyte, Robert Feysse and son William Wheyte. Witn. sir Herry Quen vicar, John Peter, John Bedell.

223.
Robert Shepherd/Scepard of Tylbrok. 1529, pr. 1 Mar. 1528/9. (3: 2)

Burial in churchyard of All Halloys, Tylbrok; for his mortuary as use and custom is; to Our Lady of Lincoln 2d.; to high altar 2d.; he requests two trentals of masses for his soul and all Christian souls; to the church 2 torches and 6s. 8d.; to the bells 12d.; to Our Ladye half a pound of wax.

His house is to be sold and his son John is to buy it, paying what another would give. To Alys Sheperd his best pan; to wife Annys the residue to be used for the welfare of his and all Christian souls.

Exors. John Schepard, John Byworthe. Witn. sir Steven Atkynson, John Day, Thomas Lamme and others.

224.
John Lord. 1 July 1527, pr. 1 Mar. 1529/30. (3: 2d)
    Burial in churchyard of St. Peter in Thurle.
    To Christopher Spury of Thurly, his nephew, the house or tenantry lying in Fleet Whoodhend with yard, close, land and meadow belonging to it, that is two acres in Borse close, two acres enclosed, and an acre containing 5 lands in 3 sundry places in Church Field, half an acre in Mill Fyld, three acres in Rydyng, the which house, meadows and lands testator purchased of Phylyppe Roody sometime servant to sir Pwyntell, vicar of Thurly.
    To wife Elizabeth three "yves of besse" (hives of bees) to be delivered as soon as his testament is made.
    To the high altar 4d.; to the bells 6d.; to the sepulchre 4d..
    The said Christopher and his heirs and assigns, whoever has the house and the land, shall yearly keep a *dirige* and mass for souls of testator and all Christians, for which the priest is to have 4d., and on the same day 12d. is to be distributed to 12 poor people in the parish, if there be so many, or else to poor people outside the parish.
    Exor. nephew Christopher who is to have all goods and to do with them as he thinks best. Witn. Harre Gale smith, Thomas Brown husbandman, William Tatam scholar.

225.
Thomas Slade of Keyshoo. 9 Feb., pr. 1 Mar. 1528/9. (3: 3)
    Burial in churchyard of Keyshoo; for mortuary as custom of the town; to high altar for tithes negligently tithed or forgotten 12d.; for an honest priest to sing or say 30 masses for testator and all Christians immediately after his death 10s.; to bells of Keyshoo church 12d.; to the five lights there 10d..
    To wife Elizabeth all household stuff, 4 kyne, two bullocks and 40 sheep. Wife Elizabeth and William Slade, testator's son, are to have the profits of all lands and tenements, woods and pastures in Keyshoo for six years after his death to pay debts and legacies.
    At the end of the six years sons Thomas and Richard are to have 5 marks in money besides such cattle as they have now of their own; daughters Margery, Johan and Agnes are to have 5 marks each towards their marriages and to marry them. If any of the two sons or three daughters die before the six years is ended or before the

daughters marry, then their portion is to be divided among the survivors.

After the six years son William Slade and the heirs of his body are to have the same lands and tenements, and if he die without issue, they go to Thomas, and if Thomas die without issue, to Richard and the heirs of his body, and if all three sons are childless, then the property goes to the right heirs of the testator.

Wife Elizabeth, after the six years, is to have during her lifetime an annuity of 26s. 8d. charged on the properties, to be paid half yearly, that is to say on the feasts of the Annunciation and of St. Michael the Archangel, in full satisfaction of jointure and dower. She is also to have testator's tenement with croft adjoining called Towoldes for her to dwell in as long as she remains unmarried, testator desiring her to be kind and loving to his children and heirs, and desiring his son William to be good and loving to his brothers and sisters in order to obtain testator's blessing.

Exors. wife Elizabeth and son William Slade. Overseer: testator's brother Edward Slade who is to give exors. advice and counsel. Witn. brother Edward Slade, William Alkyn' the elder, William Jenkyn, John Money and Robert Sumpter of Keyshoo.

226.
Thomas Bonham senior of Carleton. 24 Feb., pr. 1 Mar. 1528/9. (3: 3d)

Burial in the churchyard of Our Lady in Carlyton; to the parson there or his deputy for tithes forgot [*amount omitted*]; for his mortuary, after the custom of the town; to the gilding of the rood 20s..

To wife Elizabeth all houses, lands, meadows, pastures, "laysurys" homages, rents and services within Carleton, Chelyngton and Turvey for her life, reversion to his two daughters to be divided equally between them. To her also all moveable goods in the three parishes, subject to his gifts to the daughters, and the residue.

To his daughters Anne Grovys and Elinor Bonham, all his houses etc. equally between them after the death of testator's wife; to Anne Grovys £6 13s. 4d. and to Elinor Bonham "towards her marriage" £6, from his moveables.

His feoffees, Henry Grovys and Richard Page, are to procure a deed of feoffment to the above uses, recorded by sir John Carter, Alexander Ferrer, William Betherey, etc..

Exors. wife Elizabeth, Henry Grovys "which Henry Grovys I wyll shalbe contented with hys wyfys bequest". Supervisor Richard Page. Witn. sir John Carter testator's curate, Richard Page, William Mychell, Thomas Betherey, Edmund Wotton.

227.
John Warwycke/Warweke of Renhall. 1 Feb., pr. 1 Mar. 1528/9. (3: 4)
   Burial in churchyard of All Saints, Rounhall; for his principal, his
best horse; to mother church of Lincoln 3d.; to high altar 3s. 4d.; an
honest priest is to sing a trental for his soul; to the church of All Saints
at Rownhall 2 torches; to the bells 12d..
   To son John 26s. 8d., a young "ekforthe" (heifer) with a "ewgh" (ewe)
and a lamb; to both daughters 20s. and a ewe and a lamb; to servant
Johan a lamb; for every godchild a bushel of barley to be given them at
the next crop; to Richard Fellde and Richard Rusche 12d. each; to John
Mylward 20d.; to son John a shod cart provided that his mother mar-
ries someone who has a shod cart.
   Residue to wife Isabel to the bringing up of his children. Exors. John
Mylwarde and wife Isabel. Witn. sir John Wyon clerk, Thomas Wyon,
William Forthe, Harry Cleyton.

228.
Hugh Lecton/Layghton of Southell'. 17 June 1529, no note of probate.
(3: 4d)
Testament Burial within the church of All Hallowysse of Southell' "nere
unto my father". For his mortuary his best thing after custom of the
town; to high altar for tithes and offerings forgotten 12d.; to Our Lady
of Lincoln 4d.; to the gilding of Our Lady's tabernacle in said church
3s. 4d.; his wife is to have a trental sung in Southell' church for souls
of testator, his father and mother and all good friends, immediately after
his death.
Will To wife Elizabeth his head place where he dwells with all lands,
pastures and meadows, with appurtenances, until his daughter comes to
the age of 18, wife to keep it in repair during these years. If daughter
should die before she is 18 then everything is to remain to the next heirs
according to will of testator's father. To wife yearly for life 20s. to be
paid out of testator's lands and tenements. To his sister Alysse his tenement with the hempland near his head place until his daughter is 18,
and should his sister die before daughter is 18 then the tenement to go
to his wife until daughter is of age.
   To wife all household stuff for her lifetime, and on her death his 2
chests and a featherbed with all that belongs to them to daughter. If his
daughter die before her mother, then the 2 chests and the featherbed to
go to sister Alyce, if she is living, and if not then to Edmund Lete, his
sister's son.
   To the repair of the highway towards Ralph Barber's 3s. 4d..
   Residue to wife Elizabeth. Executrix wife Elizabeth. Supervisor sir
William Strenger "he to have for his labor" 3s. 4d.. Witn. sir William
Strenger parish priest, Thomas Bate, John Brygled, Thomas Kyrkeby.

229.
William Hewere/Haywer of Lutun, husbandman. 28 Apr. 1529, pr. Apr.
1529. (3: 5)

Burial in the churchyard of Luton; to mother church of Lincoln 6d.;
to high altar in Luton for tithes forgotten 20d.; for upkeep of church of
Luton 6s. 8d.; for upkeep of church in Kynges Walden 3s. 4d.; for
upkeep of church in Abbots Walden 3s. 4d.; for upkeep of church in
Purton 3s. 4d.; two trentalls of masses are to be said in the church of
Luton one for testator and the other for his wife.

To son John testator's place in Brache Hood Hynd in Kynges
Walden. To son Rychart testator's place in Kynges Walden called
Coldans, also all household stuff not bequeathed elsewhere, as
bedding, brass, pewter, with all other things, and testator's best gown.
To William Euere, son's son of Robert Euere of Luton, testator's
copyhold in Exstun (Hexton) and if William die without issue it is to
go to Thomas Euere son of old William Euere. To son Thomas testator's second gown. To John the son of Thomas Euere testator's blue
gown.

Exors. sons John and Rychart, to whom the residue. Witn. sir Robart
Byschoppe, William Welch, John Tynbys.

230.
Thomas Stepeng/Stepyng of Luton. 20 Aug. 1529, no date of probate.
(3: 5d)

Burial in church of Our Lady of Luton; for mortuary as is the custom; to high altar for tithes forgotten 12d.; to church of Lincoln 6d.; to
a priest to pray for souls of testator and his friends for a quarter of a
year 30s.; to every standing light in the church 2d.; at his burial 3 masses
to be solemnly sung by all the choir and they are to have for their
labours as the use and custom is, and are to do the same at "my mon-
thys mynd".

To daughter Alice £3 6s. 8d.; to his child "that my wyffe goys withall" 40s.; to his sister Margaret 13s. 4d.; to his sister Elizabeth 5s.; to
wife Annes the residue to use for health of souls.

If the child "in hys mothers belye" be a boy, he is to have testator's
house and all lands at Stevenage, but if he die without issue this house
and lands to John Steppyng, testator's brother.

Exors. wife Annes and Edward Hill, he to have 6s. 8d. for his labour.
Supervisor Robert Smyth. Witn. sir Thomas Baston his confessor,
Thomas Hill, Valentyne Stoppyng.

231.
John Darlyng of Stevynton. 24 Mar. 1529/30, pr. 7 Apr. 1529 [sic]. (3: 6)

Burial in churchyard of Our Blessed Lady in Stevynton; for his mortuary as custom requires; to mother church of Lincoln 8d.; to the high altar 20d.; to the sepulchre light 6s. 8d.; to the bells and torches 2s.; to the body of the church 20s.; to the rood loft 3s.; to Stadgysden church 6s. 8d.; to Turvey bridge, Steferd bridge and Bydnam bridge 20d. each; his wife Margaret Derlyng is to have a trental sung for testator and another for Alys Derling his mother. Wife to give Walter, testator's servant, 20s. at Michaelmas next.

To brother Robert Derling and to Richard his son the house that they dwell in with 2 tenements belonging to it and 54 acres of "fynable" land, also a messuage joined to the place testator dwells in "toward the churchward".

To his wife Margaret all his purchased land.

To Richard Derling son of Robert Darlyng all testator's other lands within the fields of Stevynton and without.

Margaret his wife to dwell in the house where testator dwells for the term of her life, and to have the parlour with the "spens at the hye deske" at her pleasure, and also the other parlour that testator lies in, and she is to be able to come and go through the hall and be in it "when that sche lyst and no creature to lett her".

Margaret is to provide an obit once a year for souls of testator, his father and mother and all Christians, and Richard is to continue this after death of Margaret. If Margaret wishes to sell the purchased land given to her, Richard shall have the first offer at a cheaper price than anyone else. Richard is to find a priest to sing for testator and his friends for one year when he finds it most convenient.

To wife Margaret all goods not bequeathed elsewhere to dispose of as she wishes for health of souls of testator, herself and of all Christians.

Exors. brother Robert Darlyng and Galfryde Loveday weaver, who are each to have 3s. 4d. for their trouble. Supervisor sir Thomas Botell, testator's ghostly father, who is to have 6s. 8d. for his trouble. Witn. sir Thomas Newtun chaplain, Nicholas Herper, John Bertun.

232.

John Edward (Edworth *margin*) the elder of Henlowe. 4 Apr., pr. 7 Apr. 1529. (3: 6d)

Burial in the churchyard of Our Blessed Lady in Henlowe. For his principal his best beast; to the high altar 2 bushels of barley for tithes forgotten; to the church of Lincoln 3d.; to the brotherhood of Our Lady in Henlowe half a quarter of barley; to the bells a bushel of barley; to the torches a bushel of barley; to the sepulchre a bushel of barley; to Margaret Underwode 2 bushels of barley.

To Annys Edward his wife for her lifetime 2½ acres of free land which testator bought, reversion to testator's son William. To Annys also for her life and then to son William the copyhold that testator dwells in, but if William should die Annys can do what she likes with it.

To son William the copyhold "that was Stonles" and if he die before marriage, then to wife Annys. All moveables in the fields and town to be divided equally between Annys and William.

Exors. wife Annys and son William and brother-in-law Richard Underwode. Witn. Rychard Malcot vicar of Henlow, William Jacobe.

233.

John Moreton of Amptell. 13 Mar. 1528/9, pr. 7 Apr. 1529. (3: 7)

His soul "to Almyghty god" and body to be buried in Amptell churchyard. For his mortuary his best good as is the custom; to the high altar of Lincoln 4d.; to All Souls light in Amptell 12d.; to Stevynton church 6s. 8d.; to Elstow Abbey 6s. 8d.; to the "Anker" (anchorite) of Northampton 10s.; to Amptell church for tithes unpaid 9s. 4d..

He wills to wife Johan all his lands and tenements in the parish of Maldon for 14 years, and then equally between his two children, each being heir to the other, and if both children die, then to Joan for life. Hugh Pavy and Rauffe Moreton are to be executors and feoffees in the land to the above uses. If his children marry and their husbands wish to sell some or all of the land, it shall first be offered to Rauffe Moreton at 20 nobles less than the price to anyone else, and it cannot be sold to another party if Rauffe Moreton wants it.

His executors are to sell a messuage in Langhforth parish the money to be used at their discretion provided they buy 3 kine to be a stock at Maldon to support an obit for testator and his friends for ever.

If wife and children all die, then the lands etc. to go to Rauffe Moreton and his heirs, and they are to cause a priest to sing for testator in Amptell church for a whole year.

To wife Joan, all other goods, and she is to have the custody of all testator's lands while she remains a widow, but if she remarry then the executors are to administer them paying her the yearly value for the 14 years.

Exors. Hugh Pavy and Rauffe Moreton, each to have 6s. 8d.. Witn. sir John Combe, Hugh Pavy, Rauffe Moreton, Thomas Fowlciam, Thomas Mershe, John Shefeilde.

234.

John Kyne of Lytlington. 1524, pr. 6 Apr. 1529. (3: 7d)

Burial in churchyard of All Halowys in Lytlyngton. To mother church at Lincoln 4d.. To John Butler, testator's daughter's son, and to his heirs and assigns, his house in Wodende; to William Butler, his daughter's son, and to his heirs and assigns, half a yard land lying next to Brogborowe Pasture; to Joan, testator's daughter's daughter and her heirs and assigns, a quarter land lying next to William Butler's.

If the lands are sold John Butler is to have them "within the price" before anyone else. John Butler is to have the half yard land and the quarter yard land for a year after testator's death "without any denying".

To the vicar sir Peter Dente 12d. to pray for testator's soul.

Residue to executors. Exors. wife Marget Kyne and John Buttler. Supervisor the vicar sir Peter Dente. Witn. Thomas Gelion, William Buttler the elder.

On (3: 8) comes the first part of no. 274 below, crossed through.

235.

Thomas Pentlowe. 15 Jan. 1529/30 [*sic*], pr. 6 May 1529. (3: 8d)

Burial in churchyard of Our Blessed Lady, Keyshoo; for mortuary after custom of the town; to the high altar for tithes forgotten 2s.; to mother church at Lincoln 2d.; to the bells 12d.; to the five tapers of Jesu 12d..

To Richard Pentlowe, testator's eldest son, 40s. and the best shod cart and the black colt and 6 ewes; to Thomas, his second son, 40s. and the next shod cart and the bay colt with a star in the forehead and 6 ewes; to daughter Em 40s. and a cow with a calf. To testator's mother, if she goes away from his wife, a quarter of wheat and three quarters of barley.

Residue to his wife Jone Pentlowe to use for his soul. Executrix Jone Pentlowe. Overseer Water Pytcokes and John Rolte who are to have 2s. each. Witn. sir William Bowydon vicar of the town, Gregory Deye clerk.

236.

Robert Butler of Edworth. 18 June 1528, pr. 6 May 1529. (3: 8d)

Burial in the church of St. George the Martyr of Edworthe before the Trinity, and to the church "for my lying there" 6s. 8d.; for his principal after the use and custom of the country; to the church at Norell' 6s. 8d.; to a priest to sing for souls of testator, his friends and all Christians for one half-year £3, which is to be done in the church of Edworth immediately after the burying.

To son Jaspere two of his best oxen, one brown cow and one gray horse; to daughter Alfray a couple of steers, one of them a black steer and the other a "bulkyn"; to daughter Dorithe 40s.; to daughter Barbara 40s.; to daughter Francys 4 marks; to the child his wife Elyng is carrying whether a manchild or a womanchild £3 6s. 8d., and should the child die under age the money is to go to Elyng; to daughter Affra £3 6s. 8d..

Residue to wife Helyng who is to be executrix. Overseers Edmund

Bolmen' chaplain, master Nicholas Brograve, Witn. William Cowpar, Robert Hobkyng, Edward Limere.

237.
William Sorrey of Studham. 10 Apr., pr. 6 May 1529. (3: 9)
Burial within the churchyard of St. Mary of Studham; for mortuary as the manner of the town; to high altar 4d.; to all the lights in the church 6d..

To wife Jone, after the death of Margaret Clarke testator's mother-in-law, all lands and tenements in the parish of Studham which should come to testator by right of Hugh Sorrey his father, to her for life, and after her death to testator's son William and his heirs and assigns for ever.

Residue to wife Jone who is to be executrix. Witn. sir Roger Geffrey, John Roben', Thomas Weste.

238.
John Strayt of Cadyngton. 3 May 1529, no note of probate. (3: 9d)
Burial in churchyard of Cadyngton; to mother church at Lincoln 2d.; to the high altar at Cadyngton 20d.; two trentals of masses to be sung in same church for souls of testator and all Christians; to the rood light 4d.; to Our Lady's light 4d.; to the great bell 3s. 4d..

To wife Margery one half of moveable goods; to son Thomas the other half except for certain things which appear in testator's will.

To daughter Jon 40s., an acre of wheat, an acre of barley and another of oats; to Richard Pays an acre of wheat, an acre of barley, an acre of oats; to Anges Talarre a sheep; to Margaret Stret a sheep; to Johan Ferybey 6 sheep; to daughter Anges 10 sheep; to daughter Johan 10 sheep.

To wife Margery half testator's house and lands with son Thomas until Thomas is 20 years, if she remains single. If she remarries Thomas and his issue are to have all except her "morow part" (dower). If Thomas die childless, the house and land to go to testator's brother Robert, he paying to testator's two daughters £6 13s. 4d..

To Thomas Watterton a sheep; to Edward Dermar a sheep.

Residue to wife Margery and son Thomas who are executors. Overseer testator's brother Robert who is to have 3s. 4d. for his trouble. Witn. sir Thomas Elneston vicar of Cadyngton, Thomas Warton, Richard Taloner, Thomas Bysslay.

239.
John Hokyll the elder of Henlow. 16 May 1529, no note of probate. (3: 10)
Burial in churchyard of Our Blessed Lady in Henlow; to mother

church of Lincoln 4d.; to high altar of Henlow for tithes forgotten 4d.; to brotherhood of Our Lady in Henlow a quarter of malt; to the bells one stone of hemp; to the rood light 2 bushels of barley; to the sepulchre light half a quarter of malt; to the torches a bushel of barley.

To wife Margaret all goods and household implements that she brought with her when she was married, 20 ewes and 20 lambs as they run out of the fold by chance, 5 kine and 2 bullocks, 10 quarters of barley. To her also the £5 of money that testator had with her at marriage which is to be paid half at St. Andrew's day next following and half at the St. Andrew's day twelvemonth; to wife a pair of beads with the rings and the jewels that are on them, 2 silver spoons and 2 pewter porringers.

To son John testator's copyhold called Balardys and his feather bed; to son William his next best bedding. All other bedding to be divided equally between wife and two sons.

To son John testator's best brass pot and to William the next best, and to each of them 12 pewter, and to each 10 ewes without lambs next Michaelmas. The residue of the brass, pewter and latten to be divided between wife and two sons. Should one son die the other is to be his heir.

Residue to testator's mother Annys Hokyll, and executors are Annys Hokyll and testator's brother John Hokyll. Witn. Wylliam Jacobe, John Edward, Wylliam Hokyll and sir Richard Malcot, vicar of the same town.

240.
John Baleit chaplain of Wyboston near Eton (Socon). 20 May 1524, pr. 1 July 1529. (3: 10d)
Latin Burial before the window in which St. James and St. Robert are depicted, where the vicar chooses. For his mortuary as is the custom; "Item pro temporali x.s." for temporalities 10s.; to the high altar of Eaton 4d..

To the chapel at Wyboston two vestments and one missal which is called a cowcher and one manual and one chest.

Residue to executor Thomas Cheissam. Supervisor the vicar of Eaton to whom 3s. 4d. for his work, and testator leaves him a book "qui vicitatrix lauduhilius de vita Christi". Witn. James Stevenson vicar of Eaton and sir John Talar.

241.
Thomas Burton of Podyngton. 30 June 1529, pr. 2 June 1529 [*sic*]. (3: 10d)
Burial in Podyngton churchyard; for mortuary as the law requires; to mother church at Lincoln 2d.; to the sepulchre, bells and torches 8s.; to the high altar in Podyngton 12d..

To brother William Burton testator's black coat; to John Strant his blue coat; to William Pygbryke a russet coat; to John Burton a red doublet and a pair of hose; to William Cleyton a pair of hose; to William Tall a black coat.

To wife Joan Burton all lands and tenements in Suldroppe and Henwyke for life. After wife's death to testator's daughter Alice Stranton 7½ acres and half a rood with a pykyll called Goys Lard in the fields of Henwyke and Podyngton parish and a cottage in the town of Erececestr' (Irchester); to daughter Margere Pygbrek a messuage with appurtenances in town and fields of Soldropp. If Alice Strayton and her children die then all the lands shall come to Margery Pygbreke and her children, and if Margery and her children die, all lands to go to Alice Strayton and her children.

To wife Joan Burton the surplus of all his goods for her lifetime and at her death what remains equally between Margery and Alice.

Exors. Joan Burton and John Straton. Witn. William Tall, William Cleysten.

242.
James Baysse/Bays. 1 June 1526, pr. 12 June 1529. (3: 11)

Burial in the churchyard of Our Lady in Steventon; for mortuary as custom requires; to mother church at Lincoln 4d.; to the maintenance of the "wacheys" of the brotherhood priest of the Trinity in Steventon £4, that is every year 6s. 8d. during the time the sum lasts, and if the brotherhood does not continue, then testator is to be sung for by an honest priest for the souls of testator, his father, mother, wife and all Christians by the quarter or the half year as it shall be most agreeable to Thomas Lane.

To Peter Lane 6s. 8d.; to wife Joan the residue of his goods, moveable and unmoveable, to pay and receive debts. Exors. Joan Baysee and Thomas Lane, the latter to have 6s. 8d. for his labour. Supervisor sir Thomas Newenton who is to have 20d. for his pains. Witn. Geffery Lewday, William Standlege, Ronia' Goldeston.

243.
William Eleot/Elyot. 5 July 1529, no date of probate. (3: 11d)

Burial in the chancel before the Blessed Sacrament in Farnedeche church; to the mother church of Lincoln 4d.; to the bells in Farnedeche 2s.; to the church of Farnedeche a vestment to cost 26s. 8d.; to the sepulchre yield in Farnedesh 6s. 8d..

To brother John Eleot 2 beasts and 10 sheep; to John's son William 4 score sheep; to Annys Eleot 2 beasts and 10 sheep; to Elinor her sister 2 beasts, a bullock and 10 sheep; to Thomas Eleot 4 beasts for his cart with a plough and plough gears.

To brother John testator's house in Farnedeche for his lifetime to keep testator's obit once a year. After John's death the property to go to John's son William to hold it to the use of William's own child, if the child lives. If the child die, then William to have property making sure that the obit is kept on the Monday in Procession week and continues as long as the house stands, the parson to have 4d. for the *dirige* and requiem mass, the parish to have a recreation when they come out of the field with bread and drink and cheese for children to the value of 16d..

Sir John Napton to sing for testator once this quarter. William Eleot, testator's brother's son, has the choice of everything and to be executor, as he has testator's trust. William Eliot to have the counsel of testator's supervisors, sir John Napton and sir John Henmarsch the vicar of Podyngton to dispose of the residue for testator's soul. If they do not agree, sir John Napton and sir John Henmarch are to dispose of the residue for testator's and all Christian souls. Witn. Rychard Clyfton, Rychart Foscot.

244.
William Hale/Hayle the elder of Maston Mortene, yeoman. 1529, no date of probate. (3: 12)

Burial in the church or churchyard of Maston as his executors decide; for his mortuary after the custom of the town; to the mother church of Lincoln 4d.; to the high altar in Maston church for tithes negligently withheld 12d.; to the high altar in Howghton church for tithes witheld 8d.; to an honest priest, to be named by executors, a quarter's service to sing in Maston church for the souls of testator and his father, mother and friends; to Our Lady in the chancel of Marston 3 sheep; to Our Lady of Bedlam in Marston church one sheep; to the Trinity in Marston church 2 sheep; to the two saints before me on the right hand of the choir door 2 sheep; to the wealth of the town for the easement of the poor folk when charge shall come to the town, 3 kine to be let at 16d. a year, whoever hires them to make good the stock; to the church of Howghton Conquest 20s. to be paid within 5 years of testator's death; he leaves a cow to the mending of Hasyllwood Lane from testator's house to the Abbot Wod Gate; to the church of Flitton 6s. 8d. and also a cow to maintain St. John's light in the chancel; to the Trinity in Flitton church a sheep; to the church of Pulloxhill 3s. 4d. to be paid within 3 years of his death; to the monastery of Redyng (Reading) 10s.; to the town of Wotton 3s. 4d.; to daughter Annes Archer £5.

His executors are to find testator's son's son, Thomas Hayle, to school at Potton for 2 years with such cattle as his father left him, and testator bequeaths to him and his issue 20 acres of land in Howghton Field which land he bought of Richard and Henry Punter, and if

Thomas Hayle dies without issue then the property to go to William Hayle and his male issue. To son William Hale the residue of all testator's other lands and tenements according to the deeds made in jointure with his son's first wife.

Residue to his executors, wife Annes and son William, to do with as they please. Witn. sir William Cockes curate, sir Briant Thomas, Robert Odell and Henry Archer.

245.
Thomas Smyth of Sutton. 20 Sept., pr. 27 Sept. 1529. (3: 12d)
Burial in churchyard of All Hallows in Sutton; for his mortuary as is the custom; to the mother church at Lincoln 4d.; to the high altar for tithes forgotten half a quarter of rye; to the church of All Hallows Sutton a "Bro" [*sic*]; to the bridge of Sutton 6s. 8d.; his wife Elizabeth is to give 10s. to a priest to sing a trental of masses in the parish church of Sutton to pray for souls of testator, his father and all Christians.

To wife Elizabeth for her life all his free and copyhold land in the town and fields of Sutton, and if Elizabeth is with child by testator it shall inherit after her death "and she to gyffe yt 20s. sterling", but if Elizabeth is not with child, on her death the lands are to be sold and the money used for souls of testator, his father and all Christians.

Executrix wife Elizabeth who is to dispose of the residue for souls. Overseer Thomas Haggys who is to have 3s. for his pains. Witn. sir Thomas Hays clerk, Nicholaus Plummer, Thomas Lyner/Lyver.

246.
William Ensam. 4 Aug. 1529, no date for probate. (3: 13)
Latin Burial in the churchyard of All Saints at Shitlyngton; to the high altar for tithes forgotten 2 measures of barley; to St. Hugh of Lincoln 2d..

His house with appurtenances is to go after the custom of the manor, that is to wife Joan for her life, and then to his sons, one after the other.

Residue to wife and children. Executrix wife Joan. Witn. William Cherche, Edward Wyet, Thomas Same.

247.
John Front of Colmorth, Bedfordshire, within the diocese of Lincoln. 1 Aug. 1529, no date of probate. (3: 13d)
Burial "within holly sepulture" wherever "it shall plese god to depart my sowll frome my sinfull body"; for mortuary as the custom of the country "in redemption of my greveys offencys to Godward"; to the high altar in Colmorth for tithes forgotten 8d.; to the mother church at Lincoln 4d.; to the bells of Colmorth 8d..

To "each of my children by the deliverance of my wife" 20s., that is to John, Thomas, George, Herry, Edmund, Grace, Elizabeth and Alice, in all £8. To daughter Anne Cockelyng a cow, and to Anne, her daughter, a calf.

Residue at the disposal of wife Elizabeth who is executrix. Supervisor William Fitzhugh. Witn. Gregory Bun, John Dryver, Richard Crosse.

248.
John Gere of Sharnebrok. 29 Aug., pr. 7 Oct. 1529. (3: 13d)

Burial in St. Peter's Church before the rood; to the mother church of Lincoln 4d.; to the high altar 12d.; to the sepulchre light 12d.; to Our Lady light 8d.; to St. Roke 4d.; to the torches 12d.; to the bells 12d.; to the Trinity 4d.; to the lamp before the rood 4d.; to Our Lady of Grace 4d.; to the rood in the wall 4d.; to Our Lady of Comfort 4d.; for testator's burial and for his wife's 6s. 8d.; for a trental to be done in this church 10s..

To Margere his mother and to his children his moveable goods; to his son William his houses and his land, and if he and testator's daughter die, then his mother to have them for her life. To daughter Margery the two acres of land that testator bought of John Kent and the one acre bought of William Hayberne.

Exors. mother Margery and Edward Lenton. Overseer master Gray of Kempston to whom 6s. 8d. for his pains. Witn. cousin John Gery, John Odei the elder, William Weste.

249.
Geoffrey Meryell of Keyshoo. 21 Sep., pr. 7 Oct. 1529. (3: 14)

Burial in the churchyard of Our Blessed Lady at Keyshoo; best beast for mortuary; to high altar for tithes forgotten 8d.; to mother church at Lincoln 2d.; to the five tapers of Jesus 4d.; to the bells 8d..

To son William Meriell testator's house in Litell Stocton, butting on Fremannys Green, 20 cows, 20 lambs, 2 kine, 2 calves, a "bulchyn", his black colt, a dun yearling, his best blue gown and best doublet and second doublet, 2 quarters of barley and 2 quarters of pease. To each of William's children a cow.

To daughter Elizabeth Merell' 7 quarters of malt, a white heifer, 2 calves, 2 of his best coffers, a bed and all that belongs to it, 6 platters, 6 pewter dishes and 4 sheep.

To godson Geoffrey Preston a new lamb and a calf; to godson Geoffrey Conyngam a new lamb and a calf. To servant Edmund Turner 2 quarters of barley, 2 quarters of pease, 4 sheep and a weaned calf. Residue to wife Alys Merell.

Exors. wife Alys and son William Meryell. Overseer son-in-law Steven Conyngam. Witn. sir William Bowydon vicar or Keysoe, John Rolth, Gregory Dey, Robert Gressam.

250.
Thomas Pepyat of Sondon. 24 Oct. 1529, no date of probate. (3: 14d)

Burial in Sondon church before the image of Our Blessed Lady; to mother church of Lincoln 4d.; to the high altar of Sondon 12d.; to the church of Sondon 13s. 4d.; to Our Lady's light at Sondon church 20d.; to the other light 20d.; to the bells of Sondon 3s. 4d.; to the church of Harlington 6s. 8d.; to the church of Stratley 6s. 8d.; to the brotherhood of Kings Houghton 2s.; to the brotherhood of Todington 2s.; to the friars of Bedford 6s. 8d.; to the friars of Echin (Hitchin) 6s. 8d.; to an honest priest to sing for souls of testator and his friends for 3 years in Sondon church £14; to every godchild a sheep; to the repair of the highway about Sondon £10.

To wife Joan all lands for her lifetime, to be kept in repair, and after her death to testator's son Richard and his assigns, and Richard is to pay out of the lands within the space of 14 years to testator's daughter Cristian the sum of £20. Residue to wife Johan Pepyat and Robert Preston, executors, and he is to have 20s. for his pains.

Supervisor son Richard. Witn. sir John Walter, John Edreche, Richard Hebbes, John Welles.

251.
William Fan of Elnestow. 1528, date of probate deleted. (3: 15)

Burial in churchyard of Elnestow; for mortuary as custom of the town; to the mother church of Lincoln 2d.; to the high altar 4d.; to the torches 3s.; to his lady abbess and her convent at Elnestow 6s. 8d.; five masses are to be sung at his burial.

To Elizabeth Pundy a quarter of barley; to Richard the son of Robert Fane a quarter of barley; to Margaret Lowell half an acre of barley and 2 bushels of malt; to each of testator's children after the death of his wife 20s. and such goods as his wife leaves to be divided among them; to brother Edward Fan 6s. 8d. to use for testator's mother.

To wife Elizabeth a cart and pair of wheels, the house where testator lives, and 5 acres of land for the term of her life, and after her death to daughter Alys, and should Alice die, then to one of his other children. Whoever has the house and lands to keep testator's obit yearly at the cost of 3s. 4d., and if all the children die, the house and lands to be sold and the money used for souls of testator and his friends that the property came from. Residue to wife Elizabeth.

Exors. wife Elizabeth Fan, brother Edward Fan and Thomas Fayre "thay for do for me like as they wolde be done fore" and Edward and Thomas each to have 20d. for their pains. Witn. sir Thomas Harward, William Bolard and William Shalte.

252.
Humphrey Basse/Basshe. 23 Sep. 1529, no note of probate. (3: 15d)
Burial in the churchyard of Sharnebroke; to mother church of Lincoln
2d.; to high altar of St. Peter's Sharnebroke, a bushel of barley; to the
sepulchre light 2 bushels of barley; to the bells 2 bushels of barley; to
the torches a bushel of barley; a trental of masses to be sung for souls
of testator and all Christians.
To his two children 2 kine, and the residue to wife Elizabeth.
Executrix wife Elizabeth.
He wills that wife Elizabeth is to enjoy both goods and lands for her
life, and if the child "she goys withall" is male and outlives her, he is to
have the land, but if it be a woman child the land is to be "departeyt"
as custom and use require.
Supervisor William Cobbe of Sharnebrok. Witn. sir William Colbonys
curate, William Cobbe, John Pulley.

253.
Richard Filde of Barton in the Claye. 13 Oct., pr. 25 Nov. 1529. (3: 16)
Burial in the churchyard of St. Nicholas in Barton; to mother church
at Lincoln 2d.; to the high altar 2s. 4d.; to the gilding of St. Thomas
20d.; to the bells 20d.; to the highway 12d..
To eldest son Layrence Fylde the house where testator dwells with all
that belongs to it after death of wife. To son Thomas Filde after death
of wife the house that Richard Huckill lives in with appurtenances.
Residue to wife.
Exor. Richard Huckill. Witn. sir William Parysse parson of Barton,
John Godley, John Prior, Richard Haull.

254.
Stephen Balle of Turvey. 26 Oct. 1529, no note of probate. (3: 16d)
Burial in churchyard of All Hallows of Turvey; to mortuary accord-
ing to custom of the town; to the high altar 12d.; to the bells 12d.; to
the torches 12d. and 6s.; to the bridge 2 bushels of barley; a trental of
masses to be said in Turvey parish church for souls of testator and all
Christians.
To each child of John Ball of Wooborne a sheep; to servant Richard
Ball a cow bullock; to testator's five children Stevyn, Thomas,
Margaret, Elyn and Elizabeth £3 6s. 8d. each to be paid to Stevyn and
Thomas at the age of 20, and to Margaret, Elyn and Elizabeth at 17
years. If any die before these ages their share to be divided equally
among the survivors.
To son Stevyn, after the death of testator's wife Agnes, the Whyt
House in Stockers End called Walkers with appurtenances, he paying to
son John Ball 26s. 8d. and to son William £2 13s. 4d.. Should Stevyn

die without issue the house and the obligations attached to it go to son William, and then to son Thomas.

Testator forgives son John Ball the 26s. 8d. he owes him.

Wife Agnes and the children who occupy the house with her shall pay testator's father William Ball 20s. a year for as long as he lives.

To son Thomas Ball the close at Pynchynckes Crosse after Agnes' death. Should he die before Agnes, then it is to be divided equally among the other children then alive, that it William, Stevyn, Margaret, Elyn and Elizabeth.

Executrix wife Agnes. Supervisors John Gefrey, John Hilles who are to have 3s. 4d. each for their labour. No names of witnesses.

255.
Thomas Couper/Cowper of Litlyngton. 1529, no note of probate. (3: 17)

Burial in churchyard of All Hallows at Litlyngton; to mother church at Lincoln 4d.; to high altar for tithes forgotten 2 bushels of barley; to the bells and torches 8d.; to every saint in the church a quarter of wax; 10s. for a trental to be sung for testator's soul in Litlyngton church 10s.; to mending the highway to the Church End Street 3s. 4d..

To each of his children a cow and a heifer and to his own children £4 each and if "other of thame dye the last to have bothe"; and to each of them a great brass pot.

Residue to wife Joan and to John Couper testator's father, executors, to dispose of for the health of souls. Witn. Thomas Feler.

256.
William Busche/Busshe of Kynges Howghton. 8 July 1529, no note of probate. (3: 17)

Burial in church of Kynges Howghton; to mother church of Lincoln 2d.; to high altar 12d.; to the maintenance of the bells 12d.; to the torches 12d.; to every "gatherde" light in the church 2d.; to the church of Tyllsworth 6s. 8d.; to the church of Mylton Brian 12d.; ten loads of stones are to be laid in the highway from Houghton to Calcot "were as most nede is".

To his brother Richard Busche 10s.; to each of his three sons 3s. 4d.; to Thomas Busche 10s.; the residue to be used for the wealth of souls of himself, his friends and all Christians.

Exors. William Wizthehede, Robert Haukynges to whom 10s. each. Overseer: master William Fossey vicar of the said town, to whom 10s.. Witn. John Eme, Richard Haukyns.

Testator wills that for 14 years after his death the 20s. which William Wyzthede should pay him each year for the house and lands which testator sold to him, as appears by the indenture of conveyance made between them, shall be used as follows: 10s. on an obit in Houghton church "as on prestes and clarkes and on bredde and hayle" with all necessary things pertaining to an obit, under the supervision of the then vicar and churchwardens, to pray for souls of testator, his parents and benefactors. The other 10s. is to be used for a trental of masses to be said in Houghton church under the same supervision to pray for the same souls.

257.

Joan Harve/Harey, widow, of Bedford. 26 Oct., pr. 22 Dec. 1529. (3: 17d)

Burial in the churchyard of Polles, Bedford; to the high altar of Polles for tithes forgotten 4d.; to the mother church of Lincoln 1d..

To her son Richard Harve the friar, a pair of sheets, a mattress, a blanket, a bolster, 2 platters, 2 candlesticks, a coverlet and a chaffing dish.

She bequeathes to master William Thomas bailiff of Bedford, her son John Harve "he to kepe hem as hys owne chylde and so to fynde hem mette and drenke and clothyng as he kepe on of hys owen childerne" and to this end she bequeaths him all the goods that she has in this world.

Executor William Thomas bailiff of Bedford. Witn. sir Thomas Pye, Richard Wyan, John Gedeing the clerk.

258.

Thomas Laurens. 1529, pr. 10 Jan 1530/1. [*sic*] (3: 18d)

Burial in the churchyard of Westinge; for mortuary as is the custom; to mother church of Lincoln 4d.; to the high altar for forgotten tithes half a quarter of malt; to the bells 12d..

To son Richard 2 kine and a colt and 6s. 8d.; to son John a cow, a colt and 6s. 8d.; to son Harry an acre of land abutting on Weke Close and a cow; to son William an acre of land abutting on Henys Crosse and a cow; to daughter Alys a cow and 6s. 8d.; to daughter Isobel a cow and 6s. 8d.; to daughter Margaret a cow and 6s. 8d. and to daughter Lucy a cow and 6s. 8d..

Executrix testator's wife. Overseer Thomas Smyth; Witn. sir John Turner, William Dey, William Upton, Thomas Dix.

259.

John Hurndall. 7 Jan. 1529/30, pr. 14 Jan. 1530/31 [*sic*]. (3: 18d)

Burial in churchyard of Aspley Gysys; his mortuary as customary.

To wife Katherine the house where he dwells for her lifetime, and on her death the house is to go to his daughter Joan Hurndall. Should Joan die, the house is to be sold and the money used for the souls of those

THE   EAST   VIEW   OF   BEDFORD-PRIORY.

THIS Priory was dedicated to St Paul, and was founded before the Norman Conquest for Canons Secular or Prebendaries: but in the Reign of K: W: I. one of the Canons having kill'd a Butcher on a fray, they were forc'd to remove from thence to a place call'd Flewnham, where Rose Wife to Papauus Baron of Bedford built a Priory to receive them.

6. The Franciscan Friary in Bedford in 1730 by the brothers S. and N. Buck, who mistook the building for the remains of Newnham Priory. Joan Harvey of Bedford (no. 257) in 1529 left to her son Richard Harvey, a friar, some household goods including his bedding.

who provided it. To William Gelian his best coat, best doublet and best hose. Residue to wife Katherine.

Executrix wife Katherine. Witn. sir Richard Grenwode, William Clowde.

260.
John Coston. 9 Dec. 1529, pr. 14 Jan. 1530/1. [*sic*] (3: 19)

Burial in the churchyard of Podington; for his mortuary "my best godde"; to mother church of Lincoln 4d.; to high altar of Podington 12d.; to church of Podington 6s. 8d..

To son Richard Coston and the heirs of his body, a messuage with the appurtenances in the town and fields of Podyngton, and all goods moveable and immoveable, and he is to pay testator's sons Thomas and William Coston £5 each in the space of three years, i.e. at All Hallows day following testator's death £3 6s. 8d. between them, and so on from year to year until the £10 is paid.

To son Ranolde Coston £6 13s. 4d.; to son Michael Coston £6 13s. 4d.; to daughter Jone Coston £6 13s. 4d.; to be paid when they marry, and if any of them marry within three years after testator's death then the money to be paid in portions as set out above.

Wife Ellen to continue with son Richard "ther to have hyr leveinge onestly if she plese beinge wedow", and if she does not remain a widow or does not stay with Richard she shall have £6 13s. 4d. and go where she pleases.

If any child cause any strife or variance or dispute over his will they shall have nothing. Richard is to see that testator's wishes are carried out and his debts paid.

Exors. William Burton, Thomas Denys, each to have 6s. 8d.. Witn. sir John Henmarsche vicar of Podington, Richard Coston, William Cleyten and others.

261.
Margery Wytte of Colmorth, widow. 2 Jan., pr. 14 Jan. 1529/30. (3: 19)

Burial in Colmorth churchyard; her mortuary as customary; to mother church at Lincoln 2d.; to bells of Colmorth 12d.; to the church light 12d.; to Lenmans bridge 6s. 8d.; to the causeway 6d..

To John Thode 6s. 8d. and to his son John a sheep.

To John Gardener the son of Walter Gardener the house and appurtenances in the Churche End, and if he should die childless, the house to go to his sister Joan, and if she die then to John Thode the son of John Thode, and if all die then the house is to be sold and the money used for the souls of testator, her husband and all Christians.

To William Fysson son of Jeffrey Fysson the house etc. that her husband bought of Thomas Buttell and the land that he bought of John

Buttelle. To Jeffrey Fysson and his wife, testator's house, land and appurtenances in Peney's End, and after their death this is to go to Robert Fysson the son of the said Jeffrey Fysson.

To Joan Gardner a pair of sheets, one of flax and the other of hemp, a coverlet, two platters, two candlesticks and a brass pot.

Residue to Jeffrey Fesson. Executor Jeffrey Fysson. Overseer master Fitzhuhes. Witn. sir Gregory Bune parish priest, Robert Butmar, John Thode.

262.
John Sanderson of Barton in Clay. 1529, pr. 14 Jan. 1529/30. (3: 19d)

Burial in churchyard of St. Nicholas at Barton in Clay. To the mother church of Lincoln 2d.; to the high altar of St. Nicholas 12d.; to poor people in bread at Easter yearly 12d.; to the highway 6s. 8d.; for a trental 10s..

To son Thomas testator's house with appurtenances with the residue. If he die then the property is to go to testator's brother Richard, and if Richard die also, then the house is to be sold for the benefit of the souls of testator and his friends.

Richard is to have the house with all the stuff within and without and to make the most he can of the land, paying the lord's rent, and keeping the child at "sckowlle" [school] and supporting him till he be of age, and then delivering the house and stuff over to testator's son Thomas. If Richard wastes the property, then Thomas Kepeys is to take it into his own hand, including taking the profits and supporting the child until he comes of age.

Exors. Thomas Kepeys, testator's brother Richard Sanderson. Witn. sir Richard Lavunder, John Cowper.

263.
Margaret Darlynge of Stevinton, widow. 15 Nov. 1529, pr. 24 Jan. 1530/1 [sic]. (3: 20)

Burial in churchyard of Our Blessed Lady in Stevynton beside her husband. For her mortuary as customary; to high altar of Lincoln 4d.; to high altar of Stevinton 20d.; to sepulchre light 12d.; to the body of the church 3s. 4d.; to the bells 12d.; to the torches 12d.; to the rood light 2s.; to Our Lady chapel 3s. 4d.. To the town bridge, Harwolde bridge, Stefford bridge, and Bednam bridge 12d. each. A priest is to sing for testator "a yere contenent" and to have 8 marks for his pains, and sir Thomas Botoll the vicar of Stevinton is to have the 8 marks and to pay the priest quarterly as he deserves it.

To Margaret Annis a bushel of malt; to Margery Perynge a bushel of malt; to Margaret Barton a bushel of malt; to testator's servants Agnes Talor and Alice Gogen a platter, a pewter dish, a saucer and a candlestick each and to each a pair of sheets of which one flaxen, one of hemp.

To Edmund Cornewell a quarter of barley; to William Darling brother of testator's husband, 4 sheep; to William Jeys of Turvey all her crop of wheat, barley, malt, beans and oats, and he is to give Simon Jud, his brother-in-law, 10 marks. To Richard the son of Robert Darling 20 sheep, and the rest of the sheep are to be divided between William Jeys and Simon Jud. To William Jeys 2 beasts and to Simon Jude one beast.

One cow is to be sold and the money arising divided among five poor folk.

To Richard Darlynge a "bulchin" bull calf.

Two cows are to be let for hire and the money to be used for a *dirige* and mass for souls of testator and all Christians on her year day. When the beasts get old the curate of the town is to sell them and buy a young cow and a bullock so as to keep testator's year day for as long as it may.

Richard Darling is to buy all testator's closes, lands and pastures and to give the money to a priest to sing for souls of testator, her husband, their fathers and mothers and all Christians.

To sir Thomas Botull a platter; to William Jeys two mashing vats and 4 of the best brass pans, and to Richard Darlinge 2 of the next best pans. To Simon Jud and to Agnes Jeys the folding table and the aumbry. To Agnes Jeys the best brass pot, the second best to go to Simon Jude.

To Agnes Jeys and to Simon Jude the coffers. To Richard Darling the chest and 2 brass pots. To sir Thomas Botall two of the best sheets. To William Jeys 3 hogs. To Richard Darling one hog. To William Jeys 3 chaffers, 2 kettles and a pan. To servant Agnes Caller a pan. To John Barber a bay horse. To Edmund Cornewell a grey horse. The young horse and the sorrel are to be sold and her executors are to have the money to fulfill her will.

To William Jeys the tilth of her land. To Richard Darling 2 old candlesticks and a bag of hay in the haybarn. To Walter Westemerlond 2 bushels of barley. To sir Thomas Botall her best candlestick. To sir Thomas Newnton a pair of sheets. To Agnes Jeys a feather bed, a quilt and all the coverlets, testator's silver spoons, a great spit, a pair of cobirons, a shod cart, all her woolen yarn, a powdering "kymnell" (tub), a wort "kymnell", and all the hay in the little house.

To Richard Derling a bare cart, half the plough gear, half the cart gear and all her augers except one or two to William Jeys. To Richard Darlynge an ark (chest). Simon Jude is to be guided by William Jeys till he is old enough to be married. The residue is to be divided between William Jeys and Simon Jude to be used for souls of testator and all Christians.

Exors. sir Thomas Botell vicar of Steventon, to have 6s. 8d. for his pains, and William Jeys of Turvey. Supervisor to be master Gostwik, commissary, and he to have 6s. 8d.. If he does not wish to be supervisor, then sir Thomas Neunte, who shall have the 6s. 8d.. Witn. Geoffrey Loveday, Walter Hobkins, Edmund Cornewill.

264.
Roger Withebrede of Eversholt. 19 Jan., pr. 24 Jan 1529/30. (3: 20d)
Burial in churchyard of Eversholt. For his mortuary his best beast after the custom of the town; to the mother church at Lincoln 2d.; to the high altar 4d.; to Our Lady altar 4d.; to the Trinity altar 4d.; to St. Nicholas altar 4d.; to the rood light 4d.; to the maintenance of the bells 4d..

To wife Jone the house that testator dwells in and all appurtenances for her life, and after her death they shall go to Richard Whytbrede, testator's eldest son and to his heirs, he to pay to the next eldest son John 20s.; to his brother Harry Whytebrede 20s.; to his brother William 20s.; to his brother Thomas 20s.; to his brother Roger 20s.; to his brother Nicholas the youngest son 20s.; and also to his sister Ezabell 13s. 4d. and to his sister Marion 13s. 4d.. This money is to be paid immediately the house and lands come into Richard's hands, as each attain the age of 21. Should Richard die before his mother the house and lands to go to the next son John, he to pay the bequests to brothers and sisters, and so on from one to another.

Residue to wife Jone, to dispose of as she pleases for the health of their souls. Exors. testator's brother William Gregory and his son Richard Whytbrede. Witn. sir William Dicson curate of Eversholt, John Brackeley.
Probate granted to Richard Whytbrede.

265.
John Holmes of Sandey. 14 Dec. 1529, pr. 24 Jan. 1530/1. [*sic*] (3: 21)
Burial in St. Swithune's churchyard, Sandey; for mortuary best beast as customary; to high altar for tithes forgotten 10s.; to mother church at Lincoln 4d.; to St. Katheringes light 20d.; to the sepulchre light 20d.; to the gilding of St. Thomas' tablernacle 20s.; to the bells 3s. 4d.; a priest is to sing a trental for testator in Sandey church within a year of his death.

To sister Annes a cow; to daughter Agnes 40s. to be given her at years of discretion, and if she die before this, a priest is to sing for souls of her and testator and of their good friends in Sandey parish church.

Residue to the discretion of wife Alys and Richard Boston. Exors. wife Alice and Richard Boston, who is to have 6s. 8d. for his pains. Witn. Thomas Draper, William Kateynge.

266.
Thomas Chessam of Margate (Markyate) in the parish of Studham. 6
Jan. 1529/30, pr. 24 Jan. 1530/1 [*sic*]. (3: 21d)

Burial in the church of St. Mary Stodham; for mortuary as manner
is of the town; to the high altar for tithes forgotten 12d.; to Our Lady
light 8d.; to the torches 8d.; to the bells 8d.; for a trental to be said for
souls of testator and all Christians 10s.; there is to be an annual charge
of 2s. out of the yearly value of his house to provide an obit for the
souls of testator and his wife for ever in Studham parish church.

To daughter Agnes one feather bed with a bolster and one coverlet
"and they to be nexte the best" and one "harneste" girdle; to sir Ralph
the son of his wife 3s. 4d..

To wife Jone for life testator's house and property in the town and
fields of Great Gansden, provided she remains single. If she remarries
then this to go to testator's right heirs.

To testator's son all his lands and tenements and he is to give to
Agnes, his sister, 20s. when he comes into possession.

Residue to wife Jone. Exors. wife Joan, John Wyght of Margate who
is to have 6s. 8d. for his labours. Witn. sir Roger Geffrey, Richard
Talor, William Myles.

267.
Edmund Thode. 6 Jan. 1529/30, pr. 14 Feb. 1530/1. [*sic*] (3: 21d)

His soul to Almighty God and his body for burial in churchyard of
All Hallowys in Ranolde; for his mortuary his best horse after the old
custom; to the mother church of Lincoln 2d.; to the high altar of
Ranolde for forgotten tithes 20d.; to the reparations of the church and
steeple 3s. 4d..

To each of his three children 40s., a cow and a sheep, and if any die,
the others are to have their part. His wife is to have the use of the
money and the cattle until the children come of age. To testator's
brother John a bullock; and to each godchild a sheep.

Residue to wife Agnes to pray for souls of testator and all
Christians. Executrix wife Agnes and brother Thomas. Overseer master vicar "my gostly father" "to be god to my chylderne and to my
wyffe". Witn. sir John Stuckeley vicar, Thomas Todye, Richard
Jurdane.

268.
Henry Fremann of the parish of Deane. 2 Feb. 1529/30. pr. 14 Feb.
1530/1 [*sic*]. (3: 22)

Burial in Deane churchyard; mortuary after custom and manner of
town; to mother church of Lincoln 4d.; to the high altar of Deane for
tithes forgotten 12d.; to reparation of four altars four sheep; to the bells

4 sheep; to the reparation of the leads 6s. 8d.; to an honest priest to pray for the souls of testator, his friends and all Christians in Deane church for one year £5 6s. 8d.; to the making of a stone bridge at Desbroke in Nether Deane 10s.; and he bequeathes "amongste pore men to remaine in a stoke perpetually at the order of 2 honeste and credable men" 10s.; to every godchild a sheep.

To eldest son John Freman testator's dwelling house and appurtenances in Nether Deane and his other house called Typpers with appurtenances; to his second son Richard his house with appurtenances in Ever Deane, a close called Brod Crose in Nether Deane, 4½ acres bought of Rayner, and a house in Beston; to youngest son William Freman testator's house and appurtenances in Denford and two houses in "Rynosted", 4 horses, 2 carts with the cart gear, plough and plough gear, 40 sheep with other goods to the value of a child's part. John, Richard and William are not to sell nor give any of the houses or lands except in need or poverty. If any of them die childless the lands etc. are to remain to the next of the blood from one to another to the longest liver.

To wife Agnes 40s. yearly from John, Richard and William and her dwelling "at hyr liberte frely".

Residue to wife to use for the pleasure of God and the profit of testator's soul and to see the will performed.

Exors. wife Agnes and son John Freman. Supervisor John Delingame. Witn. Harry Grene, Roger Hyeway, Richard Curtes, William Chandler.

269.
Harry Spene of Luton. 6 Mar. 1529/30, pr. 17 Mar. 1530/31 [*sic*]. (3: 22d)

Burial in churchyard of Our Lady in Luton; mortuary as the custom of town; to mother church of Lincoln 4d.; to the high altar in Luton for tithes forgotten 8d.; 20d. among the lights in Luton church; 3 solemn masses are to be sung at testator's burial day and at his month's day according to the custom in the church of Luton.

To each of his sons 40s. 13s. 4s. [*sic*]; to his sister Alis 3 sheep; to John the son of Alis 2 sheep; to Edward Chepeman the son of Edward Chepman 1 sheep; to Johan Petet testator's god–daughter 1 sheep; to William and Edward Spene, sons of William Spene of the Goworge Ende 1 sheep each; to testator's mother Elizabeth Spene 5 loads of wood and a flitch of bacon; to brother William Spene his best worsted coat; to brother John Spane his best gown.

Residue to wife Johan and to Edward Chepeman. Exors. wife Johan and Edward Chepeman, Edward to have 3s. 4d. for his trouble. Witn. sir Robert Bischppe, Thomas Peter, John Spane.

270.
Edward Fane of Elnestow. 20 Feb. 1529/30, pr. 18 Mar. 1530/1 [*sic*].
(3: 23)

Burial in the chapel of Saint Elyne in Elnestow; for mortuary as custom of town; to the mother church of Lincoln 4d.; to the high altar 12d.;
to the torches 2s.; to the bells 20d.; to the leads of Elnestow 10s.; to the
town bridge 3s. 4d..

To Margaret Lovell' a quarter of malt; to Elizabeth Ballard 6 bushels
of malt; to Alys Fane daughter of William Fan 6 bushels of malt; to
Joan Purney 6 bushels of malt; to Hugo Clowde a bullock 2 months old;
to each godchild 4d..

To son Edward a shod cart, a bare cart and cart gear, a plough and
plough gear and four horses the price of every horse 20s., and four oxen
as assigned by his executors.

To daughter Elinor Fan 20s..

To wife his house and appurtenances for her life, keeping it in repair
"tenand lyke" and after her death this to go to son Edward Fane and
the heirs of his body. If he die childless, then to daughter Elinor and the
heirs of her body. If both die childless then the house is to be sold to
provide a lawful priest to sing a whole year in Elnestow parish church
for the souls of Thomas Monk and Elizabeth his wife, Richard Fane,
the testator and all Christians, for which he is to be paid 10 marks, and
the rest of the money is to be used in "other gode dedes of marci" as
the executors think best. Residue to use for the good of testator's soul.

Exors. wife and John Fane. Supervisor William Ballard. John Fane
and William Ballard are to have 3s. 4d. each for their labours. Witn. sir
John Kinge parish priest, William Wolmore, William Salte.

271.
William Byndall of Eyworth. 3 Feb., pr. 17 Mar. 1529/30. (3: 23)

Burial in the parish churchyard of Eyworth; to the high altar of
Eyworth 2 bushels of barley; to the rood and to Our Lady's light two
bushels of barley; to the maintenance of the bells half a quarter of barley; for a trental to be done in "Heyworth" church for the souls of testator and all Christians 10s..

To testator's father £4, a mattress, a pair of sheets, a coverlet, a bolster, a pillow and a "huche". 20s. of the £4 is to be paid within one
month of testator's death, the rest in the next half year. Also he is to
have half an acre of wheat ready sown in the field of Eyworth, as he
chooses.

12s. is to be used to buy a cow to keep an obit for the souls of testator and all Christians once a year in Eyworth church to the value of
16d. a year, that is 8d. to the vicar for the bede-roll, *dirige* and requiem
mass; 2d. to the parish clerk; 1d. for wax; 1d. for an offering; and 4d.

to the "Rangarrys" (ringers) of the bells. The vicar and churchwardens are to have the management of the cow to see the obit is kept.

To Richard Mody 2 bushels of barley; to testator's sister Alys half a quarter of barley; to Alys Chylde 3 bushels of barley; to John Palmer 3s. 4d.; to each godchild a bushel of barley.

Residue, after debts are paid and his month day kept, to be divided into two parts, one part to wife and Walter and Robert the two children of her and testator, and the other part to be divided to be divided amongst the rest of testator's children.

To wife Elizabeth everything that was her own that she brought with her before testator married her, and also 2 pairs of sheets and a huche.

Exors. John Palmar of Heyworth and wife Elizabeth. Witn. sir John Lambe vicar of Eyworth, sir James Billingford, John Laurens, Walter Fyssher.

272.
John Gardner of Colmorth. 22 Feb., pr. 17 Mar. 1529/30. (3: 23d)

Burial in Colmorth churchyard; for mortuary as custom of town; to mother church of Lincoln 4d.; to high altar at Colmorth 6d.; to the bells 3s. 4d.; to a priest to pray for souls of testator, his wife and friends and all Christians for a year £5 6s. 8d.; six pounds of wax to make 2 or 3 tapers; to help make a bridge at "Ranoll" 3s. 4d..

To wife Agnes 20 sheep to be delivered at shearing time, 3 milch beasts and all manner of stuff which belongs to her chamber with all manner of pewter, brass and latten, and a pair of cob irons with a spit.

To son John Gardener the residue of household stuff, 2 horses and all manner of carts, ploughs and all things belonging to them and a heifer.

To son William Gardner to pray for testator 40s. and a heifer; to each of his other children a sheep; to godson John Synge a sheep; to godson John Gardner a sheep; to each of his other godchildren 4d..

Residue to be divided between wife Agnes and son John "he Kepenge hur honestly as longe as she doys leve".

Exors. wife Agnes and son John. Overseer sir William. Witn. sir Gregory Bun his curate, sir William Gardner, John Gardner.

273.
Thomas Wryght'. 19 Feb. 1529/30, pr. 17 Sept (no year). (3: 24)

Burial in churchyard of Crowley; for mortuary as custom and manner of the town; to mother church of Lincoln 2d.; to the repair of the high altar of Crole church one bushel of barley; to Our Lady's altar 4d.; to St. Katerin's altar 4d.; to the bells 4d.; to the torches 4d..

He wills that his son James, after the death of his mother, pays within the next ten years to his two sisters or their assigns 20s., that is 10s.

each, or else they shall have two roods lying upon Bruke Mead Furlong, Little Busche and a pightle in Gofyn.

Residue to wife Isobel for the term of her life. Exors. son James Wryght, godson Roger Crowche who is to have 8d. for his labours. Witn. Nicholas Abbot, John Grene, William Croch.

274.
Richard Loremar of Stotfolde. 28 Jan. 1528/9, pr. 5 Oct. 1529. (3: 24d)

Burial in the church of Our Lady St. Mary in Stotfold in the north aisle before Our Lady; for mortuary as custom of the town; to the mother church of Lincoln 4d.; to the high altar of Stotfold church half a quarter of barley; to the bells a quarter of barley; to Our Lady light in the high choir 2 bushels of barley; to the sepulchre light half a quarter of barley; to the rood light half a quarter of barley; to Our Lady light in the north aisle a cow; to Stotfold church towards a "forder" (load) of lead 20s.; to St. James' chapel 2 quarters of barley; to the "town Fyne of Stotfold" the house in which Awbury lives on the green for ever; "to the XV" as often as it shall be paid 13s. 4d. to be paid evermore by testator's heirs out of his lands and tenements.

His heirs are to pay out of his lands and tenements 13s. 4d. every year to keep an obit for souls of testator, his wife and his good friends. To the highways in Stotfold 20s..

Immediately after the death of his wife Elizabeth, his heirs are to hire a priest to sing for the souls of testator, his wife and his good friends in Stotfold church from Scher Thursday (Maundy Thursday) as long as 6s. 8d. lasts, and again from the Thursday before Whitsunday, for as long as 6s. 8d. lasts, for evermore at these two feasts.

To each godchild 2 bushels of barley.

To wife Elizabeth all lands and tenements for life "making no stepe nor waste" and after her death all is to go to Thomas Loremar and his heirs male, and if Thomas die without a son then to Richard Loremar his brother and his heirs male, and if he die to William Loremar testator's brother and his heirs male, and if all die without sons, then wife's executors, if they are alive or else the churchwardens of Stotfold advised by the prior of Newenham, shall sell the lands and use the money in Stotfold church for such ornaments as shall be most useful and necessary and in other charitable works, as they think best, for the good of the souls of the testator, his wife and their good friends.

To Edward Butler, his wife's son and his heirs male, the house testator bought of William Wigges, and if he die without a son, the house to revert to testator's heirs, as above. Residue to wife Elizabeth.

Exors. wife Elizabeth, and Master John Bowlys and Thomas Stepney of London, who are each to have 10s. for their labours. Overseer sir Edmund Bray and he to have 20s. for his labour. Witn. Nicholas

7. Brass of John and Alice Peddar of Salford and their sons and daughters.
John died in 1505, and his will is in *BHRS* vol. 37. The will of Alice Peddar,
proved in 1530, is no. 275 in this volume.   *Thomas Fisher.*

Loremar, Richard Thruston, Thomas Lelay, Robert Stankake, master the parson of Holcot, John Wadley, Edmund Emery.
Probate granted to executrix, master John Bowlys and Thomas Stepney refusing the executorship.

275.
Alys Pedder of Salford, widow. 20 Dec. 1529, pr. 12 May 1530. (3: 25d)
Burial in Salford church next to her husband John Pedder; for mortuary as the law wills; to mother church at Lincoln 6d.; to high altar in Salford church half a quarter of barley; to the bells 20d.; to the lamp before the rood a cow; to the lights before Our Lady in the chancel, Our Lady of Pity and St. Katerin, two kine, which with the other cow mentioned above are to be under the control of the churchwarden now and in the future, that with the increase of them the lights may be maintained for ever.
To the church of Salford a quarter of malt; to the light before St. Nicolas 2 bushels of barley; to the light before St. Christopher 2 bushels of barley; to the chapel of Our Blessed Lady of Wolbur 3s. 4d.; to the church of Holcot 3s. 4d.; to the church of Cramfelde 3s. 4d.; to the church of Mulso 3s. 4d.; to the church of Broughton 3s. 4d.; to the church of Medelton Keynes 3s. 4d.; to the church of Wavendon 3s. 4d.; to the church of Asplay Gyes 3s. 4d.; to the fraternity of Saint Margyt of Fenestratford 3s. 4d.; to the fraternity of Our Lady of Newport Pannell 3s. 4d.; to the friars of Dunstable 5s.; to the friars of Bedford 5s.; to each godchild a sheep or else 12d..
To John, William, Robert and Thomas Pedder the sons of Thomas Pedder testator's son, a bullock each, and if any die unmarried then his part to be given to his brothers who are alive; to Agnes her son's daughter a bullock; to each child of John White of Calcot two sheep, and if any die unmarried his part to be given to those that live; to each child of Thomas Cowper two sheep, and if any die unmarried his part to be given to those that live; to each child of John Robyns a bullock and if any die unmarried his part to be given to those who live.
To Alys Pedder her son's daughter, on the day of her marriage, £4, and if she die unmarried the £4 to be given to her sister M—— for her wedding day; to Agnes daughter of Thomas Whith a cow, and on her wedding day 13s. 4d.; to Alys Robyns on her wedding day £3 and if she die unmarried the £3 to remain to the use of her sister Mary; to Mary Robins on her wedding day 20s..
To each child of Harry Pedder two sheep, and if any die his part to remain to the use of the others who live; to Harry Pedder two oxen; to Thomas Pancost two bullock steers; to John Whiet of Calcot two oxen and £7 to be claimed from Thomas Whit of Manfeld, his brother, which he had borrowed from testator, and if he does not pay, John Whit is to

take an action against Thomas, in the name of testator's executors.

To Thomas White son of John Whit a bullock; to Thomas Whit son of Thomas Whit, to Richard Whit and to Elizabeth Whit a bullock each and if any die unmarried, his share to go to those living.

To testator's son sir William Pedder 20s.; and the residue to son Thomas Pedder.

Exor. son Thomas Pedder; overseers John Robins, Richard Eton each to have 6s. 8d.. Witn. Richard Newman, John Cesse, Thomas Hull, William Leche.

276.
Richard Puttnam. 20 May 1530, no note of probate. (3: 26d)

Burial in Toternow churchyard; to the high altar 8d.; to the glazing of a window in Toternoo 6s. 8d.; to Alis Nevell sister of testator, 13s. 8d.; to William Cowche testator's best doublet; to John Cowche his best coat.

To wife Elizabeth £10 on condition that she does not "let, trobell nor vex" testator's uncle John Puttnam from testator's house in Edisborow (Edlesborough, Bucks.) which testator sold to him with all the lands belonging to it, and if she does trouble him she is to get nothing.

Residue to uncle John Puttnam to bring testator "honestly in erth" and to do for the souls of testator, his friends and all Christians. Witn. sir Thomas Bottisford vicar, John Gefford, William Haryett, Thomas Aschewell.

277.
John Pryse of Flutwike. 29 Mar., pr. 12 May 1530. (3: 27)

Burial in Flitwike churchyard; to the mother church of Lincoln 12d.; to Our Lady's light in the chapel 4d.; for mortuary as customary; to the church porch at Flitwick 4d..

To son Robert a calf, a ewe and a lamb; to son William a calf, a ewe and a lamb; to daughter Anne a calf, a ewe and a lamb. Testator's wife is to keep these three calves two years. Residue to wife.

Executrix his wife. Supervisor Ranold Collope. No mention of witnesses.

278.
Thomas Browne. n.d., pr. 14 June 1530. (3: 27)

Burial in the churchyard of All Hallows, Kyngys Howghton. To the high altar for tithes forgotten a bushel of malt; to the torch light 2d.; to All Hallows light 2d.; to Our Lady light 2d.; to the gilding of Jesus half a bushel of malt.

To wife Julian his house with all implements and appurtenances and all his land except for one acre. To son William the one acre lying at the Morter Pitts, and a calf.

To son John a cow, and testator's house and lands after the death of wife, and if John die childless then William is to have all. If both die childless, the house and land are to be sold, and half given to a priest to sing for them, and half to be used for charitable works chosen by his executors, such as making of high ways or repairing of the church.

Exors. wife Jelian and Thomas Sponer, he to have 12d. for his trouble. Witn. Richard Howis, William Peret, William Turner.

279.
Thomas Knygh of Birchemore parish. 3 Apr., pr. 26 May 1530. (3: 27d)
Burial in the chapel of Our Blessed Lady of Woburne; to the chapel of Our Blessed Lady of Woburne 10s.; to the mother church of Lincoln 2d.; to the parish church of Birchemore 13s. 4d.; to the brethren of Woburne Abbey 13s. 4d.; to the friars of Bedford 20d.; to the friars of Dunstable 20d..

The residue to wife Agnes and brother-in-law Edward Stonton to be used for the health of souls of testator, his friends and all Christians. If Agnes die childless all such goods as she has from me are to be given to the children of Edward Stonton at the discretion of Edward Stonton or his assigns.

Exors. wife Agnes, and Edward Stonton. Witn. Robert Salford curate of Birchemore, John Cooke of Woburne.

280.
Gregory Compton. 26 May 1530, no note of probate. (3: 27v)
Burial in Bromham churchyard. To Thomas Morgan his best coat; to Nicholas Morgan a quarter of malt that he owes testator, and he is to be good and true to testator's soul; to Thomas More a coat "next the best" and half a quarter of malt, to be true to his soul; to brother Robert a colt and a cow; to brother William a colt and a cow; to father-in-law the third part of testator's crop, to be good to his mother, and the tilth of his land which his master dressed for him. His executors are to do a trental for souls of himself and his father. Residue to brothers Robert and William.

Exors. Nicholas Morgan, Thomas Mur. Witn. Thomas Berd, Margere Grene his mother, Elius Morgan.

281.
John Russell of Stephinton. 26 Nov. 1529, no note of probate. (3: 28)
Burial in Our Lady churchyard at Steventon; for mortuary as custom requires; to mother church at Lincoln 4d.; to the high altar at Steventon 16d.; to Steventon church roof 6s. 8d.; to the sepulchre light 12d.; to the rood light half a pound of wax; to the Trinity light half a pound of wax; to Our Lady light in the chapel half a pound of wax; to St. John light

half a pound of wax; to Our Lady of Pity half a pound of wax; to the lights of Our Lady and St. Peter in the choir a pound of wax; to the bells half a quarter of barley; to four bridges that is Turvey, Harwolde, Bedenham and Stafford 2 bushels of barley each.

To son Robert a cow, 2 sheep and 2 hives of bees "at his mother's deliverans"; to daughter Annes 2 sheep and 2 hives of bees, to daughter Margery Purrey 13s. 4d.; and the residue to wife Alis.

Executors wife Alis and son Robert. Supervisor sir Thomas Botall who is to have 4s. for his labours. Witn. Robert Taylor, Nicholas Talor, Robert Ratwell.

282.

George Acworth of Todington. 31 May 1530, no note of probate. (3: 28d)

Burial in the church of Luton near the sepulture of his father; to the cathedral church of Lincoln 4d.; to the high altar of St. George at Todington 8d.; to every other one of the altars in the said church 2s.; there shall be 14 priests and 9 clerks at his burial and each priest shall receive 12d. and his dinner, and each clerk 8d..

Wife Margaret is to pay testator's daughter Frances the £10 which testator promised her at her marriage; to daughter Anna Cornwell £3 6s. 8d.; to son George his damask gown; to son Thomas his "senet [or seuet] of golde" and his gown furred with "fownys"; to daughter Joan, after death of his wife, 3 silver goblets and one covering, his best salt with the cover, and 12 silver spoons; to John Cornewell his gown furred with fox.

If his brother Thomas continues with testator's wife Margaret he shall have his keep and 26s. 8d. in money, and if Thomas leaves Margaret she shall give him £3 6s. 8d. "and so to be discharched of hem for hever".

To Laurence Wharton 40s.; to Elizabeth Browche 40s.; to Gilbert Myris 6s.; to William Lincolne 6s. 8d.; to John Ward 6s. 8d.; to Thomas Minor his tawney coat without sleeves and his best "lacke" hose; to John Horsley his best "kyndell" coat and to his wife Katherine Horsley one of the weaning calves; to Ciceley Simson 2 kine; to Miles Foreste a cow and a calf; to William Abbot his best russet coat and to Anne Abbot his wife a cow; to sir John Bage 3s. 4d..

Residue to wife Margaret, who is to be executrix. Supervisor the right worshipful Sir Henry Grey, to whom testator gives his dun gelding. Witn. sir William Browge, sir John Bage, William Abbot, John Horsley. Given at Todington.

283.

John Massam of Bedford. 10 Feb. 1529/30, no note of probate. (3: 29)

Burial in churchyard of St. Paul in Bedford; to the high altar for tithes forgotten 20d.; to the mother church of Lincoln 4d..

To wife Elizabeth his tenement in Bedford for her life, and after her death to testator's daughter Elizabeth and her children, and should she die childless, then the house is to be sold to provide a priest to sing for the souls of himself, his wife and all Christians, as testator's curate and ghostly father thinks best, in whom he puts a special trust to see this done.

He wills that his feoffees "that stand in strenth" of his house give an estate to testator's wife and daughter when necessary, without "trobell or let".

Residue to wife Elizabeth and to daughter Elizabeth to be divided between them, his wife to have the first choice in all things.

Executors to be testator's wife Elizabeth and his brother Fethgeffray to aid and comfort her, and to collect debts, for which he is to have half the debts and "dweteys belonging the bell that I send him to London" in return for his work. Supervisor "the forsaid curat". Witn. Master John Bard "vicar of Polles", sir Thomas Negaus, William Berd, Richard Burton.

284.
John Lord of Potton. 20 June 1530, no note of probate. (3: 29d)

Burial in parish churchyard of Potton; to high altar for tithes forgotten 12d.; to the bells 2s..

To wife Margaret for life, the cottage where testator lives, with all his arable lands lying in the fields of Potton. His son John is to till and "compose" (compost) the land yearly, and carry all such grain grown on the same to the use of wife for her lifetime, at his own expense, provided that she finds seed each year for the same, and the felling is at her own charge.

To wife Margaret all moveable household stuff in his cottage to do with as she pleases, and all such grain as grows on testator's own lands together with half an acre of pease, a rood of wheat and a rood of meslin, which testator hired from son John. To her also two beasts, a ewe and a lamb, and all testator's clothes except his best gown and jacket.

To son John Lorde all other moveable stuff (not household goods) and the messuage where he lives, on condition that "he be of god and honest behavior and thryvenge". If not, Walter Worlich is to sell it and use the proceeds for charitable purposes. To son John also testator's best gown and best jacket.

To Elizabeth ?Fyne, his cottage in Gamlagay on condition that she and her husband allow testator's son John to enjoy the messuage testator bought of them in Potton. If at any time they make any claim on this estate, testator's executor's are to sell the cottage in Gamlegay and use the money for souls.

To son-in-law Robert Johnson 13s. 4d. and to Agnes his wife one harnessed girdle. Residue to son John.

Exors. son John and Walter Worlich. Witn. sir William Atkinson,
Richard May.

285.
John Franckling the elder of Maston. 1530, pr. 24 June 1530. (3: 30)

Burial in churchyard of Maston; to high altar a bushel of barley; to
Our Lady within the chancel a bushel of barley; to St. Thomas a bushel
of barley; to the bells two bushels of barley; to the rood light a bushel
of barley; to St. John a bushel of barley.

All the implements in his house which were once his father's are to
remain to the use of testator's son William, and failing William, to son
Thomas. To son Thomas a dun horse.

To son William and his heirs testator's house, close and all arable
land and meadow belonging to it, and if William die childless then to
Thomas and his heirs, and if Thomas die childless to daughter Jone for
her lifetime, and then to testator's brother John and his heirs.

To his wife Elizabeth the house which has been left to William until
he reaches the age of 21, and she is to repair such houses as are now
upon the ground.

His executors are to divide his cattle between his wife and children.
His wife is to have the crop on the ground to support his children.
Residue between his wife and his children, at the discretion of his execu-
tors.

Exors. Robert Odill, Richard Parkinges. Witn. Brian Medelton priest,
Thomas Mowse, Thomas Morys.

286.
Thomas Packe of Steventon. 17 June, pr. 8 Aug. 1530. (3: 30d)

Burial in the churchyard of Our Blessed Lady of Steventon; to the
mother church at Lincoln 4d.; to the high altar at Steventon 3s. 4d.; to
the rood light a pound of wax; to the two tapers of the sepulchre two
pounds of wax; to the five tapers in Our Lady chapel "to be repared
agane and to burne styll ther"; to the torches two pounds of wax; to the
bells 12d..

To wife Johan all the goods that she brought to testator which are
left, and also 6s. 8d. and two kine, a black cow and a red hued cow; to
son Thomas Pack his best brass and a spruce coffer; to cousin Richard
West a calf weaned this year; to cousin Margery West a brass pan with
all other trash; to testator's daughter Margaret a coffer with a "virgins
barrell"; to Margaret West aforesaid two bee hives and testator's best
cow; to Simund West, his son-in-law, two bee hives and a cow; to John
Barbor a bee hive and to his wife another bee hive. Residue to son

Thomas Packe and to cousin Margery West to use them for the good of souls of testator and all Christians.

Exors. son Thomas Packe and cousin Robert Packe. Supervisor sir Thomas Botell vicar of Steventon, who is to have 3s. 4d.. Witn. sir William Gybon clerk, Johan Williams, George North.

287.
Jane Trat widow of Richard Trat of Milton Harnes. 24 June, pr. 8 Aug. 1530. (3: 31)

Burial in All Hallows churchyard, Mylton Harnes; to the high altar of All Hallows church for tithes and oblations forgotten 20d.; to maintaining a light before St. Katherine a ewe and a lamb; to maintaining a light before Our Lady in the north aisle of Allhallows church a ewe and a lamb; to the church of Allhallows testator's great chest so that it be not sold; to the finishing of the work about the church 6s. 8d..

To daughter Jane a coverlet and a bolster; to god-daughter Katherine Lintford a shearhog sheep; to god-daughter Alis Lintford a pewter platter and testator's best cap; to godson Thomas Tappe a lamb hog. To son John Trat the residue of her goods to dispose of for the health of the souls of the testator and her ancestors.

To son John all messuages, lands, tenements, pastures, meadows and leys in the town, fields and parish of Mylton for life, and at his death the lands and tenements are to be sold to Jane Est testator's daughter at the market price, and this money is to be used to find a priest to sing for the souls of Richard Trat and Jane his wife as long as it lasts.

Residue to son John, to use for the wealth of her soul. Exors. John Trat, William Gylmen. Supervisor Phillip Parker. Witn. Francis Lews, Robert Tappe, Richard Lancaster.

288.
John Crowley of Luton. 30 June, pr. 8 Aug. 1530. (3: 31d)

Burial in Luton church; to the high altar for tithes forgotten 3s. 4d.; to mother church at Lincoln 6d.; to every standing light in the church 4d..

To son Richard testator's house in the South End of the town of Luton with all appurtenances; to son Thomas testator's house and land in the parish of Wotton in the Vale; to brother William 20 quarters of barley; to brother Thomas 20 quarters of barley.

The residue is to be divided equally into three parts: the first to testator's wife Annes; the second to his five children, John, Richard, Thomas, William and Annes Crowley in equal portions; the third to his executors to pay testator's debts and to use in deeds of charity for the health of his soul.

Executors Thomas Monyngham, William Aukke (or Ankke) each of whom to have 20s. for his labours. Witn. sir William Baston testator's confessor, John Thrall, John Weye, John Day, William Dyer.

289.
Richard Fyssher of Potton yeoman. 30 Mar., pr. 16 Sep. 1530. 3: 32)
Burial in the parish church or churchyard of Potton, as his executors and supervisor decide; to the high altar of the parish church for duties forgotten 3s. 4d.; to the bells 3s. 4d.; to the sepulchre light 3s. 4d.; to the torches 16d..

To wife Annes the house which testator inhabits and all other lands and tenements with appurtenances in Potton parish for her life, without impediment of waste. She may do as she wishes with his moveable goods. After her death all lands, rents and tenements with their liberties are to go to Richard Rysse and his wife or his heirs, together with the meadows and pastures in the town of Potton, and Richard Rysse shall pay £60 for it within 6 years after death of testator and his wife "of wiche sume I have resaved in part of payment of the said Richard Rysse £6 14s.".

Testator excepts from the above bequests his house with the croft adjoining in Horslay Stret, about 2 acres with house and croft, which he leaves after the death of his wife to Thomas Awbre and his wife for life, and they shall pay 6s. 8d. yearly to every obit kept in Potton church for the souls of testator and his wife. If this is not paid the brotherhood of Potton is to take it and observe the obit for testator and his wife. After the death of Thomas Awbre and his wife the house and croft are to go to the brotherhood and guild for ever to pray for testator, his wife, and all his kinsfolk and friends.

To the brotherhood of Potton £10 to be prayed for.
To brother Hugh Fysscher 40s.; to Hugh Barker and his children 40s.; to testator's sister Margaret 40s.; to Agnes Boram 20s.; to William Fysscher testator's close called Schepecot close after wife's death; to god-son Thomas Burgon £6 13s. 4d..

On his burial day he leaves 40s. to be bestowed for the health of his soul as his executors advise, and another 40s. to be given to priests to sing masses for his soul within 3 days after his burial.

To his wife all his household stuff for life and after her death one half to his kinsfolk and one half as his wife chooses for the health of her soul.

Residue to his executors and supervisor to order it for the health of the souls of testator and his wife.

Exors. wife Annys, together with Richard Clarke and Alan Dalane, both of whom are to have 20s. for their labour. Supervisor Richard Rysse who is to have 20s. for his labour. Witn. Master William Atkynson vicar of Potton, Master Charles Witton of Christ's College

Cambridge, Richard Manlay, Alan Caverley, Joan Gad, Thomas Albery, William [?]Cheller.

290.
John Bromham the elder of Cleifton. 28 May 1515, pr. 8 Aug. 1530. (3: 33)
   Burial in All Hallows churchyard Clifton; to the high altar of Clifton church for tithes and oblations forgotten a bushel of barley; to the mother church of Lincoln 2d.; to the bells a bushel of barley; to Elizabeth his wife his "heid tenement weche I dwellin" with all lands and appurtenances belonging to it for her lifetime, and all his household stuff and all his cattle. John his son and his heirs are to have the house and lands after the death of his wife. The residue to his son John.
   Executor son John. Witn. sir Richard Sparling, Robert Audley, Thomas Ensham.

291.
William Deane of Todington. 15 Aug. 1530, no note of probate. (3: 33)
   To be buried "within cristen beriall"; to high altar of parish of Todington for tithes forgotten 4d.; to the light of St. George within the chancel 4d.; to the light of Our Lady within the chancel 4d.; to the light of St. Katerin 4d.; to the rood light 4d.; to St. James' light 4d.; to the brotherhood of Assherege [Ashridge, Herts.] to sing half a trental of masses for testator's soul 5s..
   Executor Thomas Clarke of Todington who is to dispose of the residue as he thinks best for testator's soul. Witn. sir John Denet curate, sir John Bagerd, John Barker, William Wells.

292.
William Burre of Eyton (Bray). 20 Jun. 1530, pr. 13 Nov. 1530. (3: 33d)
   Burial in Eyton churchyard; to mother church of Lincoln 2d.; to the high altar 3s. 4d.; to the Trinity light 4d.; to the sepulchre light 4d.; to Our Lady light 4d.; to St. Nicholas' light 4d.; to the bells 4d.; to the torches 8d.; to the highways 3s. 4d..
   To each of his children's children 4d.; to all other his godchildren 1d. each; to daughter Juliana Warlose a bushel of wheat and a bushel of malt; to John Pirton his best gown; to Elene Pirton his daughter 2 ewe sheep "to increase to the behuffe of her childerne".
   To wife Joan the tenement where testator lives with 8 acres of land, and another tenement called Belsers in the East Street with appurtenances for her lifetime. If she marries then she is to have the tenement where testator lives and the 8 acres of land for her lifetime, but the tenement called Belsers is to go to testator's son Raffe. To his wife also all

his lands and tenements with the copyhold called Palmers for life, if she stays single. After her death the house called Belsers in East Street with the lands are to go to his son Raffe Burre and to his heirs, and the house where testator lives with the 8 acres of land and the copyhold called Palmers to go to Edmund Cooke, the son of Richard Cowke of Eyton, and if Edmund die without heirs male, this land and houses are to go to John Cowke his brother and to his heirs male, and if he dies without heirs male then to Richard Cowke, brother of John and to his heirs male, and to all the heirs male of testator's daughter Alis the wife of Richard Cowk. For lack of male heirs, the lands and houses shall remain to testator's son Ralph Burre and his heirs for ever. It is agreed that Richard Cowke, the father of Edmund, John and Richard shall pay £5 to testator's wife Joan to perform his will, pay his debts, and to have 3 trentals sung within 3 years in Eyton church for the souls of testator, his wife and all Christians. Joan Burre is to keep an annual *dirige* with the bede-roll in Eyton church and is to keep his tenements in repair during her life.

Residue to wife Joan to dispose for the health of his soul.

Exors. wife Joan and son-in-law Richard Cowke. Overseer Master Thomas Tomlingson vicar. Witn. Henry George, John Fuller, Richard Broke, Raffe Burre, sir John Hewet.

293.
Robert Squere of Astwik. 8 Oct. 1530, no note of probate. (3: 34)

Burial in the church porch of Astwik, beside his father; to the high altar for tithes forgotten 12d.; to mother church of Lincoln 2d.; to the maintenance of Astwike church one quarter of barley.

To wife Annes all his household stuff, corn and cattle, four of his best horses and all his lands for her life, as long as she remains single, and after [*words omitted*]. To John his son the elder, 7 acres of land in both fields for him and his assigns after death of wife. To son Henry 7 acres of land in both fields after death of wife. To son Nicolas 7 acres of land in both fields after death of wife. To son Henry 2 horses and the newest shod cart. To son Richard a shod cart and 2 horses. Sons Richard and Henry are to have and occupy testator's farm for his years, between them paying the rent and finding the seed.

Wife Annes is to pay testator's daughter Elizabeth Jeffe 40s.. Son Henry is to have one "lese and a backe" to graze his beasts upon, but testator wills that he does not inherit them.

To Squer and John the younger, testator's sons, both testator's closes and the residue of his lands in Astwike fields, and they are to find a priest to sing for the souls of the testator and his good friends for half a year, and to do two trentals costing 20s., and to keep one obit yearly in Astwike church for ever, giving 3s. 4d. at the obit.

William Rowffe the elder and John Cowper of Astwike are to divide his lands equally between all his sons according to his will after the death of his wife.

Exors. sons Richard. Squer and John. To daughter Joan 40s. within his wife's lifetime. To his maid Annes a quarter of barley after his death, and a cow after the death of his wife. To John Adone a yearling after testator's death.

Witn. sir Edmund Bowman, William Reffe the elder, John Cowper, William Brekeley, William Tomson.

294.

Master William Westerdaile bachelor of canon law and parson of the church of St. George in Edworth. 18 Aug. 1530, note of probate but no date. (3: 34d)

Burial in the chancel of the church before the high altar; to mother church of Lincoln 12d.; to the fraternity of the guild of Bekelliswade 20 marks, to be paid to the guild priest as long as it lasts, on condition that the wardens of the guild maintain the farms and tenements belonging to the fraternity during this time and give an account of them to testator's executors.

To the chapel of St. Peter of Holme 6s. 8d.; to the chapel of Straton 13s. 4d.; to the church of Edworth one chalice worth £3; for his funeral expenses at the discretion of his executors.

To Robert Milward of Edworth 2 quarters of barley; to William Wodward of Edworth 2 quarters of barley; to William Taylor and Joanne his wife and his heirs a tenement in Bekellswad called Birtes with three half yardlands "that the said William hath". To testator's kinswoman Alice Martiall and her heirs one tenement in Shortmede Strete next the tenement once Haywardes. To Annes Swenoo daughter of William Swenoo, and her heirs, a tenement in Bekillswaid that Richard Wryght lives in, and the house with the yard that was Byrchefordes, when she is 17 years old, and meanwhile his executors are to receive the profits of it, and if she die before the age of 17, then his executors are to sell it for the health of the souls of testator and all Christians.

To the fraternity of Bekellswaide one messuage in the Backe Layne, sometime Langfords of Bekellswaide, next the messuage once Henry Cowper's, with the land belonging to it.

To William Sells, to be paid in money to buy him 2 oxen, 20s.; to Joanne Lymer in money 6s. 8d.; to his servant Elizabeth Sawnder a kirtle, two smocks, two kerchiefs and in money 3s. 4d..

To William Swenoo and his heirs half a burgage in Bekellswaide which lies between Thomas Kettes and testator's own ground, and also 40s. provided that he is content with the will and does not trouble testator's executors, but if he does trouble them, the executors shall use the 40s. for testator's soul.

Residue to Master Francis Pegotte, William Colmorth gentleman and Henry Whithed to use for the souls of testator, his father and mother and all Christians.

Exors. Master Francis Pegotte, William Colmorth, Henry Whithed, and Master Pegot to have 26s. 8d., William Colmorth 20s., and Henry Whithed 20s.. Witn. sir Water Wyghton, sir Edmund Bowman, Francis Moris, William Selles.

295.
John Harding the elder of Aspley Gyse. 29 Oct. 1530, no note of probate. (3: 35)

Burial in the churchyard of the parish church of Aspley; to the mother church of Lincoln 4d..

To maintain a light before St. Peter in Aspley church for ever one cow for a stock; to the church of Husbande Crowley one cow for a stock for ever from the rent of which the present vicar and his successors shall have 6d. every Whitsonday for *dirige* and bede-roll, the residue to Our Lady light; to Our Lady Chapel in Woborne one cow to maintain a light before her for ever; to the church of Litell Brekhill one cow for a stock to maintain a light before Our Lady of Pity there; to All Hallows Bow Brekehill a cow to maintain a light before Allhallows; to Wandon parish church one cow for a stock to maintain a light before Our Lady for ever; to an honest priest to sing for the souls of testator, his wife and all Christians in Asply church for a year £5 6s. 8d.; to every priest of the convent of the monastery of Woburne 4d..

To Robert Harding, son of John Harding, on his father's death, one house with appurtenances in Litell Brekehill called Danells house; to William Harding, son of John Harding, one house in Little Brekhill called Daniells house [*sic*].

To Ellen Estamforth one house in Hosburne Crowley with appurtenances called Stokes Howse and if she die childless it shall go to Henry Estamforth, her brother, and if he die childless then it shall go to testator's son John Harding and his heirs.

To John Harding the younger, testator's son's son, a copyhold in Litell Brickhill of 4 nobles a year.

To Ellen Estamforth 2 kine, one pot and one pan; to every godchild one sheep; to Henry Estamforth 2 sheep; to Bery Lane 40d..

To testator's daughter Luce half a hundred sheep, an acre of rye, a half acre of wheat, a shod cart, one cow, one mare and the residue of his household stuff to be divided equally between John and Luce.

To Richard Bull of Woborne and his wife "all seche stuffe as is lying in ther howse at Woburne". To Thomas Kent 2 steers.

Residue to son John Harding. Exor. son John Harding to dispose of goods for his soul's health. Overseer sir Richard Birche vicar of Husband Crawley, and he is to have for his labours 20s.. Witn. sir Richard Birche, Robert Hunt, John Potter.

296.
Michael Mosse of Kinghes Houghton. 12 Oct. 1530, note of probate but no date. (3: 35d)
    Burial in Allhallows churchyard in Houghton; to the mother church of Lincoln 2d.; to the high altar of Houghton church 12d.; to every gathered light in Houghton church 2d.. Residue to son John and Richard Typladye. Exors. son John and Richard Typladye to dispose of testator's goods for the health of his soul, and Richard is to have for his labours 3s. 4d..
    To wife Joan testator's house and lands for her life, and after her death to son John and his heirs and assigns. Son John is to be guided by Master William Fossey vicar of Houghton and by Richard Typlady.
    Overseer Master William Fossey who is to have 40d.. Witn. John Gud, Richard Welbe, John Smyth.

297.
Thomas Tomms otherwise called Thomas Mody of Hach' in the parish of Northivell. 16 Aug. 1530, note of probate but no date. (3: 36)
    Burial in churchyard of Our Lady Saint Mary in Northivell; for his principal after the custom of the parish; to the high altar of Northivell 3s. 4d. and a pair of sheets; to Our Lady in the chancel 5s.; to the church of Northivell a quarter of barley; to the torches a quarter of barley; to the bells half a quarter of barley; to St. Anne in the chapel of Northivell church a brown cow; to the mother church of Lincoln 6d.; a priest is to celebrate for as long as 10 marks lasts, for the most part in the chapel of St. Anne; to the college of Our Lady in Northivell three half-acres of barley and an acre of pease; to the church of Blounham 3s. 4d.; to the church of Sanday 3s. 4d.; to the church of Temsford 3s. 4d.; to the church of Northivell 3s. 4d.; to the mother church at Lincoln 6d..
    To every godchild a bushel of barley; to Broke Lane 12d.; to John Tomms a quarter of malt, a quarter of pease. 2 hogs, 4 yards of russet and a yard and a half of kersey, 4 sheep and a horse; to John Tomms the elder 2 kine one red and one black, and a colt and "the mony that cane be maid of a shode cart"; to William Fyssher a ewe and a lamb; to the poorest people in Northivell 12 bushels of malt; to John Mauddying a russet coat; to William Tylbroke a sleeveless coat; to Elizabeth Smyth a pair of sheets, 2 pewter dishes and a coverlet; to Alice Topsale, 2 pairs of sheets, a coverlet and a brass pot and 2 platters and "the courser materesse"; for ten masses "to distrubut" for testator's soul

4d.; to Gyrford Lane 12d.; to Richard Gray of Langford a black cow; to Margaret Gray a weaning calf; to John Gray a cart body and a plough with the share and 2 hogs. Residue to executors to be used for the health of testator's soul.

Exors. Robert Persell, Robert Carter, Richard Greye and each to have 6s. 8d. for his pains. Supervisor sir William Swetbone who is to have 5s. for his pains. Witn. John Tomms, Walter Sharpe, William Fyssher.

298.
John Fresbey of Potton. 8 Nov. 1530, pr. 20 Oct. 1530 [*sic*]. (3: 36)

Burial in the parish churchyard of Potton; to the high altar for tithes forgotten 6s. 8d.; to the bells 12d..

To wife Annes for the term of her life the house testator lives in with the close to the Dowhowse and after her death to Bertlmew Fresbey testator's son and his heirs, and if he die childless then to second son William Fresbe.

To wife Annys the house called Lilleys until son William is 24 years old, which then goes to William and his heirs. If either son die under 24 then the survivor to have both the houses with their appurtenances, provided that his wife has them for life. If both sons die childless then both houses are to be sold by Walter Worlys or his executors and the money is to be divided equally among testator's daughters, provided as much of the profits as is deemed necessary by his executors is used for the health of his soul.

To wife Annes the lease and years of Cawdwell land which testator bought of Master John Burgoyn.

His office of the bailiwick of Potton he leaves to his wife Annes and he wills she shall occupy it by "the overseght, consent and agrement" of Walter Worlich.

To daughter Elizabeth Fresbey a cow, 4 sheep, a mattress, a pair of sheets and a coverlet; to daughter Annes Fresbe 6 sheep and one calf; to daughter Alice Fresbey 20s. provided she be of "onest" behaviour.

To John Fresbe testator's father, every year as long as he lives 26s. 8d. to be paid half-yearly, and 5 marks to be paid within 5 years. Residue to wife Annes.

Exors. wife Annes and Walter Worlis. Witn. sir William Atkynson vicar of Potton, Thomas Pokerell.

GLOSSARY

Ambry, Aumbry: cupboard or place to keep food.
Ark: wooden chest or bin for dry stores.
Auger: tool for boring holes in wood.
Beads (pair of): a string of beads used to keep count of prayers.
Bede roll: list of benefactors to the church, for whose souls the faithful were asked to pray.
Camlet: originally a costly eastern fabric, afterwards imitations and substitutes.
Canvas: A fine unbleached cloth made of flax or hemp and used for sheets and clothing.
Chafing-dish: a vessel to hold burning charcoal or other fuel, for heating food.
Chantry: an endowment for the maintenance of one or more priests to say mass for the souls of the founders or other particular persons.
Charger: large flat dish for serving meat.
Cobbard: two iron bars having knobs at the upper end to rest upon the andirons.
Cob-iron: one of the irons on which a spit turns.
Cleat, "cletes": wedge-shaped piece of wood.
Cope: a vestment of silk or other material resembling a long cloak made of a semi-circular piece of cloth.
Counterpoint: a quilted cover for a bed, a counterpane.
Damask: a rich silk fabric woven with elaborate designs and figures, often of a variety of colours.
Diaper: a linen fabric woven with a small and simple pattern, formed by the different directions of the thread.
Dirige: the first word of the antiphon at matins in the office of the dead, and used as a name for that service.
Fenestral, "fenestre": small window, often made of paper, cloth or canvas.
Foins: trimmings or garments made of the fur of the beech-marten.
Frieze: a coarse woollen cloth with a nap, usually on one side only.
Frontlet: something worn on the forehead, an ornament or band.
Fustian: a coarse cloth of cotton and flax.
Gaud: one of the larger and more ornamental beads placed between the decades of "aves" in a pair of beads or rosary.
Handles, "handillys": wooden devices in which teasels were set for raising the nap on cloth.
Harnessed: mounted with silver or other metal.
Hog, Hoggett: generally sheep of either sex from six months old until the first shearing.
Kendal: a species of green woollen cloth (from Kendal in Westmorland, the place of manufacture).
Kerchief: cloth used to cover head.
Kersey: coarse narrow cloth, woven from long wool and usually ribbed.

179

Latten: a mixed yellow metal, resembling brass.
Mark: 13s. 4d. in money.
Mortmaining: providing that lands granted to an ecclesiastical body were thenceforth exempt from various civil dues and taxes, as regulated by the Statute of Mortmain.
Mortuary or principal: a gift or offering due by custom to the incumbent of a parish from the estate of a deceased parishioner.
Obit: office (usually a mass) performed in commemoration of, or on behalf of the soul of a deceased person, on the anniversary or other mind day of his death.
Pillowbere: pillowcase.
Placebo: in the Latin rite, the name commonly given to vespers in the office for the dead, from the first word of the first antiphon.
Posnet: a small metal pot or vessel for boiling, having a handle and three feet.
Pricket: candlestick with a spike on which the candle was impaled.
Principal: *see* Mortuary.
Pug or Puxes: a second-year ewe lamb or lambs.
Rail: neckerchief worn by a woman.
Russet: russet-coloured, a reddish brown.
Shod cart: a cart having wheels edged with metal.
Standards: permanent furnishings or fixtures to remain in a house.
Strike (of barley): a bushel.
Tabernacle: canopied niche or recess in a wall or pillar, to contain an image.
Tenter: wooden framework on which cloth was hung with weights after milling.
Trental: a set of thirty requiem masses, said on the same day or on different days.
Trundle (Trendle): round lump of wax.
Tunicle: ecclesiastical vestment.

ABBREVIATIONS

B.H.R.S.   The Bedfordshire Historical Record Society
Exors.   Executors
Pr.   Proved
Witn.   Witnesses

INDEX OF PERSONAL NAMES

In the indexes the number given is that of the will, unless otherwise stated.
Under personal names, italic type denotes a testator.

Abbot(t), Agnes, 26; Ann, 282; Elizabeth, 26;
    Henry, 26, John, 11, 26, 206; Nicholas, 26,
    273; William, 198, 282.
Abolton, Abotton, John, 172; Katharine, 115;
    Richard, 115.
Abyngton, Geoffrey, 87; John, 179.
Achurch, John, 75.
Acotton, Thomas, 169.
Acworth, Frances, 282; George, 62, *George, 282*;
    Joan, 282; Margaret, 282; Thomas, 282.
Adam(s), Maud, 111; Robert, 111; Thomas, 49;
    – – –, 197.
Adone, John, 293.
Akirk, William, 9.
Albany, Alice, 78; Elizabeth, 78; Henry, 78;
    Joan, 78; *John*, 78; sir Robert, 78; William,
    78.
Albright, William, 103.
Alcok, Thomas, 171.
Aldrige, Aldrich, Aldrith. Thomas, 160, 165,
    186.
Alec, Robert, 133.
Alee, A Lee, Agnes, 90; *Robert, 90.*
Alkyn, William, 204, 225.
Allen, Alen, Aleyn, Alyn, Bartholomew, 194;
    Edmund, 104; Henry, 163; Hugh, 104;
    Joan, 157; James, 17; Joan, 130; John, 17,
    42, 157, *John, 130*; Richard, 157; Robert,
    128, 157; sir Robert, 125, 149; *Roger, 17*;
    Thomas, 17, 130, 157; William, 17, 29,
    William, 157; sister, 165.
Amery, Amere, Amore, *see also* Emery, Agnes,
    74; John, 94, 118, 180, 199; *William, 74.*
Amps, William, 162.
Amyot, Richard, 131.
Andrew, John, 143.
Angold, John, 11.
Annis, Margaret, 263.
Ap David, Mathew, 115.
Archebold, sir Bartholomew, 139, 140.
Archer, Archar, Agnes, 60, 85, 244; Christian,
    60, 85; Henry, 60, 85, 244; John, 85;
    Richard, 60, 85; *Thomas, 60*, Thomas, 130.
Ardren, Alice, 154; Margaret, 154; William,
    154.
Arnold, Elizabeth, 10; Margery, 10; *Matthew,
    10*, Matthew, 145; Richard, 10.
Asshwell, Aschewell, Hasshwell, sir John, 170;
    John, 136; Richard, 212; Robert, 158, 164;
    Thomas, 276.

Astlyn, John, 68.
Atkyns, William, 212.
Atkynson, Alice, 195; Margaret, 195; *Richard,
    195*; sir Steven, 223; William, 195, sir
    William, 35, 86, 195, 284, 289, 298.
Atpownd, Margaret, 112; *Thomas, 112.*
At Slow, William, 174.
Aukke, William, 288.
Aulaby, Aunaby, Aunelby, Agnes, 81; Amy, 81;
    Jane, 81; John, 81; Margaret, 81; *Thomas,
    81.*
Awbury, Albery, Awbere, Awbre, John, 14;
    Richard, 72; Thomas, 289; – – –, 274.
Awdley, Audley, John, 90; Robert, 290.
Awngell, John, 54.
Awnncell, William, 146.
Awnsty, John, 94.
Awstyn, John, 180.
Aylbourne, Thomas, 9.
Aynsam, Eynsam, Alice, 146; *John, 146*,
    Mathew, 146.

Bager, Bage, Bagerd, sir John, 101, 282; John,
    291.
Bak– – –, John, 2.
Baker, John, 50, 100, 119, 170, 179, 193;
    Robert, 148.
Bakster, John, 178.
Baleit, sir *John, 240.*
Ball(e), Agnes, 184, 254; Edith, 184; Elizabeth,
    254; Ellen, 254; Joan, 184, 191; John, 184,
    194, 254, *John, 191*; Margaret, 191, 254;
    Richard, 184, Richard, 191, 254; *Stephen,
    254*; Thomas, 191, 254; William, 191, 194,
    254.
Ballard, Bolard, Elizabeth, 270; William, 251,
    270.
Bamford, sir Thomas, 135, 196–7.
Barbour, Barber, Barbur, *see also* Momford
    alias Barbour, Bartholomew, 125; Ellen,
    149; John, 113, 134, 159, 263, 286;
    Margaret, 149; Margery, 159; Ralph, 228;
    Richard, 145; Thomas, 149, 159.
Bard, master John, 283.
Bareff, Edmond, 63; Emma, 63; John, 63;
    Margery, 63.
Barford, Berford, Burford, sir John, 211;
    William, 44, 108.
Barker, Hugh, 289; John, 291.
Barklet, Thomas, 146.

181

Moris, Morys, Francis, 294; Thomas, 285; William, 114.
Mortymer, *William, 40.*
Modelay, sir John, 52.
Mose, John, 15.
Mosse, Joan, 296; John, 296; *Michael, 296;* Ralph, 170, 179.
Mowse, Mowce, Thomas, 94, 180, 285.
Mullinsworth, Mullisworth, Mullesworth, Anne, 201; John, 201; sir Thomas, 56, 69; son, 201.
Mundes, Elizabeth, 205; Isabel, 205; *Richard, 205;* Robert, 205; Thomas, 205.
Mux, John, 152.
Myles, William, 266.
Myris, Gilbert, 282.

Naksey, Robert, 185.
Napton, sir John, 243.
Neele, John, 88.
Negus, Negaus, John, 3; sir Thomas, 283.
Nevell, Alice, 276.
Newman, Numman, Richard, 64, 168, 275; Robert, 197.
Newold, John, 128, 149; William, 219.
Newton, Newenton, Newntun, Neunte, Emma, 139; sir John, 42; sir Thomas, 231, 247, 263.
Nicholl, Nicholas, 75, 83.
Nightyngale, Nightynggale, Thomas, 46, 212.
Nik, sir Adam, 193.
Nith', John, 87,
Niton, Margaret, 84.
Nogare, Thomas, 213.
Norres, Noresse, Richard, 23; William, 18.
Norrett, Alice, 62; *Thomas, 62.*
North, George, 286.
Norton, John, 50; William, 50.
Nott, Agnes, 71; John, 71; Richard, 71, *Thomas, 71.*

Odam, John, 168.
Odei, John, 248.
Odell, Odill, Wodell, *see also* Hodill, Harry, 173; Jane, 91; Joan, 173; John, 132, 173; Robert, 244, 285; *William, 173.*
Offode, Amy, 105; Elizabeth, 105; *William, 105,* William, 177.
Okeley, Henry, 199.
Oldershew, Margaret, 168.
Oliff, Richard, 57.
Ordway, Christian, 111; Joan, 111; John, 167.
Osborne, Osbourne, Alice, 109; Geoffrey, 189; Joan, 109; John, 109, 211; *Thomas, 109;* Thomas, 209.
Osmond, Thomas, 210; William, 109.
Ostok, Margaret, 42.
Otway, William, 199.
Oviall, Thomas, 52.

Packe, Pake, Joan, 134, 286; Margaret, 286; Robert, 51, 134, 286; *Thomas, 134, 286.*

Page, John, 183; Lucy, 208; Richard, 226.
Palmer, Palmar, John, 68, 74, 271; – – –, 197.
Pancost, Thomas, 275.
Parell *see also* Percell, Agnes, 171; Edmond, 171; Joan, 171; *Walter, 171.*
Parissh, Parrisse, Parysse, John, 58; Thomas, 41; sir William, 253; William, 58.
Parker, Henry, 2; Phillip, 287.
Parkinges, Parken, Richard, 11, 285.
Parre, sir William, 157.
Parson, Thomas, 17.
Paswater, Thomas, 135, 137.
Patenham, Agnes, 119; Alice, 119; Elizabeth, 119; Henry, 119; *John, 119;* Richard, 119; William, 119.
Patenson, sir John, 39.
Patwyn, Patewyk, Agnes, 92; Alice, 92; Richard, 92; *Thomas, 92.*
Pavy, Hugh, 153, 233.
Pays, Richard, 238; Thomas, 92.
Pech', Richard, 47.
Peck, Pek(e), Edward, 202; Henry, 100; Joan, 100; John, 38; sir John, 50; *John, 100;* Margery, 100; Richard, 100; Thomas, 100, sir Thomas, 186.
Pecok, Pecoke, Picok, Pycok, Alice, 53; *Joan, 53;* John, 139; Rainold, 53, 54; Richard, 53, 99; Thomas, 53, 99; Walter, 53.
Pedder, Agnes, 275; *Alice, 275;* Harry, 275; John, 95, 275; Matthew, 93; Robert, 275; Thomas, 275; sir William, 275; William, 275.
Pegotte, Pegot, master Francis, 294.
Pell, William, 106
Pemberton, Sibyl, 201
Pentlow, Emma, 235; Joan, 235; Richard, 235; *Thomas, 235;* William, 175.
Pepyat, Christian, 250; Joan, 250; Richard, 250; *Thomas, 250.*
Percell, Parcell, Parcellis, Percellis, *see also* Parell, Agnes, 171; Christian, 201; Edmond, 63, 171; Joan, 47, 171; John, 47; *Margaret, 201;* Robert, 47, 64, 297; Sibyl, 201; Thomas, 201; *Walter, 171; William, 47.*
Percevall, *Ellen, 120.*
Perott, Perrot, Peret, Joan, 138; John, 138; *John, 167;* Margaret, 167; Roger, 167; Thomas, 111, 167; William, 59, 167, 278.
Peryn, Perynge, John, 99; Margery, 263.
Pestell, John, 94.
Peter, John, 150, 222.
Pett, *John, 181;* Thomas, 103, 181; William, 181.
Petide, Thomas, 34, 111.
Petit(t), Elizabeth, 111; Joan, 110, 269; *John, 110;* Maud, 110; Thomas, 269.
Philipp, John, 29.
Picke, Thomas, 116.
Piers, Joan, 197.
Pierson, Robert, 205.

INDEX OF PLACES

Potsgrove, church, 59.
Potton, 35, 82, 86, 143, 195, 213, 244, 284, 289,
298; church, 35, 80, 82, 86, 195, 284, 289,
298; bailiwick, 298; causeway, 86; Church
Street, 195; Dowhowse, 298; Horslay,
Horselow Street, 195, 289; Lilleys, 298;
Mill, 86; Schepecot close, 289. *see also*
fraternities.
Pulloxhill, 27; church, 27, 244.

Ravensden, 193; church, 99, 171, 193.
Renhold, 198, 227, 267; church, 171, 189, 198,
227, 267; proposed bridge, 272.
Ridgmont, 174; Segenhoe church, 174;
Brogborough, 174.
Riseley, 150, 175, 201, 221, 222; church, 150,
171, 175, 201, 221, 222; Coles land, 150;
West End, 221; Wyllysworth Hill, 150. *see
also* fraternities.
Roxton, 152, 158, 164, 176; church, 152, 158,
164, 176; Cross, 164; Joys tenement, 176;
Chawston in, 158, 176, and manor, 176.
Stoughton Bridge, 158.
"Rynosted", ?Ringstead, Northants., 268.

St. Neots, Hunts., 63; bridge, 53. *see also*
franternities, religious houses.
Salford, 275; church, 275.
Sandy, 29, 64, 160, 165, 265; church, 11, 29, 160,
165, 186, 196, 265, 297; highways, 186;
Beeston in, 29, 165, 186; Christian's
Orchard, 186, bridge, 186, torches, 186;
Girtford in, 64, 186, bridge, 186, torches,
186.
Sharnbrook, 3, 37, 168, 185, 190, 248, 252;
church 3, 168, 248, 252; highways, 168;
Calfulende, 168; Clenyogges bridge, 3, 168.
see also fraternities.
Shefford, 64, 144, 162; chapel, 6, 144; bridge
toward Clifton, 162; bridge toward
Hardwik, 162.
Shillington, 7, 10, 123, 126, 146, 246; church, 7,
10, 123, 126, 146, 246; almshouses, 146;
Shillington Bere, 10; Brekles House, 10;
Nether Stondon in, 7, 126. *see also*
fraternities.
Souldrop, 37, 241; church, 3, 37, 168.
Southill, 28, 64, 72, 202, 228; church, 28, 145,
202, 228; highway, 228; Gese Hery', 145;
Brownes place, 202. Broom in, 72, 127, 145.
Southoe, Hunts., church, 196.
Stagsden, 15, 70, 155, 210; church, 15, 22, 155,
210, 231; Church End, 15; Mables, 22;
house called Russell, 15; Wekend, 22; West
End, 15.
Stanbridge, church, 59.
Staughton, Great, Hunts., 38, 63; church, 63,
171; Brosse Bridge, 63; Pery in, 63.
Staughton, Little, 214, 249; church, 171, 214;
Church Field, 214; Dynge, 214; Fremannys
Green, 249; Willhamoate, 214. Steppingley,

153; church, 9.
Stevenage, Herts., 230.
Stevington, 2, 51, 114, 129, 134, 213, 216, 231,
242, 281, 286; church, 2, 51, 114, 134, 213,
216, 231, 233, 242, 281, 286; Cokkes lane,
51, Lovit croft, 216; Shortcroft Green, 51;
Westcroft, 51. *see also* fraternities.
Stotfold, 205, 272; church, 205, 274;
highways, 274; town fine, 274; the
Fifteenth, 274.
Streatley cum Sharpenhoe, 50; church, 50, 250;
Myddilstretes and Lygravis, 50;
Sharpenhoe in, 50.
Studham, 92, 109, 237, 266; church, 92, 237,
266; Markyate in, 92, 266.
Sundon, 250; church, 250; highways, 250.
Sutton, 143, 245; church, 143, 245.
Swineshead, church, 171.

Tadlow, Cambs., 80.
Tempsford, 11, 31, 64, 215; church, 11, 31, 165,
215, 297; causeway between Church and
Lampat end, 215; causeway at Lampat
Bridge, 215; Bullys Bridge, 11; Little
Marsh, 31; Little North Field, 11;
Lombardes Place, 31; Pease furlong, 31;
West Mead, 31. *see also* fraternities.
Thurleigh, 74, 185, 224; church, 168, 171, 224;
Borse close, 224; Church Field, 224; Fleet
Whoodhend, 224; Mill Fyld, 224; Rydyng,
224.
Tilbrook, 71, 223; church, 71, 223; Lekes, 71;
Richards, 71.
Tilsworth, 116; church, 59, 116, 256;
Acurbusshes, 116.
Tingrith, 9, 153.
Toddington, 9, 62, 212, 282, 291; church, 101,
116, 212, 282, 291; chapel of St.
Bartholomew, 59; Chalton in, 59; Herne
in, 101.
Totternhoe, 104, 110, 136, 276; church, 136,
276; Burlettes Bush, 136; Cartersway, 136;
Cowpers, 136; Cokkysthorn Hill, 136;
Otehill, 136; Shortte Neme, 136;
Taggyshedelong, 136; Welhede Way, 136;
Welhedmyll, 136.
Turvey, 43, 56, 69, 132, 183-4, 191, 203, 226,
254; church, 43, 56, 69, 132, 183-4, 191,
203, 254; bridge, 43, 56, 69, 96, 132,
183-4, 191, 216, 231, 281; Brige End, 183;
Camfeldes, 191; High Street, 183; Hillys,
191; Pikkshill, 56; Pynchynckes Cross, 254;
Town, 191; Whyt House in Stockers End,
254.

Warden, 84; church, 165. *see also* religious
houses.
Watton, Yorks., 16; church, 16.
Wavendon, Bucks., church, 275, 295.
Wellingborough, Northants., 203; bridge,
206.

SUBJECT INDEX

117, 119, 145, 149, 154, 159, 162–3, 173, 176, 179, 183, 188, 192, 194–5, 197, 201–2, 214, 221, 257, 261, 263, 271, 297–8; silver, 197; skillet, 188; spit, 32, 117, 176, 197, 263, 272; spoons, 41, 83, 97, 111, 115, 130, 154, 201, 213, 239, 263, 282; standards, 67, 155; stool, 32; table, 6, 10, 19, 32, 101, 111, 115, 123, folding, 263; table cloth, 6, 32, 41, 179, 188, 201; tester, 115; towel, 6, 32, 41, 111, 176, 179, 188, 201; trestles, 32; trough, 116; tub, powdering and wort, 263; vat, mashing, 263, wort, 207; vessel, 13, 34, 115, 202, garnish vessel, 176; yarn, woollen and flaxen, 11, 218.

Jewellery, chain, gold, 213; jewels, 239; rings, 239, gold, 115, gold engraved, 213, gold signet, 213, silver, 115, wedding, 115, 197, 201.

Land tenure: ancient demesne, 218; copyhold, 9, 10, 59, 67, 72, 120–1, 145, 149, 163, 174, 213, 229, 232, 239, 245–6, 295; feoffees, 6, 9, 11, 30, 37, 41–2, 44, 49, 59, 62–4, 80, 103–4, 128, 133, 156, 158, 164, 171, 196, 205, 214, 226, 233, 283; freehold, 9, 59, 72, 232, 245; leasehold, 41, 54, 56, 62, 76, 122, 293, 298.

Lights: torches, *passim*; before the rood, sacrament, sepulchre and Our Lady St. Mary, *passim*; the Plough light, 82; before images of: All Saints, 7, 42, 154, 163, 173, 220, 278, 295; All Souls, 20, 84, 112, 153, 233; St. Ann, 59, 113, 173; St. Anthony, 62; St. Christopher, 62, 275; St. Erasmus, 62, 104; St. George, 62, 291; King Henry VI, 59 62; St. Hugh of Lincoln, 246; St James, 94, 291; Five Tapers of Jesus, 249; St. John, 94, 244, 281, 285; St. Katherine, 26, 59, 113, 151, 163, 184, 186, 193, 265, 275, 287, 291; St. Laurence, 173; St. Loy (Elege), 62, 104; St. Margaret, 22, 59, 113, 146; St. Martin, 59, 113; Our Lady St Bethlehem, 244; Our Lady of Comfort, 248; Our Lady of Grace, 7, 120, 248; Our Lady of Pity, 7, 11, 15, 42, 49, 59, 107, 149, 184, 275, 295; Our Lady of Todyngton, 116; Our Blessed Lady of Woburn, 102; the White Lady of Newnham, 170; St. Mary Magdalene, 59, 113; St. Michael, 62; St. Nichols, 26, 94–5, 102, 104, 113, 207, 275, 292; St. Osyth, 62, 102, 111; St. Peter, 11, 281, 295; St. Roke, 248; St. Sunday, 59, 62, 104, 154; St. Thomas, 59, 104, 113, 285; the Trinity, 62, 95, 102, 116, 132, 163, 168, 207, 216, 244, 248, 281, 292; Twelve Apostles, 62, 113.

Malt, 10–12, 38, 42–3, 52, 56, 59, 62, 67, 83, 93, 95–6, 103, 111, 113, 117, 122, 124,

126–7, 131, 136, 142, 159, 163, 167, 200, 211, 216, 239, 249, 251, 258, 263, 270, 275, 278, 280, 292, 297.

Marriage: dower, 11, 25, 29, 65, 134–5, 238–9, 271; gifts for 61–2, 66, 80–2, 87, 103, 142, 153, 162, 171, 174, 196, 212, 225–6, 260, 275, 282; remarriage, 13, 21, 27, 92, 99, 135–6, 145, 152, 162, 165–6, 168, 179, 192–3, 225, 227, 233, 238, 260, 293; settlement, 244.

Mortuary or principal, *passim*.

Mill, 84, 86, 213.

Occupations and offices (ecclesiastical): abbess, 41, 83, 251; abbot, 170; anchorite, 233; brother, 64; canon, 24, 115, 170; cellarer, 170; children, 41; clerk, 30, 41, 51, 109, 115, 153, 181, 204, 235, 257, parish clerk, 112, 159; curate, *passim*; friar, 6, 41, 96–7, 257; novice, 115, 170; nun, 41, 44, 115; priest and parish priest, *passim*; prioress, 127; quirister, 64; scholar, 35; sister, 115; student, 41, 198; subprior, 6, 115; vicar, *passim*.

Occupations and offices (secular) and status: apprentice, 27, 36, 152; bailiff, 72, 154, 219, 257, 298; baker, 78; butcher, 123; commissary, 263; draper, 97; esquire, 62, 80, 128, 219; gentleman, 80, 119, 174, 201, 215, 294; goldsmith, 133; husbandman, 224, 229; knight, 73, 80, 201, 282; mayor, 78, 119, 133; maid, 293; mercer, 96; notary, 111, 129; servant, 41–3, 66, 80, 103, 146, 171, 202, 209, 219, 224, 227, 249; shepherd, 212; singleman, 7; smith, 96, 100, 111, 204, 224; weaver, 152, 231; widow, 31, 35, 41, 61, 111, 203, 261; 263; yeoman, 244.

Orchard or garden, 28, 168, 186.

Religious houses: Ashridge, Herts. (Bonshommes), 291; Barking, Essex (Benedictine nuns), 42, 107; "Belvere" ?Beaulieu, Hants. (Cistercian), 153; Bushmead, Eaton Socon (Augustinian canons), 63, 156, 171; Caldwell, Bedford (Augustinian canons), 148, 192, 196, 298; Chicksands (Gilbertine canons and nuns), 6, 24, 41, 97, 115; Dunstable (Augustinian canons), 41, 62, 81, 88–90, 110, 142, 218; Elstow (Benedictine nuns), 12, 23, 41, 44, 83, 121, 149, 196, 233, 251; Haliwell, Middx. (Augustinian canonesses), 127; Newnham, Goldington (Augustinian canons), 37, 96–7, 153, 156, 170, 192, 196, 274; Reading, Berks. (Benedictine monks), 244; St. Neots, Hunts. (Benedictine monks), 54, 156, 218; Warden (Cistercian Abbey), 64, 145, 165, 170; Woburn (Cistercian Abbey), 279, 295.

Roads, highways, maintenance and repair, 9,